Architecting AI Solutions on Salesforce

Design powerful and accurate AI-driven state-of-the-art solutions tailor-made for modern business demands

Lars Malmqvist

BIRMINGHAM—MUMBAI

Architecting AI Solutions on Salesforce

Copyright © 2021 Packt Publishing

Associate Group Product Manager: Alok Dhuri

Senior Editor: Rohit Singh

Content Development Editor: Tiksha Lad

Technical Editor: Pradeep Sahu

Copy Editor: Safis Editing

Project Coordinator: Manisha Singh

Proofreader: Safis Editing

Indexer: Manju Arasan

Production Designer: Nilesh Mohite

First published: October 2021

Production reference: 1081021

Published by Packt Publishing Ltd.

Livery Place

35 Livery Street

Birmingham

B3 2PB, UK.

ISBN 978-1-80107-601-2

www.packt.com

To Damiana, Ada, and Pino. To my mother, Inger Bejder, and the memory of my father, Finn Malmqvist.

– Lars Malmqvist

Contributors

About the author

Lars Malmqvist has spent the past 12 years working as an architect and CTO within the Salesforce ecosystem. For the past 5 years, he has been particularly focusing on advanced AI solutions. He has worked on over 40 Salesforce implementations, ranging from simple out-of-the-box scenarios to advanced, bespoke, multi-cloud solutions for large global brands. He is a 23x certified Salesforce CTA with degrees in computer science, mathematics, and technology management and an MBA from the University of Cambridge. Currently, he works as a senior manager at Accenture and is in the final stages of completing a PhD with a focus on deep learning.

I would like to thank my wife, Damiana, for her undying support and my children, Ada and Pino, for their constant inspiration.

About the reviewers

As a Salesforce solution architect, **Madhav Kakani** delivers exceptional value to customers by designing high-performance solutions and leading successful implementations of Salesforce CRM to automate sales, marketing, and business-critical processes.

His work entails negotiating solutions to complex problems with multiple parties and agendas, managing technical scope and client expectations, and managing development and change following the Salesforce governance framework.

He has been working on the Salesforce platform for 15 years, and in addition to leading projects, he has also done numerous implementations using different technologies available on the platform, namely Apex, Visualforce, Aura Lightning Components, Lightning Web Components, and Flows.

Rafael Gutierrez Castillo is a Salesforce architect with multi-cloud implementation experience. With ten years of working experience, he started his career in the education industry, developing leadership programs for university students.

He has worked in different positions within the Salesforce ecosystem, including business consultant, tester, solution consultant, and solution architect.

Working as an associate manager at Accenture, he designs solutions that bridge the gap between business processes and technology and advises companies on their digitalization and transformation journeys. With 20 Salesforce certificates, he is passionate about building automation processes, solution design, process management, and development of leadership skills.

Ashvin Bhatt is an enterprise architect, technical writer, trainer, and speaker with more than 10 years of experience on the Salesforce platform and working on various clouds. He has trained 500+ people on Salesforce through various initiatives. He is a certified application architect and holds a wealth of experience on various Salesforce products. He is a co-organizer of Salesforce Architect Summit and has been a speaker at various events, such as Dreamforce and TDX.

He has worked in a variety of domains, such as high-tech, advertising, manufacturing, health, insurance, and pharma, to name a few. He believes in sharing his knowledge through community-led initiatives to help foster learning and innovation.

Table of Contents

Section 2: Out-of-the-Box AI Features for Salesforce

2

Salesforce AI for Sales

3

Salesforce AI for Service

4

Salesforce AI for Marketing and Commerce

5

Salesforce AI for Industry Clouds

Section 3: Extending and Building AI Features

6

Declarative Customization Options

7

Building AI Features with Einstein Platform Services

8
Integrating Third-Party AI Services

Section 4: Making the Right Decision

9
A Salesforce AI Decision Guide

10
Conclusion

Assessments

Other Books You May Enjoy

Index

Preface

Salesforce is one of the world's leading enterprise software platforms. Businesses across the world rely on it to run increasingly critical parts of their business. **Artificial Intelligence (AI)**, principally in the shape of machine learning models of ever-increasing scale and complexity, is equally becoming influential in many areas of business operations and strategic decision-making.

The Einstein platform is Salesforce's answer to how to marry the core functionality of their product offerings with the need for sophisticated AI-based solutions to improve, automate, and enlighten business processes. In this book, we will explore this platform in terms of what it can and what it can't achieve, so that you as an architect can make the right decision for your stakeholders about how to implement AI solutions on Salesforce.

We start by surveying the big picture in the introduction. Then, in the following four chapters, we dive deep into the Einstein functionality embedded into the various Salesforce clouds. We start with Sales, then move on to Service, followed by Marketing and Commerce, ending up with a look across the industry clouds.

Having learned how to use the built-in offerings, we will proceed to explore your options for when the out-of-the-box features just won't cut it. We will start by looking at declarative options, then move on to various programmatic ones, starting with those provided by Salesforce and moving on to three examples of using third-party services in your Salesforce solution.

After mastering how to build custom AI solutions on the Salesforce platform, we will end the book by condensing our learning into a decision guide. Then we will draw some final lessons and give some pointers to where you might go to deepen your mastery of the topics at hand.

Architecting AI solutions is different from traditional architecture, but it will increasingly become part and parcel of your work as an architect. I hope this book helps you to do this work well.

Who this book is for

This book is for existing and aspiring technical and functional architects, technical decision-makers working on the Salesforce ecosystem, and those responsible for designing AI solutions in their Salesforce ecosystem. Lead and senior Salesforce developers who want to start their Salesforce architecture journey will also find this book helpful. Working knowledge of the Salesforce platform is necessary to get the most out of this book.

What this book covers

Chapter 1, AI Solutions on the Salesforce Einstein Platform, starts by clarifying why it is a good idea to build AI solutions on Salesforce and what business and technical benefits this approach can have. It will then present a bird's-eye view of the various components that will be discussed throughout the book, present a basic architectural view of Salesforce Einstein, and then continue with a discussion of how architecting AI solutions is different from architecting traditional solutions. The chapter ends by previewing the structure of the parts and chapters to come and giving a preview of the Pickled Plastics Ltd. scenario that will be expanded throughout.

Chapter 2, Salesforce AI for Sales, covers the core Sales-related AI options in Salesforce. It will go through Einstein Lead and Opportunity Scoring, Einstein Forecasting, Einstein Activity Capture, and Einstein Conversational Insights, and covers the main features and configuration options. For each topic, there will also be a discussion of the pros and cons and what options an architect has if the limits of the feature are reached. As part of each feature discussion, it will reference the scenario that is used throughout the book to give a real-world grounding.

Chapter 3, Salesforce AI for Service, covers the core Service-related AI options in Salesforce. It will go through Einstein Bots, Case Classification and Routing, Einstein Article Recommendations, and Einstein Reply Recommendations, and covers the main features and configuration options. For each topic, there will also be a discussion of the pros and cons and what options an architect has if the limits of the feature are reached.

Chapter 4, Salesforce AI for Marketing and Commerce, starts by going through the integration architecture between core Salesforce, Marketing, and Commerce clouds to show how one needs to think differently about architecting across multiple clouds. It will then focus on the features of first Marketing Cloud Einstein and then Commerce Cloud Einstein. These will be covered in slightly less depth than the Sales and Service features due to the large number of features to cover, but will still be covered in sufficient depth to make an architectural assessment of their potential inclusion in a solution.

Chapter 5, Salesforce AI for Industry Clouds, covers how Einstein has been brought into Salesforce's various industry clouds, including the Health, Financial Services, Manufacturing, Consumer Goods, Education, and Non-profit clouds. As most of these features have been created using other elements rather than being unique, this is more a showcase for how Einstein features can be used than a discussion of new technical material.

Chapter 6, Declarative Customization Options, shows how you can use generic Einstein declarative features to create your own solutions, as well as discussing when that can be the right approach. It will first show some of the many ways you can embed and configure Einstein Next Best Action, then walk the user through making a good prediction with Prediction Builder, and finish with creating a story using Einstein Discovery.

Chapter 7, Building AI Features with Einstein Platform Services, will take you through three examples of using the Einstein Platform Services APIs to create custom AI solutions for the platform. Along the way, it will also discuss the architectural choices and trade-offs involved. The examples will move from an image classifier to a form text recognizer to a sentiment analysis application, all integrated into a normal Salesforce Sales or Service workflow.

Chapter 8, Integrating Third-Party AI Services, takes you through three examples of custom development, in this case using external third-party services as part of normal Sales/Service workflows on Salesforce. For each example, the architectural setup and the relevant choices in relation thereto will be discussed. The first example will show automated translations with the Google Translation API, the second will extract information from documents attached to a Case, and the third will train a custom prediction model using Amazon SageMaker.

Chapter 9, A Salesforce AI Decision Guide, presents a summary of all the key architectural decisions and trade-offs that are relevant to the technologies discussed in the book. It will start by introducing the guide and how to use it, then move on to a discussion of common use cases for AI technologies. For each use case, it will make architectural suggestions based on the key dimensions of the particular use case. It will then do a similar thing, but focusing instead on common technical requirements and constraints that may impact the architectural choice to be made.

Chapter 10, Conclusion, summarizes the main points of the preceding section. First, it will remake the case for using out-of-the-box declarative features when this is possible and summarize the substantial architectural benefits of doing so. Then it will revisit the key considerations for going above and beyond these features and the ways this can be done. It will end by giving some hints for other resources that can be consulted should the reader wish to go further in various directions.

To get the most out of this book

This book assumes you are familiar with the basics of using the Salesforce web application. You need to be working on a recent version of a modern browser such as Chrome or Edge to do the exercises. You can find a full list of recommendations and considerations here: `https://help.salesforce.com/s/articleView?id=sf.getstart_browser_recommendations.htm&type=5`.

Software/hardware covered in the book	Operating system requirements
Salesforce Einstein Platform	Any OS that can run a modern browser
Einstein Platform Services	Any OS that can run a modern browser
Tableau CRM: Einstein Discovery	Any OS that can run a modern browser

You will need to sign up for a fresh Tableau CRM-Enabled Developer Edition Org to follow most of the examples in this book. You can find instructions for getting access to one of those by using the following link: `https://trailhead.salesforce.com/content/learn/projects/quick-start-einstein-analytics/sign-up-for-an-analytics-org`.

If you are using the digital version of this book, we advise you to type the code yourself or access the code from the book's GitHub repository (a link is available in the next section). Doing so will help you avoid any potential errors related to the copying and pasting of code.

Download the example code files

The code for the chapter can be found here:

`https://github.com/PacktPublishing/Architecting-AI-Solutions-on-Salesforce`

We have other code bundles from our rich catalog of books and videos available at `https://github.com/PacktPublishing/`. Check them out!

Code in Action

The Code in Action videos for this book can be viewed at `https://bit.ly/3DerU2h`.

Download the color images

We also provide a PDF file that has color images of the screenshots and diagrams used in this book. You can download it here: `https://static.packt-cdn.com/downloads/9781801076012_ColorImages.pdf`.

Conventions used

There are a number of text conventions used throughout this book.

`Code in text`: Indicates code words in text, database table names, folder names, filenames, file extensions, pathnames, dummy URLs, user input, and Twitter handles. Here is an example: "Also create a text variable named `recordId`, available for input, to receive the ID of the context case."

A block of code is set as follows:

```
#train/test split
train_data, test_data = np.split(model_data.sample(frac=1,
random_state=432), [int(0.8 * len(model_data))])
print(train_data.shape, test_data.shape)
```

Bold: Indicates a new term, an important word, or words that you see onscreen. For instance, words in menus or dialog boxes appear in **bold**. Here is an example: "Now go to flows and create a **Record-Triggered Flow**. Set the object to **Case Comment** and run the flow after creation, as shown in the following screenshot."

> **Tips or important notes**
> Appear like this.

Get in touch

Feedback from our readers is always welcome.

General feedback: If you have questions about any aspect of this book, email us at `customercare@packtpub.com` and mention the book title in the subject of your message.

Errata: Although we have taken every care to ensure the accuracy of our content, mistakes do happen. If you have found a mistake in this book, we would be grateful if you would report this to us. Please visit `www.packtpub.com/support/errata` and fill in the form.

Piracy: If you come across any illegal copies of our works in any form on the internet, we would be grateful if you would provide us with the location address or website name. Please contact us at copyright@packt.com with a link to the material.

If you are interested in becoming an author: If there is a topic that you have expertise in and you are interested in either writing or contributing to a book, please visit authors.packtpub.com.

Share Your Thoughts

Once you've read *Architecting AI Solutions on Salesforce*, we'd love to hear your thoughts! Scan the QR code below to go straight to the Amazon review page for this book and share your feedback.

https://packt.link/r/1801076014

Your review is important to us and the tech community and will help us make sure we're delivering excellent quality content.

Section 1:
Salesforce and AI

In this section, you will learn the background material needed to understand the rest of the book (which assumes a pre-existing Salesforce background), how architecting for AI solutions is different from traditional architecture, as well as getting acquainted with Pickled Plastics Ltd., the running scenario used to exemplify features throughout the book.

This section comprises the following chapter:

- *Chapter 1, AI Solutions on the Salesforce Einstein Platform*

1

AI Solutions on the Salesforce Einstein Platform

In this chapter, we will see why it is a good idea to build **AI solutions on Salesforce** and what business and technical benefits this approach can have. We will then take a bird's eye view of the various components that will be discussed throughout the book, present a basic architectural view of Salesforce Einstein, the AI platform embedded in Salesforce, and continue with a discussion on how architecting AI solutions is different from architecting traditional solutions.

This chapter ends by presenting **Pickled Plastics Ltd.**, a scenario that will be expanded throughout the book to help reinforce the real-world applications of the technology.

In this chapter, we're going to cover the following main topics:

- Why would you build AI solutions on Salesforce?
- What are the main components of Salesforce AI?
- What are the elements of Salesforce Einstein?
- What's special about architecting for AI?
- Presenting Pickled Plastics Ltd.

By the end of this chapter, you will know how to think about architecting AI solutions on Salesforce.

Technical requirements

There are no explicit technical requirements for this chapter, but you may find it useful to have an analytics-enabled developer org available to review points as we go through. This can be requested using the form here: `https://developer.salesforce.com/promotions/orgs/analytics-de`.

Why would you build AI solutions on Salesforce?

AI is at the heart of the Salesforce platform. There isn't a cloud or prominent feature today that doesn't have predictive or analytical capabilities available. Right now, you can build advanced AI solutions using clicks, not code, across most major Salesforce applications. To some extent, this is surprising. Salesforce is a relative latecomer to the world of AI.

The Einstein platform, which is Salesforce's collective name for its various AI and analytical features, did not exist until 2016. However, once it got going, the pace of evolution has been breathtaking. In 2016 alone, Salesforce acquired 10 companies, many of which were rolled into its AI capability.

In 2019, they acquired Tableau, an undisputed market leader in analytical software. Tableau CRM, the name given to the product combining Einstein Analytics and Tableau, is poised to become the *de facto* standard for analyzing CRM data. Even in academic AI research, Salesforce has become a force to be reckoned with, presenting groundbreaking research on natural language processing and computer vision. It is one of the first companies committed to a vision for responsible AI, encompassing the five trusted AI principles that AI should be responsible, accountable, transparent, empowering, and inclusive.

Overall, Salesforce has made an impressive commitment to including AI features across its product portfolio and doing so in a way that honors the platform by allowing extensive point-and-click-based configuration and more in-depth code-based customization. However, this begs a simple question: *Why do I need AI capabilities in my CRM in the first place?* Given the already extensive customization and configuration capabilities of Salesforce, do I need to complicate the picture with **artificial intelligence (AI)**? As you may guess from the fact that you're reading a book about these features, my answer is a resounding yes. In the next section, I will summarize why you need integrated AI features in your CRM platform.

The value of intelligent CRM data

For most large companies today, CRM is one of the vital arteries through which critical business data flows. Put bluntly, it is the system that knows about customers. The more we know about customers and the better we can use that knowledge to serve their needs, the better our businesses will do. If we learn more about customers, we can sell them products that better fit their needs at the exact time they need them. We can address their questions and concerns proactively both before and after purchase. Not least, we will be able to respond to changes in the market so that our products and services remain relevant over time.

These points have always been true, even before there was such a thing as CRM software. What CRM has enabled companies to do is track their relationship with customers in a way that far surpasses traditional methods. Similarly, an AI-enabled CRM far surpasses a conventional CRM in building and strengthening customer relationships over time.

The first important reason for that is the *increasing complexity* of the relationships that companies have with consumers. Today, you need to track interactions across digital and physical channels, in-store purchases, promotional events, social media, email campaigns, website visits, online orders, mobile notifications, and potentially a whole plethora of apps and dedicated digital experiences. Some of these may also have real-world components that may generate more relationship data, such as with wearable technology. This complexity means that it is increasingly difficult for a salesperson or customer support representative to look at the customer's profile and understand what is going on and what action is appropriate at a given point in time. They need help to make sense of the actual relationship and make the right decision when dealing with the customer.

Taking this up a level, complexity of relationships generates previously unseen levels of fast-moving data in various formats that do not necessarily respond well to traditional BI/reporting treatment. Managers and marketers, therefore, can no longer rely on the conventional way of analyzing and interpreting data. They need help to aggregate, simplify, and make actionable the treasure trove of behavioral insights found in customer data. The ability to precisely target consumers and interact with them in a genuinely personalized way is at the core of why you need AI in your CRM.

On a more practical level, AI allows the automation of a wide range of traditional CRM tasks, freeing up resources to help make use of the new opportunities generated by complex and varied data. Use cases such as automated report generation, data cleanup, quality management, handling simple sales, and service requests through automated channels (such as chatbots and automating routine process steps via RPA-like technologies) all offer immediate efficiencies.

While, in theory, these technologies need not sit inside the CRM, a native capability that enables you to gain access to these tremendous benefits easily is, in most cases, a no-brainer. With a native capability, you do not have to move data around, transform it, or manage yet another set of complex integrations. You can build on your existing team's skill sets rather than have to learn entirely new technologies and limit off-platform choices to only the areas where you can make a genuine business case.

Some examples

While the Einstein platform is relatively new compared to the Salesforce platform, it has been around for long enough that we can have a look at a few cases where these benefits have been realized.

U.S. Bank is the fifth-largest bank in the United States, with 73,000 employees. They are a long-term user of Salesforce and also an early adopter of the Einstein platform. They adopted the Einstein platform's predictive capabilities across several functions within the bank, explicitly to address the issues of fast-moving and varied relationship data. By increasing the volume and quality of their data, they can see patterns that they wouldn't have been able to identify manually.

This information is brought to the front line by adding predictive analytical capabilities to the interface seen by front-line officers, enabling them to make better sense of the relationship and make the right decision with the customer.

Accenture is the largest IT services company in the world, with more than 500,000 employees. Within the company's CRM, the Einstein platform is used to visualize and predict information relevant to winning more deals. By embedding Einstein capabilities into lightning components shown in the relevant part of the CRM, users get highly relevant and accurate information that helps them clarify the steps to take for a given opportunity and a prediction of the current win rate.

Stonewall Kitchen is a US-based specialty food company with wholesalers across 42 countries and its stores in the US. From an AI perspective, Stonewall Kitchen has gone all-in on personalizing the online retail experience. Based on the Einstein platform, they have developed a product recommendation engine that is so good that 78% of customers who get a recommendation end up adding that recommendation to their cart, and 41% go on to buy. From an e-commerce perspective, these are awe-inspiring numbers.

These are just a few examples of how different companies have leveraged the Einstein platform to improve their ability to engage with customers and serve them better. These examples, however, are just the beginning. As a relatively young platform under constant development, we can expect genuinely great solutions to come to light in the future. Maybe after reading this book, you will work on some of them. Having gained an understanding of why using the Salesforce Einstein platform may be a good idea, we will now continue to look at the components that make up the platform.

What are the main components of Salesforce AI?

The most important fact about the Einstein platform is that while it is an entity in its own right, it is also an integral part of the complete Salesforce platform. That means, first and foremost, that the core CRM data model that powers the rest of the Salesforce feature set is directly available to the Einstein platform's AI features. That also means that the core security model, user interface, administrative functions, and so forth that make up the Salesforce CRM can be used by and straightforwardly use the Einstein features. This fact is crucial to maximizing the benefit of working on CRM instead of integrating third-party solutions. The following diagram gives an overview of the platform architecture:

Figure 1.1 – Einstein platform architecture

The architecture diagram starts at the bottom level, with programmatic services that require advanced programming skills to implement, and proceeds up the stack to the pre-built solutions, which can be activated at the click of a button.

The Platform Services layer

The **Platform Services layer**, sometimes referred to as **myEinstein**, is the part of the Einstein platform that directly builds on top of the core data model to provide customizable capabilities for prediction and analysis. Overall, in keeping with the Salesforce platform, these can be divided into declarative services that you can configure via the administrative user interface and platform services that enable programmatic access to the platform:

- In the first category, we find, for instance, **Einstein Prediction Builder**, a point-and-click interface for making predictions about the value of fields on CRM records. This feature has extensive configurability and allows substantial tweaking of what data is used for prediction and how the system will evaluate the prediction. This feature can be maintained administratively and does not require a data scientist or a developer to implement it.

- In the second category, we find, for instance, the **Einstein Vision** feature. Einstein Vision is a programmatic API-based deep learning model that you can train for your particular use cases. For example, you could train a model to detect instances of your brand imagery in visual imagery. This feature requires considerable programming skills and machine learning knowledge to implement well.

Tableau CRM (previously called Einstein Analytics)

The analytics capabilities of **Tableau CRM** are prodigious, and they make use of many of the Einstein platform features that are discussed in this book. When considering the Einstein platform, this is often seen resting as a separate layer on top of the services layer. It is, however, well outside the scope of this book to go into any detail about this area. It deserves a large volume of its own. It is also principally focused on analyzing data to gain insight rather than using it for the types of AI-centric use cases we will be considering. Some of the pre-built solutions that we will learn about have analytics elements in them, but we will cover the specifics as and when required in these cases.

The Lightning Platform

The **Lightning Platform** in and of itself does not have any AI capabilities. However, you can't meaningfully operationalize the other features without them, so it deserves a mention in the overall architecture. Typically, you might bring in the predictive capability in the UI, for instance, as a field on a record that is set based on a machine learning model, or in a more elaborate scenario as a custom component, visualizing the information in a way that is particularly relevant to the context record.

However, in many cases, you may want to use the AI features directly in automation, such as a flow or process builder. A simple example might be a model that classifies incoming support cases based on which might likely escalate. If that probability is above a certain threshold, automation might alert relevant managers and assign the case to a special queue for velvet-glove treatment.

Einstein products

The last and increasingly largest category of features is found within specific **Einstein products**. These are prepackaged AI and analytics offerings that address particular use cases in particular clouds. It is more the rule than the exception for a Salesforce cloud to have a dedicated Einstein product offering, although some are better developed than others. There are many of these, they vary wildly, and more are added at a rapid clip release after release.

We will be going through many of these in later chapters, so we do not need to labor the point here. These solutions are, broadly speaking, less configurable than the Platform Services, but they are the obvious place to start if they fit your use case.

Third-party options

While it is generally advisable to use the platform options whenever possible, sometimes you reach a point where they do not offer the functionality you require. In those cases, you have two options:

- First, you can look at AppExchange and see if someone has created a pre-built app for you to utilize.
- Second, you can integrate third-party APIs into your solution. We will examine three options for this in *Chapter 8, Integrating Third-Party AI Services*, and give detailed guidance on when it is appropriate to go down that route. However, you should go down this route only when there is a much stronger fit for your requirements from going off-platform than staying on it.

With this foundation in place, let's move on to looking at the platform's various components in detail.

What are the elements of Salesforce Einstein?

This section will serve as a crash course in the various elements of the Einstein platform. It also serves as a handy reference for the content that will be coming in future chapters. All the features shown in the following diagram will be elaborated on further on in the book.

The chapters are standalone, so if anything catches your fancy, feel free to skip ahead to that section. I do, however, recommend that you take the time to finish this introductory chapter, as it sets the scene for the rest of the book.

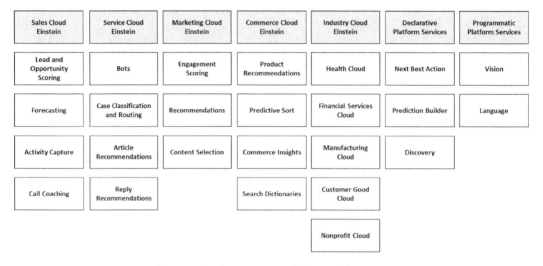

Figure 1.2 – An overview of Einstein elements

We will start by considering the components of the Einstein platform related to sales.

Einstein for sales

Sales are the first use case that springs to mind when you think of Salesforce. It is, therefore, not surprising that this is an area with a strong AI offering as well. The following sections will introduce you to the various elements in play.

Einstein Lead and Opportunity Scoring

With **Einstein Lead and Opportunity Scoring**, you get an out-of-the-box way to apply AI to filter leads and opportunities within your CRM so that you can focus on the most likely to succeed and not waste scarce sales resources. Practically, that means each lead or opportunity is assigned a numeric score that indicates their attractiveness. Attractiveness in this context implies the likelihood that it will convert from a lead to an opportunity and from an opportunity to a sale.

While each model used for scoring is unique to the specific customer, the underlying model framework is fully automated. Salesforce automatically builds the model based on the data available in the lead and opportunity objects. You have minimal control over how this model is built, but you can use the score for various additional automated purposes. That might include alerting relevant people when a score crosses some threshold, automatically subscribing leads to a given customer journey in Marketing Cloud based on their lead score, or automatically stopping and archiving records where the score drops too low.

Einstein Forecasting

The need to increase forecast accuracy is near-universal. Very few organizations get their forecasts consistently correct. It is, therefore, not surprising that Salesforce has included an automated forecasting capability in Sales Cloud Einstein. Much like lead and opportunity scoring, **Einstein Forecasting** automatically analyzes data in individual Sales Cloud objects, mainly Opportunity but also others, and generates a set of predictive models to explain the outcomes.

Based on the best model, it generates several dashboards where you can see the forecast broken down by teams, with a confidence interval and information about key factors influencing the forecast. You can also see trend information based on the forecast and Einstein's prediction of future developments.

Einstein Activity Capture

Einstein Activity Capture is a way to automate some of the drudgery involved in matching emails and calendar events to Salesforce contacts and accounts. Once installed, it automatically matches emails and calendar events in your email client to existing accounts and contacts, saving you a considerable headache.

The synchronization details and how fields are mapped across can be a little tricky, but it's well worth it for the reduced manual work. Architecturally, it is also slightly different from most Salesforce offerings in that it stores information in a public cloud rather than on Salesforce itself. This has implications both for how you can use the data and for compliance.

Einstein Conversation Insights

Einstein Conversation Insights is one of the most exciting offerings in the Sales Cloud suite. It offers part-automated sales coaching via AI to improve the efficiency of sales teams. The critical ability is for AI to identify key moments within a conversation, such as the mention of a product or a competitor brand. Managers can then review this moment directly without the need to revisit the entire conversation.

That capability allows sales coaches and managers to handle a much higher volume of calls and substantially improve the feedback given to sales staff. The product also allows for analytics on top of the voice call data to see aggregate information about calls over time. Technically speaking, this is a bit more difficult to set up as it requires integrated telephony to be viable. However, there are many good options for doing this, including both native and third-party solutions.

Einstein for Service

Service is almost as commonly used on the Salesforce platform as Sales. The Service AI offering has many unique and interesting features that can help you enrich your solutions. In the following sections, we will explore how.

Einstein Bots

Chatbots are becoming ubiquitous as a channel for both sales and service. It is, therefore, not surprising that Salesforce has introduced its own bot framework directly within the Einstein platform. That means you now have the capability of building bots and exposing them via Salesforce chat, external websites, or social media channels.

The bot learns by example using natural language programming, which is to say that you define the limits of the dialogue that the bot will be able to participate in and the actions it will be able to take, but that you need to provide a certain amount of input for it to be effective. You can create chatbots without Einstein. However, it will not be able to make any kind of inferential leap. Bots can undertake a wide variety of actions on your behalf and can also escalate to a human operator if they get confused.

Einstein Case Classification and Routing

One of the most common activities within any Service Cloud implementation is working out ways to effectively route cases to the right people at the right time. Salesforce has a variety of options to deal with this area, depending on the level of complexity. Now one of them comes with AI.

Einstein Case Classification and Routing is a pre-built feature that allows easy creation of a machine learning model that enables predicting certain case fields based on other information in that record. Effectively, this will allow you to set the value of pick lists and checkboxes based on the model's best guess derived from historical data. This, in turn, will enable you to route cases based on that information using the usual methods. Thereby, companies can save the manual effort in the call center spent on classifying incomplete records.

Einstein Article Recommendations

Einstein Article Recommendations is another feature that focuses on eliminating drudgery. Searching through the knowledge base and attaching relevant articles to a case is one of the most common parts of the customer service agent's day job. The purpose of article recommendations is to partially automate this by Einstein automatically searching for similar cases and relevant articles and suggesting them directly without the need for agent interaction.

It works by building a machine learning model on top of the case object and the knowledge object. You have the option of telling it what fields to learn from and what fields are more important than others, and once this is done, agents will start seeing improved article recommendations that they can simply accept to have them tied to the case.

Einstein Reply Recommendations

Many chat interactions are quite repetitive, and **Einstein Reply Recommendations** leverage this fact to generate automatic reply options for customer service agents that they can use to help make chat interactions faster and more effective. Once activated and trained, the reply recommendations mode suggests replies in real time based on the current state conversation. Agents can either post these directly or edit them before posting.

Replies are generated using an advanced deep learning-based natural language processing model customized using historical data from past chats. It can, therefore, only be used where a substantial amount of historical data exists.

Einstein for Marketing

Marketing Cloud is arguably the leading digital marketing platform on the planet. The need to precisely target audiences with the right message at the right time is one that positively begs for an AI approach. We'll explore how Salesforce has risen to this challenge in the following sections.

Einstein Engagement Scoring

Einstein Engagement Scoring is a deceptively simple feature that uses a pre-built machine learning model to segment your subscribers based on their tendency to engage with the content you send out. The model is fully out of the box, but you have relatively wide opportunities for using it in your unique marketing scenario. Based on the engagement score assigned to subscribers, they are segmented into one of four groups:

- **Loyalists**: The best kind of subscribers. They frequently open your emails and click on the links.

- **Window Shoppers**: These subscribers open emails but have low click engagement.
- **Selective Subscribers**: Choosy subscribers, have a low open rate, but if they open, they often also click through.
- **Winback/Dormant**: Subscribers with both a low open rate as well as a low click engagement.

You can use these groups for specially targeted promotions with all your favorite Marketing Cloud tools. In particular, you can use these personas with the Einstein Split mechanism in Journey Builder to send different types of subscribers on different customer journeys automatically.

Einstein Recommendations

Einstein Recommendations is a feature that helps you by suggesting the most relevant next bit of content to share with a customer either through email or on the web. The feature automatically analyzes behavioral and affinity data related to customers and feeds this to a recommendation engine that you can use to produce personalized recommendations.

It relies on product or catalog data within Marketing Cloud, a prerequisite that not all users will have in place. It is also somewhat more heavyweight in configuration terms than most Einstein features we will be looking at. Once set up, however, it can be used directly within the Marketing Cloud Personalization Builder or Content Builder by using the pre-built recommendations component. That makes it very easy to deploy once the configuration has been completed.

Einstein Content Selection

When using **Einstein Content Selection**, email marketers can automatically customize their emails using configured business rules to maximize the click-to-open rate. Content is dynamically selected from a preexisting pool based on the underlying machine learning model's predictions and automatically tested using A/B testing to optimize even more. This allows email marketers to include the relevant component in an email template and have the AI do the rest.

Fundamentally, content selection works based on three factors:

- Customer profile
- Business rules
- Content pool

That is to say, given preconfigured business rules, a set of subscribers to send to, and a pool of content to choose from, Einstein Content Selection will try to optimally pick the most relevant piece of content on a subscriber basis. The business rules give a relatively strong element of configurability to this feature. However, as with most of the pre-built Einstein features, you have no control over the underlying model.

Einstein Splits

Einstein Splits allows you to tailor your user journeys based on AI-generated personas and other factors to give truly customized experiences for your users. Various kinds of splits can be configured to tailor the path taken by particular kinds of users, selected by machine learning models based on their underlying characteristics.

Einstein Messaging/Copy Insights

Einstein Messaging Insights gives you insights automatically generated based on the characteristics of your email sends, such as an unusually high or low response rate. They appear as notifications and allow you to drill into the details.

By contrast, **Copy Insights** uses the same underlying information to predict what subject lines will be more effective than others. That way, you can more easily craft the right message for your audience.

Einstein Send-Time Optimization

Einstein Send-Time Optimization allows you to optimize the time your emails are sent based on the historical response rate for similar emails. You use it as part of a user journey in Journey Builder, where you have the option to choose the period over which to optimize.

Einstein for Commerce

E-commerce is an area where a strong AI offering can result in direct improvements to the bottom line in an immediate way. For that reason, Salesforce's Commerce Cloud is not shying away from introducing AI features. We'll examine how they've done this in the following sections.

Einstein Product Recommendations

Einstein Product Recommendations is the core recommendation engine for e-commerce sites built on Salesforce Commerce Cloud. It leverages a state-of-the-art, AI-driven recommendation engine to show product recommendations to shoppers dynamically. The quality of product recommendations is frequently down to the historical data quality that underlies the recommendations.

One of the unique features of the Salesforce offering is sharing data between merchants, so the pooled dataset achieves a different level of scale. As for the Einstein Recommendations feature in Marketing Cloud, you need first to configure product and catalog data and a set of business rules within the configuration module. You will also need to incorporate the product recommendations in your storefront template, a fairly technical task. Once this is done, however, the recommendation engine does the rest of the work seamlessly.

Einstein Predictive Sort

One-to-one personalization is the holy grail of marketing. The more unique and well-fitted you can make the shopping experience to the individual consumer, the higher the probability that consumer will buy your product. **Einstein Predictive Sort** is a way of achieving this goal for search results. The underlying machine learning model crunches profile, clickstream, and order history on a customer-by-customer basis and tailors the ordering of search results to show the most relevant products for that particular customer further up the list. In practice, you add the predictive sort as a sorting rule, among other rules you configure, which gives you a more refined degree of control.

Einstein Commerce Insights

Basket analysis is one of the most common uses of machine learning in e-commerce. It shows you sets of products typically bought together, which can help with promotions and other cross-selling initiatives.

While the algorithms to perform market basket analysis are relatively old and relatively standardized, the ability to have this information automatically preprocessed and structured into well-designed dashboards and allow you to drill through and find the exact information you need adds significant value.

Einstein Search Dictionaries

Most internet users will have experienced the frustration of searching for one word only to have it return no results because the website you are searching on uses a synonym for the same word. This common frustration has resulted in almost all major websites that provide their own search mechanism implementing a search dictionary that defines synonyms between search terms.

Einstein Search Dictionaries takes the struggle out of maintaining such a search dictionary by automatically detecting relationships between search terms and linking them to a synonym list. As with product recommendations, this can be pooled across merchants, making the feature much more powerful.

Einstein for Industry Clouds

Salesforce has recently begun having a major focus on industry solutions in recognition that challenges vary tremendously between sectors. That means that metrics and models generating insight and predictions have to vary commensurately. In the following sections, we'll explore how that works across Salesforce's industry clouds.

Health Cloud

In **Health Cloud**, the key focus of the pre-built solution, Tableau CRM for Health Cloud, is to provide actionable insights to help customer engagement and manage patient risk intelligently to allow proactive outreach via care programs.

The offering consists of two apps:

- Analytics for healthcare
- Risk stratification

They both consist of a set of pre-built dashboards that give particular insights to managers and practitioners. The first is targeted principally at managers to visualize key metrics about the patient population and enable actionable insights; the second highlights at-risk patients based on configurable patient data, enabling an appropriate response.

Financial Services Cloud

The pre-built solution for **Financial Services Cloud** is similar to the solution for Health Cloud in providing pre-built analytical apps. However, the range of analytical apps is much broader in scope. There are pre-built analytical solutions for wealth management, insurance, retail banking, consumer banking, a dedicated wealth starter analytics app, and an app for client segmentation analytics. The common thread between these apps focuses on *customer intelligence* so that financial advisers can identify high-potential clients and take appropriate action to engage with them.

Manufacturing Cloud

The **Manufacturing Cloud** offering consists of a manufacturing analytics app that provides 14 pre-built dashboards to manage various aspects of a manufacturing business, which we'll explore in *Chapter 5, Salesforce AI for Industry Clouds*. There are dedicated dashboards to analyze product performance, the health of customer account relationships, and even the individual sales agreements made between your company and key customers. Compared to the Health Cloud and Financial Services Cloud offerings, the Manufacturing Cloud offering is broader in scope and more traditional, using less of the depth of capability that the platform offers.

Consumer Goods Cloud

Consumer Goods Cloud is also focused on providing pre-built dashboards that provide actionable insights to users. It contains a pre-built analytics app, which includes dashboards for typical consumer goods use cases, such as store performance or white space analysis. In addition, it also includes embedded dashboards that you can put directly into the user interface.

For instance, users can see the analytics generated for an individual store (such as the store's top-selling products) directly when looking at the store's standard Salesforce UI. Also, it contains dedicated dashboards that allow managers to drill into data for individual merchandisers.

Nonprofit Cloud

For **Nonprofit Cloud** users, Salesforce offers a pre-built fundraising performance analytics app. To work successfully, you need about 3 years of running data, so it's not for new adopters unless you migrate substantial amounts of data. Once you have the data, however, you get detailed analytics on both donors and giving, as well as a KPI-based performance dashboard to help you make sense of it all.

Declarative Platform Services

Declarative Platform Services allows administrators and configurators to build custom AI capabilities using clicks, not code. They are often the best way to achieve organization-specific AI functionality. We'll explore the various ways this can be achieved in the following sections.

Einstein Next Best Action

Einstein Next Best Action is one of the most powerful declarative features in your platform arsenal because it allows you to leverage all the analytical and predictive data generated by the other AI features in an action-based strategy. Simply put, Einstein Next Best Action surfaces recommendations directly in the user's normal workflow based on configurable strategies that can use key insights from your machine learning or analytical models to drive the choice. That way, you can impact user behavior at precisely the right time to drive better outcomes for your customers.

The configuration is not simple, and we will cover it in detail in *Chapter 7, Building AI Features with Einstein Platform Services*. However, the flow works by you outlining a set of recommendations that can be made to users, embedding these in action strategies, integrating the output of your predictive models to enable advanced intelligence in the decision-making, and configuring a component so that you can show these suggestions in the user interface.

Einstein Prediction Builder

Einstein Prediction Builder is probably the most powerful feature you have at your fingertips in the Einstein platform that you can access without writing a line of code. Salesforce refers to it as *custom AI for admins*, which is to some extent fair. The feature allows you to predict the outcome of Boolean or numeric fields on your Salesforce records based on historical data in the underlying objects.

You have a wide range of configuration options, including what fields to include in the prediction, what data to train on and which to exclude, and where you want to store your predicted outcome. It also comes with extensive monitoring tools that allow you to assess the quality of your prediction. However, you do not have any control over what machine learning model is chosen to predict your data.

That way, you can have the prediction running in the background for an extended period and only deploy it into the user experience when you are comfortable that it works as intended. The prediction itself, because it is stored directly in the data model, can be used throughout the Salesforce platform, including all the standard automation features.

Einstein Discovery

Einstein Discovery is where the AI features of the platform meet the analytical ones. Like Einstein Prediction Builder, Einstein Discovery uses supervised machine learning models based on existing data. However, the purpose of Einstein Discovery is not first and foremost to predict future outcomes but to gain deep insights that will allow you to change those outcomes by taking appropriate action.

In the terminology of the tool, what Einstein Discovery generates is a story, that is to say, a beautifully visualized statistical model that shows what factors contributed the most to the outcomes we have observed. For instance, we may find that color is a significant determinant of product sales in our catalog, but that one particular shade of green that sells exceedingly well in Bavaria is a death knell to a product sold in Provence.

The insights you generate with Einstein Discovery can be made actionable in several ways. This would typically be as parts of reports or dashboards, or as contextual information for a record. But it is also possible to make them directly actionable within the Salesforce platform, for instance as part of an automation.

Programmatic Platform Services

Programmatic Platform Services is the most powerful set of services you will have at your disposal when working with AI on-platform. They allow you to tap directly into the AI capabilities of the Salesforce platform by calling APIs. In the following sections, we will introduce the various options.

Einstein Vision

Einstein Vision is a powerful programmatically accessible API that allows developers to access both pre-trained classifiers and to train custom classifiers to solve a range of different use cases in the computer vision domain. The first service is image classification that enables you not only to detect cats in YouTube videos but also, for instance, to classify images in your content catalog or uploaded content from your user base to automate and enrich your business processes.

You can also use Einstein Vision for object detection, which can give you granular details about the size and location of objects in an image, something that can be very useful, for instance, in a field service setting. Finally, an OCR service can help you to convert all of that printed documentation that might still exist within your company into a digital form.

Einstein Language

Einstein Language is the second central API released as a part of Einstein Platform Services. As with the Vision API, you have the option of using pre-built models or creating custom models for your language domain. The first service, sentiment analysis, analyzes text to give an indication of the emotional valence it conveys. You can use it, for instance, to detect negative comments and respond with a support follow-up automatically or, conversely, detect positive statements to give people a thumbs up.

The intent API instead categorizes unstructured text into user-defined labels, trying to map the unstructured text into a more meaningful context that you can use for routing in automation. For instance, you can detect different topics within text messages and automatically respond to the right person for handling.

Finally, the **named entity recognition** (**NER**) API allows you to detect entities in unstructured text. For instance, you could detect every time somebody uses a currency amount and your company stock ticker symbol to detect conversations about target stock prices.

What's special about architecting for AI?

Traditional solution and technical architecture are well-established disciplines with a range of solid approaches and methodologies that can all lead to good outcomes. However, all of these methodologies are based on assumptions that are questionable, if not decidedly false, when architecting for AI solutions.

Next, I will present seven key differences from traditional architectural assumptions that you should keep in mind throughout the rest of the book and in the future when you apply the knowledge in practice.

In short, AI solutions have the following characteristics:

- Probabilistic
- Model-based
- Data-dependent
- Autonomous
- Opaque
- Evolving
- Ethically valent

While not unique to Salesforce, these considerations are essential when creating AI solutions on the Salesforce platform. Because you are given so much out of the box, it can be tempting to follow a traditional mindset in your architecture and design. This will backfire.

Probabilistic

Days before the beginning of the *2018 soccer World Cup*, researchers from the German Technische University of Dortmund, the Technical University in Munich, and Belgium's Ghent University predicted the winner of that year's trophy. They had run 100,000 simulations and had concluded that Spain was going to win. They weren't alone. Researchers from UBS, Goldman Sachs, and several other universities joined in the fun. They used a variety of approaches and predicted different winners. The only thing they shared was that they all got the winner wrong. Only a single machine learning prediction – from EA Sports, makers of the *FIFA 18* computer game – picked the correct winner of the tournament, France.

This story might seem disheartening to some. However, it is not something to preoccupy yourself with much, as long as you understand that machine learning systems are inherently probabilistic, not deterministic. In the aforementioned predictive model, Spain was given an overall 17.8% chance of winning. This was more than France's 11.2% but hardly a ringing endorsement. Therefore, we shouldn't be surprised at what happened but acknowledge that any prediction is most likely going to be wrong for one-off events.

Where AI solutions have real value, instead, is when we have repeated events occurring over and over again. If we had 1,000 world cups running one after the other, most likely Spain would have won more of them than France, and this would be actionable information we could use in our processes – perhaps to manufacture or promote more Spanish merchandise.

In our day-to-day processes, we have events happening millions of times and usually with much less variability than in a world cup. Our ability to predict is, therefore, much better. However, that can also lead to problems. A prediction that is too good can come to be taken as a certainty, and we can end up designing our systems so they fail when we encounter outliers. The key when developing AI-based solutions is to look hard at the data and the predictions and then to come to a reasonable compromise about what level of process use they will sustain.

Model-based

In contrast to traditional solutions, AI-based architectures use models rather than prescriptive code to solve a problem. This requires a shift in thinking on behalf of the architect. There is a famous mini short story by the Argentinian writer Jorge Luis Borges, called *On Exactitude in Science*. It is written in a single paragraph and can be found at the following link: `https://walkerart.org/magazine/empire-art-cartography-attained`.

A map covering the whole territory is useless, just as trying to capture all the complexity of your processes and data in a machine learning model is futile. In traditional solution design, we tend to be precise and specify all the rules and exceptions; in an AI system, that leads to your predictions not generalizing. You get good results on the data you already have and terrible results on future data. The most useful map size, just as the most useful model size, is big enough to let you see the amount of detail you need and no larger.

Data-dependent

This point is hopefully apparent based on the discussion we have had so far in this book. The quality of predictions in an AI-based system is proportional to the quantity and quality of the data used to build the models by which the system predicts.

Think back to the recommendation systems of the early internet, based as they were on synonyms and manual encodings of likeness. Let's for a moment assume that you are searching for thermal socks. The website might show you different pairs of socks based on that search, but you would be unlikely to be shown other pieces of thermal ware that you might want unless the retailer was very good at managing their catalog. Most likely, you would not be offered a good selection of other winter gear that might be relevant to your current pursuits, and certainly, the website would not customize it to your personal preference or the preference of other shoppers like you.

Love them or hate them, these features are all run-of-the-mill today, and that is mostly because certain internet companies have vast troves of data that they can use to generate such recommendations. The actual improvement in recommendation algorithms pales in comparison to the impact of more data.

Autonomous

Ethereum, the second-largest digital cryptocurrency, saw its price drop from more than $300 to as low as $0.10 in a matter of minutes on June 22, 2017. This crash was caused by a single massive sell order triggering more than 800 stop-loss orders, orders set to sell once the price hit a certain level automatically. There seems to have been no malice or wrongful action involved, merely the interplay of many automated agents acting in an uncoordinated but similar way.

If the interplay of relatively dumb rule-based agents can lead to this level of disruption, what will happen when we start to divulge more autonomy to AI-based systems? We don't know, but almost inevitably, when we start having bots and predictive automation on our key business systems, there will come a time when we start seeing unexpected behavior. Maybe our bots will begin to undo each other's work because they have conflicting instructions, or perhaps we will see messages being sent in a loop because there is a hidden circularity in one of our models.

For now, the consequences are likely to be minor inconveniences, but as these systems grow in responsibility and complexity, so will the problems. It is, therefore, essential to ensure that you have appropriate monitoring and *humans in the loop* at the right points in the process. You might be able to get away with not having it for a little while, but the long-term consequences of inaction will most likely be considerable.

Opaque

When I was starting out building machine learning models, I worked on a binary node classification problem using large graphs. I had a large set of graphs that contained different structures, and based on those structures, the nodes within the graph should be labeled either **Yes** or **No**, depending on whether the program should include the node in question in the output. I ran my initial model and was pleased with myself when I got 97% accuracy.

I then tried the model in practice, and it failed utterly. It just didn't work. I started digging around in the data and the model training, and after a (too) long time, I found the problem. Within my training data, a small number of graphs were huge (100–1,000 x the size of the other graphs) and had a structure that meant everything should be classified as **No**. These graphs represented unsolvable problem instances. When I had trained my model, what had happened was because of this overwhelming preponderance of **No** in the training set that I hadn't spotted because the unsolvable graphs had not been a part of my initial data analysis, the model had learned to say **No** 100% of the time. Because 97% of the cases were **No**, that gave 97% accuracy.

There were many failings on my part in this example:

- I didn't do proper exploratory data analysis.
- I didn't check my assumptions.
- I jumped too quickly into implementation.
- I had an inadequate evaluation framework in place.

However, what it also underscores is that AI systems can be opaque. There isn't a simple way to go into debug mode, step through the code, and work out what is happening. Therefore, the evaluation and gradual implementation of models are critical factors to consider whenever you are rolling out these kinds of systems.

Evolving

On March 22, 2016, Microsoft unveiled **Tay**, a Twitter chatbot, as an experiment in *conversational understanding*. Tay used advanced deep learning technologies to learn from conversations with real humans. According to Microsoft, the more you talked with Tay, the better he would get at conversation. Less than 24 hours after, Microsoft took Tay offline after spewing Nazi and anti-feminist rhetoric, which is too colorful to include in a serious work on technology. Effectively, after being targeted by an army of Twitter trolls, Tay had learned what they had to teach him and parroted them with alarming accuracy.

While Tay presents an extreme example, the fact of the matter is that machine learning systems learn. And they learn from the data that you feed them. Most of the models you build on the Salesforce platform will continue to learn after you deploy the initial model, and as the incoming data changes, so will the models, mostly for the better and sometimes for the worst. That may mean that your models' performance also changes over time, and you may get a question from your business users as to why. Again, monitoring the model regularly and having a plan for continuous validation is a good idea.

Ethically valent

The final factor to consider is that AI systems are ethically relevant in a way that most traditional computer systems are not. Data contains bias, and if you aren't careful, your models will reflect those biases. Google, for instance, was recently forced to apologize for their computer vision model generating racist labels. For example, a black hand holding a thermometer was assigned a label of **gun**, while an identical white hand holding the same thermometer was labeled **monocular**.

There are good frameworks and principles for addressing these problems, and Salesforce is one of the major technology vendors that has dedicated the most effort to ensuring responsible use of AI, incorporating such principles in its work.

Now, having understood how to architect for AI solutions, let's move on and meet the company whose requirements we'll be following throughout the book.

Meet Pickled Plastics Ltd.

You always learn better from an example. Therefore, when going through the technical material in this book, we shall relate it to real-world scenarios to make them more concrete and meaningful. The vehicle by which we shall do this is the fictional company **Pickled Plastics Ltd**. In this section, I will go through the company, its IT infrastructure, and its use of Salesforce. This will be the baseline environment into which we will be adding new functionality as we go through the chapters to come.

Pickled Plastics Ltd. is a UK-headquartered manufacturing company, with local sales subsidiaries in 37 countries worldwide. The company is family-owned and employs about 3,000 people, with most being either in production or sales. The company has historically been slow to adopt new technologies. Still, 5 years ago, it hired a particularly forward-thinking **Chief Information Officer** (**CIO**) and is now considered among the most technologically forward manufacturers in the UK. This has coincided with a period of high single-digit growth, which for the industry is considered excellent.

Pickled Plastics Ltd. has been a Salesforce user since 2011, but it was only with the new CIO's entry that it started taking it seriously as a significant business-critical system. Now, however, it is a serious user, with a well-established center of excellence. It has adopted the Sales and Service Cloud throughout the business and across all subsidiaries. Besides, it has an extensive Community Cloud implementation, catering to its distributors in various countries.

Outside the UK, most business is done B2B through local distributors, but in the UK itself, Pickled Plastics Ltd. also sells directly to consumers through a subsidiary called Handsome Homewares. Handsome Homewares has a standalone Salesforce environment that includes Marketing Cloud, which is used to deliver customer journeys via email marketing, and B2C Commerce Cloud, which runs a small-scale webshop. The company is considering rolling out a B2C presence in more countries, so the technology investment in Handsome Homewares is also seen to prepare for this eventuality.

In addition to Salesforce, Pickled Plastics Ltd. is heavily invested in a reasonably old SAP implementation that runs all major backend processes and financials. It has a bespoke homemade middleware platform that it maintains, although replacing this is on the long-term roadmap. It has experimented with various public clouds and is open to using these services, but has not invested heavily in any of them so far.

You can see an overview of the system landscape in the following diagram:

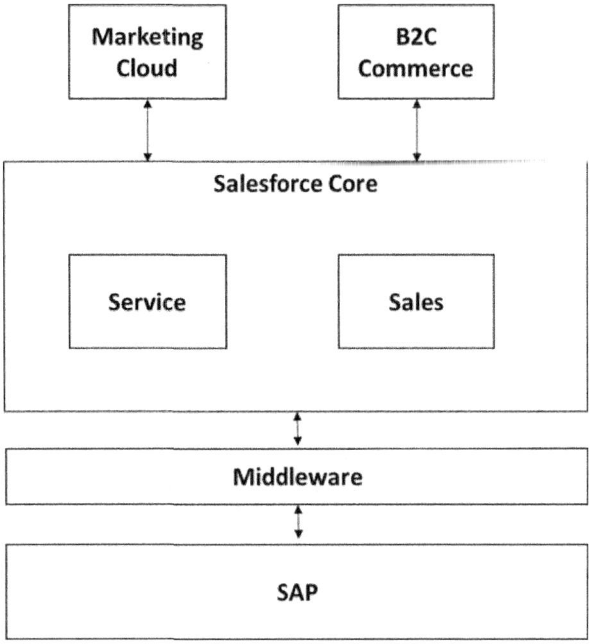

Figure 1.3 – Pickled Plastics Ltd. system landscape

The key strategic priority for the next 3 years of IT investment is AI. The company has so far not conducted any serious studies or done any real projects in this space. Still, with her usual bravado, the CIO has declared that Pickled Plastics Ltd. will have become an **AI-driven intelligent manufacturer** within 3 years. What that means is still a little unclear, but the appetite to invest in AI projects is clear.

Because of how its center of excellence is set up and the kind of capabilities it has in-house, Pickled Plastics Ltd. has a strong preference for out-of-the-box solutions. All of its existing implementations use 90%+ configurations over customization, and it has a strong preference for continuing this principle in the future. That being said, if there is a genuine need to do something different, it can make it happen. While the company does not have many deep technical resources on staff, these can be procured through long-standing vendor relationships. The preference, however, remains for out-of-the-box solutions.

Throughout the rest of the book, we shall be checking back in with Pickled Plastics Ltd. on an ongoing basis to see how the features we are talking about can help it on its journey. At the end of the book, it'll be a lot closer to realizing its goal of becoming an AI-driven business.

Summary

In this chapter, we started by looking at why we need to bring AI capabilities into our CRM. The key takeaway was that AI capabilities allow you both to personalize and improve the service you deliver to customers, both before and after purchase, in a way that represents a step change in comparison to traditional CRM. Additionally, AI allows you to automate and simplify many labor-intensive processes.

We looked at the layers of the Einstein platform and examined how we can use pre-built solutions to get a head start with AI capabilities. Equally, we looked at both the declarative and the programmatic platform services that you can use to extend the native capabilities.

Then, we took a whistle-stop tour through the different elements that make up the total Einstein offering, including sales, service, marketing, commerce, industry solutions, and platform services. This gave us a sense of both the depth and breadth of the platform as a whole.

Then, we changed tack and looked at the general question of how architecting AI solutions is different from architecting traditional solutions. We learned that seven characteristics define AI architecture, namely that AI solutions are probabilistic, model-based, data-dependent, autonomous, opaque, evolving, and ethically valent. This gave us a starting point for how to approach the deployment of these capabilities in the real world.

Finally, we learned about the fictional company Pickled Plastics Ltd., whose requirements we will be using as a reference throughout the book. And now, with the preliminaries out of the way, we will dive straight into the principal matter of the book and look at AI features for sales.

Questions

1. Why would you want to build AI features on Salesforce?
2. What are the components of the Salesforce Einstein Platform?
3. What are some of the special things about architecting for AI?

Section 2: Out-of-the-Box AI Features for Salesforce

This section will explain the out-of-the-box features available on different Salesforce clouds that can be used to implement AI solutions. We will start with the core Sales Cloud and Service Cloud offerings and then proceed to Marketing Cloud and Commerce Cloud. Finally, we will take a whistlestop tour through the various industry clouds.

This section comprises the following chapters:

- *Chapter 2, Salesforce AI for Sales*
- *Chapter 3, Salesforce AI for Service*
- *Chapter 4, Salesforce AI for Marketing and Commerce*
- *Chapter 5, Salesforce AI for Industry Clouds*

2
Salesforce AI for Sales

This chapter will cover the core sales-related **artificial intelligence** (**AI**) options in Salesforce. We will systematically go through scoring leads and opportunities, forecasting the value of sales, capturing activities from email, and analyzing conversations between staff and customers using the out-of-the-box Einstein features. For each topic, we will also discuss the pros and cons and what options an architect has if the limits of the feature are reached.

As part of each feature discussion, we will reference the Pickled Plastics Ltd. scenario that is used throughout the book to give a real-world grounding. In addition, we will do a hands-on configuration of the Lead Scoring feature in line with our scenario requirements.

In this chapter, we're going to cover the following main topics:

- Introducing Sales Cloud Einstein
- Setting up Einstein Lead Scoring and Opportunity Scoring
- Learning about Einstein Forecasting
- Diving into Einstein Activity Capture
- Examining Einstein Conversation Insights

By the end of this chapter, you will know when and how to apply Sales Cloud Einstein to your business requirements.

Technical requirements

To follow along with the hands-on parts of this chapter, please register a Sales Cloud Einstein-enabled developer org from the following link:

```
https://developer.salesforce.com/promotions/orgs/
einsteinleadscoring
```

The Code in Action (CiA) video for the chapter can be found at `https://bit.ly/3196I7M`.

Introducing Sales Cloud Einstein

The whole point of Sales Cloud Einstein is to make your sales team more effective. That means spending less time on routine chores and more time on selling and also enhancing that time by focusing it on the right leads and opportunities. Thereby, your organization will be able to close more sales and gain more revenue.

The following three key components make up this ensemble of sales productivity:

- **Einstein Lead Scoring and Opportunity Scoring**: This gives a numeric score to leads or opportunities that indicates its likelihood to convert a lead into an opportunity and an opportunity into a sale, based on the historical data you have available.

- **Einstein Forecasting**: This is an AI-enabled sales forecast to enhance the accuracy of your forecasts and give you insights into which direction your current pipeline might evolve.

- **Einstein Activity Capture**: This automates the process of linking activities from your mailbox to the right leads and contacts in Salesforce, helping you avoid wasting salespeople's time and keep data quality high.

In addition to these three components, we are also going to talk about a fourth element called **Einstein Conversation Insights**, which is not a part of the Sales Cloud Einstein license, but instead comes as part of Salesforce's High Velocity Sales app. Nonetheless, it shares the focus on improving sales efficiency along with these other apps, in this case by allowing sales managers and coaches to focus on the crucial parts of a conversation using AI that so they can review a much larger number of sales calls and give appropriate feedback to the sales team.

All of these components, however, comes with certain caveats, which we look at next:

- First and foremost, they are built with the assumption that you are using the standard Salesforce objects in more or less the standard way. That is to say, your sales process as you have implemented it in Salesforce does not substantially deviate from the way Sales Cloud works out of the box.

- You are assumed to have leads representing potential new customers that have not yet been made concrete enough to have specific opportunities. These leads convert to **Contact, Account, and (optionally) Opportunity** records using the standard lead conversion mechanism. Once an opportunity is created, it then goes through a sales process defined by a set of stages that will result in it being won or lost as a terminal stage.

  If that sounds like your sales process—and for most Salesforce users, it is likely to—then you are in luck, and the Salesforce Einstein features are likely to work well for you. However, if you aren't using the standard Lead and Opportunity objects or the standard lead conversion or sales stages, then they may not be a good fit.

  You do find organizations that, for various reasons, customize these elements, substituting custom objects or components for the out-of-the-box ones, and for these organizations, the advice has to be to steer clear of Sales Cloud Einstein unless they are willing to use these new features as an opportunity to give their legacy processes an overhaul.

Beyond that, there are a few technical requirements that need to be fulfilled to use these features in your Salesforce org, as outlined here:

- First, you need an **Enterprise, Unlimited, or Performance** edition org. You need to purchase or trial the Sales Cloud Einstein and High Velocity Sales (for Conversation Insights) add-on licenses and assign the permission set licenses to the relevant users.

- Finally, you need sufficient data in the org for the **machine learning** (**ML**) models to have something to work on. About 1 year of operational data is a good rule of thumb. Some specific features have additional requirements that we will cover as we go through the chapter, but these hold at a general level.

In the rest of this chapter, we will go through these features and cover the details of their functionality, configuration, and requirements, as well as the key points of architectural concern that should be taken into consideration when selecting the feature for a project. For Lead Scoring, we will also apply some hands-on exercises to configure some of Pickled Plastics Ltd.'s requirements.

Setting up Einstein Lead Scoring and Opportunity Scoring

In the following sections, we will cover in detail Einstein Lead Scoring and Opportunity Scoring. First, we will cover the basics of Lead Scoring, then the key use cases and configuration options. We will cover the main architectural considerations for using the feature and then move on to a hands-on example. Finally, we will look at how Opportunity Scoring differs in some minor ways from Lead Scoring.

The basics of Einstein Lead Scoring

Lead Scoring is not a new invention. It refers simply to any way in which a company may numerically differentiate which leads to prioritize for distribution to sales staff, given limited sales resources. Many companies have pre-existing models, ranging from the basic (for example, the title is **chief executive officer** (**CEO**) and *value > £1m*) to sophisticated (for example, a statistical model informed by demographic and trend data). Einstein Lead Scoring, however, is a step up in so far as it uses all your past data to create a model that presents the best fit to historical data.

It performs this analysis using all the data in the Lead object—including custom fields—and by default, it will consider all fields that you don't explicitly exclude during configuration. It also takes into consideration activities related to the leads, but it cannot consider any other objects. So, if you track some of your lead information in a custom object, for instance, you are out of luck. You will have to synchronize that information to the Lead object to have it taken into account. The same goes for any information you store on a marketing platform or in a customer data platform.

However, once the information is in the Lead object and the model parameters are configured, the rest is automatic. Einstein will try out a variety of different ML models under the hood and automatically select the one that gives the best result for your data. Once the model is built, lead scores are assigned to all the leads in the database and they are available through the **user interface** (**UI**) using a pre-built component that can be shown in both ways, upon hovering in list views and on the page layout for the lead. Refer to the following screenshot for an overview of this:

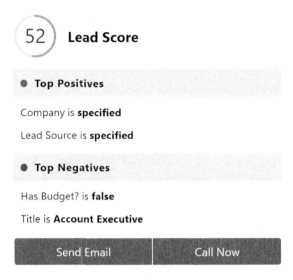

Figure 2.1 – Lead score component in list view context

In the lead score component, you can see not only the raw score but also the fields that contributed the most to the score both positively and negatively, which can be helpful for analysis. You can also use the value directly in automation, formulas, and Apex code. The model itself is updated every 10 days, but lead scores are updated every few hours or so depending on the update frequency. The following screenshot shows the lead score in the context of a Lightning page:

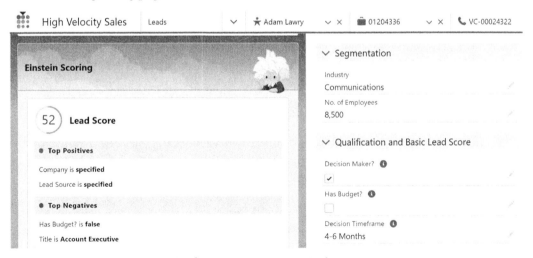

Figure 2.2 – Lead score component in a Lightning page context

As you can see from the preceding screenshot, the lead score component integrates smoothly in the normal lead layout. Now, with the basics covered, let's move on to the main use cases for the feature.

Lead Scoring use cases

The typical use cases for Lead Scoring revolve around using limited sales resources more effectively by only following up proactively on leads that meet certain minimum criteria. In addition, Lead Scoring is sometimes used to assign the best salespeople to the most promising leads.

The use cases for Einstein Lead Scoring also include optimizing sales resource allocation, but there are several additional considerations in play, as outlined here:

- First, an automated lead score can be an efficiency boost for a company that is relying on an extensive sales operations team to maintain the quality of lead data. Of course, this requires that the model is reasonably accurate, but for the sake of argument, let's take that for granted. Because the scoring model considers all the fields, it may be less vulnerable to the detail of an individual field than traditional scoring models would be. Furthermore, the manually updated factors that contribute to a traditional lead score may be derivable from other information already in the lead, and you may therefore be able to skip certain *hygienic* field updates in your lead process. All in all, automating Lead Scoring and related field updates can lead to efficiency gains for back-office sales operations teams.

- Second, you can combine a traditional lead score with Einstein Lead Scoring for a more nuanced view of your incoming leads. This allows your sales team to weigh both sources of information and therefore be better informed when making any follow-up decisions and allows you to route leads to the relevant people based on a combination of factors. This pattern can also be useful to establish trust in the automated lead score prior to further rollout.

- Third, and most importantly, an automated lead score can generate fresh insights into your sales process by pointing out relationships that may not have been obvious. For instance, you may find that buyers from textile companies respond much better to your sales efforts as long as the lead came in through a trade show channel and not the web, whereas your old model would simply have discarded the lead altogether as unpromising.

We will now consider how to configure Einstein Lead Scoring.

Configuring Lead Scoring

The configuration of Einstein Lead Scoring is straightforward, and the options you have to customize it are basic. However, before you get that far, several prerequisites need to be met in your environment.

The main considerations are outlined here:

- The first consideration is that you need 1,000 leads created in your org over the past 180 days, with at least 120 of these having been converted using the standard Salesforce lead conversion process. This requirement is not as hard as it seems, because Salesforce will default to a global model based on anonymized data from a large number of other organizations if you do not have sufficient data of your own. However, the key benefit of having the ML model fit your historic data is, of course, lost when using the global model.

- You should also take a view of the completeness and quality of the data in your Lead object. The better and more complete the data, the better the model that will be generated.

- Furthermore, you should be aware that if you use encrypted fields, these are not available for use in the ML model.

To get a personalized view of how well suited your org is for Einstein Lead Scoring, you can run the **Sales Cloud Einstein Readiness Assessor**. This will generate a **Portable Document Format** (**PDF**) report containing the evaluation of your org against all the prerequisites for the various Sales Cloud Einstein features. We will run this tool later in this chapter under the *Lead scoring at Pickled Plastics Ltd.* section, so we will defer any further discussion till then.

You can only configure the following three elements when setting up Einstein Lead Scoring:

- First, you need to tell Einstein whether you convert leads into contacts and accounts ccounts only, or if you convert them into contacts, accounts, and opportunities. This is simply providing information about the current process needed to build the ML model.

- Second, you can filter the records in the Lead object so that only a subset is considered for lead scoring. This can be useful if you want to try out the new Lead Scoring functionality on a subset of leads or you want to retain an old Lead Scoring model in parallel for certain leads while adopting the new Einstein-based model for others.

- Third, you can exclude some fields from the Lead Scoring model. By default, Einstein will include all fields, and most of the time, that is what you want. However, you may have fields that should be excluded for good reason—for instance, these may be process fields that are only filled out once a lead is ready to be converted. Including these fields would create information leakage in the model and it would cease to be useful.

We will now consider the main architectural points to keep in mind for Einstein Lead Scoring.

Architectural considerations for Lead Scoring

As an architect, you need to recommend the best feature for the customer requirement based on an assessment of the trade-offs involved. For Lead Scoring, we have already discussed a few of the salient points when we were going through an overview of the feature.

Summing up, we have discovered the following points:

- Einstein Lead Scoring is quick to set up and deploy but has limited configurability.

- The platform automatically selects the best model for you based on an internal evaluation of the options, but you have no control over and little explanation of this choice.

- Lead Scoring requires that you use the standard Salesforce Lead and Opportunity objects in something like the standard way.

- All the input data for the model needs to be present as fields on the Lead object directly.

Let's cover each of these in a bit more detail in the following sections.

Fast deploy, limited configurability

This is the archetypical trade-off for most of the out-of-the-box Salesforce Einstein features. We will see this in various guises over and over again in this book. The Lead Scoring capability can be deployed quickly, as long as you have the required historical data, and may work well for your requirements. However, the only configuration it allows is excluding fields and/or only training on a subset of the total data. If you need more granular control, for instance, because you want to train different models for different types of leads or you want to select an algorithm that is used for training, you are out of luck.

The alternatives for those who want this capability are either using a manually created Lead Scoring model or building a more sophisticated ML model on a separate system. A manual model can require a lot of data analysis from the company but often works well in practice. A more sophisticated ML model can give superior results but is fiendishly difficult for most companies to develop and operationalize. In any case, a key decision will be to balance the potential gain versus the extreme simplicity of deploying the out-of-the-box feature.

Automated model selection

As noted, there is no way to select or customize the ML model used by Einstein Lead Scoring to score your leads. That not only means a loss of control but has potential implications for explainability.

Einstein Lead Scoring will give you the major positive and negative factors contributing to the score, but not the detail behind these evaluations. If you are operating in a high-compliance environment, these two elements may weigh against a decision to adopt Einstein Lead Scoring, but for most companies, they are not going to be significant concerns.

Standard process assumption

We've already seen that you have to use the Lead and Opportunity objects in more or less the standard way for Einstein Lead Scoring to work. That means you will have to de-select this feature if you are working in an environment where the sales process doesn't use standard objects or a standard lead conversion process. It will rarely be a good business case to change existing processes solely based on adopting out-of-the-box Einstein features, although, of course, it can be part of a broader picture.

All the data must be in the Lead object

In practice, this will be one of the most common reasons to reject this feature. Salesforce only allows the scoring model to consider fields directly on the Lead object when training. That means if you have data from your marketing platforms or commerce systems, or even just other related objects in Salesforce that are relevant to a lead, then you have to replicate that data into the Lead object to use it with Einstein Lead Scoring. This may not be practical or desirable in more advanced setups.

We've now learned how and when to use Einstein Lead Scoring, so we'll now move on to a practical example using one of Pickled Plastic Ltd.'s requirements.

Lead scoring at Pickled Plastics Ltd.

Pickled Plastics Ltd. has been operating a simple lead scoring model for several years. It uses only three factors—the title of the prospect, the size of the prospect's company, and the time since the last touchpoint with the prospect. This largely works well and the salespeople are skeptical about automated models, however they are created.

Historically, most leads have come from trade shows and industry events, but recently, there has been a strong uptick in web leads, many of which are of dubious quality, and that doesn't seem to evaluate well using the manual lead scoring matrix. Therefore, the **chief information officer (CIO)** has decided to deploy Einstein Lead Scoring to quickly improve the triaging of incoming web leads. The functionality required is to create a model for web leads specifically and then assign high-quality web leads to a special handling queue that has *digital natives* manning it. Other leads will still follow the old lead-handling process. Other web leads should be ignored at this point, and salespeople should be able to use the old model for other types of leads.

To get started, we will look at the Sales Cloud Einstein Readiness Assessor, which is a necessary step to determine whether our org meets the requirements for Sales Cloud Einstein.

Running the Sales Cloud Einstein Readiness Assessor

Before setting up anything on Sales Cloud Einstein, it is a good practice to run the **Sales Cloud Einstein Readiness Assessor**. This will tell you whether you are good to go with using the features.

You should also note that while we are doing work directly in what is effectively a production org for the examples in this book, in a real enterprise org, you should test out all these steps in a sandbox before deployment to production.

To use the assessor, perform the following steps:

1. From **Setup**, enter `Readiness Assessor` in the **Quick Find** box, and then select **Readiness Assessor** under **Einstein**.

2. Click on **LOGIN WITH SALESFORCE** if you are in a production or developer org and **LOGIN WITH SANDBOX** if you are in a sandbox org, as illustrated in the following screenshot:

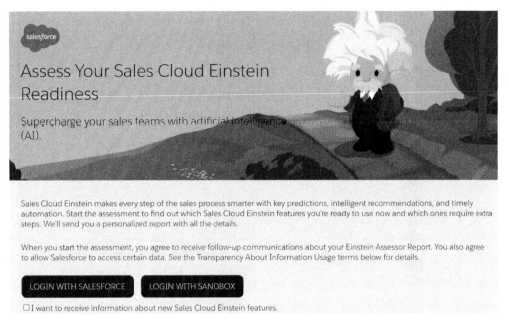

Figure 2.3 – Sales Cloud Readiness Assessor main page

3. A popup will appear, asking you to allow access on your behalf to the org. Click **Allow** to proceed, as shown here:

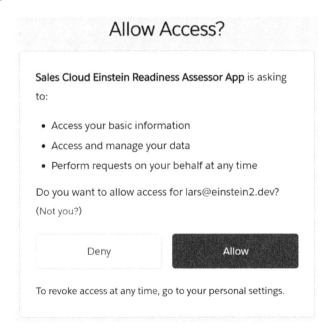

Figure 2.4 – Allowing access to the Sales Cloud Einstein Readiness Assessor app

4. Now, all you have to do is wait until you receive an email telling you the analysis is done.

Then, you can navigate back to the same page and a PDF report will be waiting for you with the status of your org against each of the Sales Cloud Einstein features, as shown here:

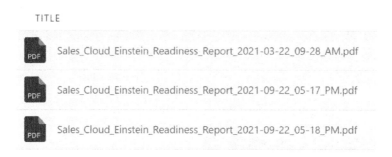

Past Assessments

TITLE

Sales_Cloud_Einstein_Readiness_Report_2021-03-22_09-28_AM.pdf

Sales_Cloud_Einstein_Readiness_Report_2021-09-22_05-17_PM.pdf

Sales_Cloud_Einstein_Readiness_Report_2021-09-22_05-18_PM.pdf

Figure 2.5 – Finished Sales Cloud Einstein readiness report for download

Having now made sure we meet the prerequisites, we will now run the **Assisted Setup** wizard, which will help us set up the necessary permission set assignments that will enable the user to use the Lead Scoring feature.

Assisted Setup for Sales Cloud Einstein

To start setting up any Sales Cloud Einstein feature, you first have to complete the prerequisite actions related to the permission set assignment. This ensures that users have the necessary licensing and permissions in place to use the functionality. You can start this process using the **Assisted Setup** function. Here's how to go about it:

1. From **Setup**, enter `Assisted Setup` in the **Quick Find** box, and then select **Assisted Setup** under **Einstein Sales**, which gets you to this screen:

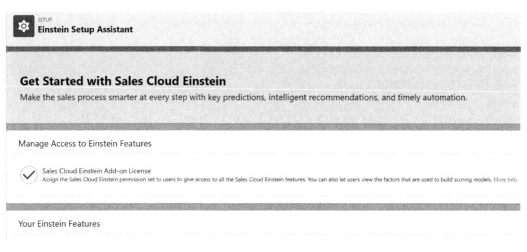

SETUP
Einstein Setup Assistant

Get Started with Sales Cloud Einstein

Make the sales process smarter at every step with key predictions, intelligent recommendations, and timely automation.

Manage Access to Einstein Features

✓ Sales Cloud Einstein Add-on License
Assign the Sales Cloud Einstein permission set to users to give access to all the Sales Cloud Einstein features. You can also let users view the factors that are used to build scoring models. More Info

Your Einstein Features

Figure 2.6 – Assisted Setup wizard start screen

2. Next, click on **Get Started** to take you to the **Permission Sets** screen to assign the right permission set to the users, as shown here:

Permission Set Overview

Description	Access to Sales Cloud Einstein	API Name	SalesCloudEinsteinAll
License ⓘ	Sales Cloud Einstein	Namespace Prefix	force
Session Activation Required	☐	Created By	salesforce.com, inc., 3/8/2021, 7:14 AM
Last Modified By	salesforce.com, inc., 9/14/2021, 11:05 PM		

Apps

Object Settings
Permissions to access objects and fields, and settings such as tab availability

App Permissions
Permissions to perform app-specific actions, such as "Manage Call Centers"

Flow Access
Permissions to execute Flows

Settings that apply to Salesforce apps, such as Sales, and custom apps built on the Lightning Platform

Figure 2.7 – Managing permission sets for Sales Cloud Einstein

3. Click on **Manage Assignments**, select the user that should have access, and click **Done**, as illustrated in the following screenshot:

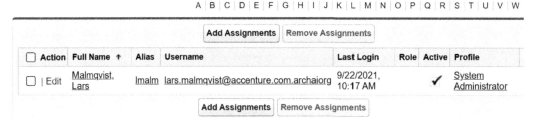

Figure 2.8 – Permission set assignment screen

4. Now, when you go back to **Assisted Setup**, you will have a tick indicating that you have completed the prerequisites, as illustrated in the following screenshot:

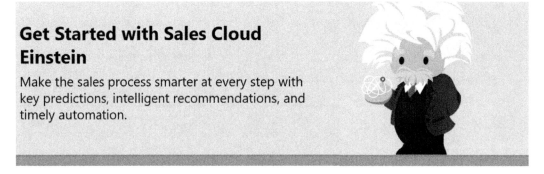

Manage Access to Einstein Features

Figure 2.9 – Sales Cloud Einstein Assisted Setup with prerequisites completed

Having completed the prerequisites, we can now finally begin the actual configuration of the feature.

Lead Scoring configuration flow

Now comes the main part of the work of configuring this feature. We will configure Lead Scoring in line with the requirements specified by Pickled Plastics Ltd.

To start, we need to prepare our developer org so that it matches the Pickled Plastics Ltd. setup. This will involve adding a custom field to the Lead object. Here is how you go about it:

1. Go to **Setup**, select **Object Manager**, and find the **Lead** object.
2. Select **Fields & Relationships** and click **New**.

Choose **Checkbox** for the type and click **Next**.

1. For **Field Name**, enter Ready_for_Conversion and click **Next**.

    Refer to the following screenshot to see a representation of this:

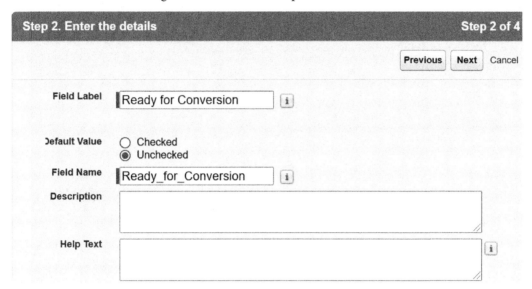

Figure 2.10 – New Custom Field screen

2. Leave the default settings for the remaining steps.

This field is used within Pickled Plastics Ltd. to indicate whether a lead is ready to be converted. It is set by a salesperson once they want to indicate that they are ready to have the lead converted. The lead is then picked up by a **quality assurance (QA)** admin, who will inspect the lead for data quality issues and convert it if it meets the minimum criteria. From an ML point of view, however, this presents a challenge. Since the field is only ever set once we know a lead is going to convert, it is a perfect predictor for that event. It would therefore compromise a model that is trying to predict leads that are likely to convert. This is called **data leakage** and is a major issue in ML. Thankfully, we can correct it easily by simply excluding this field from our lead scoring model.

To get started configuring Lead Scoring, we have to enable the feature. Here's how:

1. Go to **Setup** and search for `Lead Scoring` in the **Quick Find** box, then select **Einstein Lead Scoring**.

2. Click **Get Started** and the configuration wizard will launch, as illustrated in the following screenshot:

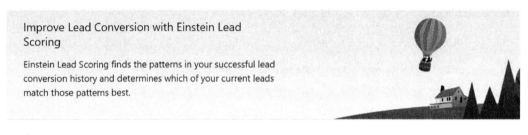

Figure 2.11 – Start screen for Einstein Lead Scoring

3. The first page of the wizard simply lays out the process and you should safely click **Custom**, as illustrated in the following screenshot:

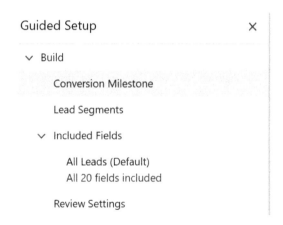

Figure 2.12 – Startup screen for Einstein Lead Scoring configurator

4. The first choice you need to make involves your sales process. You have to select whether you are converting to **Account and Contact** or **Account, Contact, and Opportunity**. Pickled Plastics Ltd. generates opportunities as part of lead conversion, so pick that option and click **Next**, as illustrated in the following screenshot:

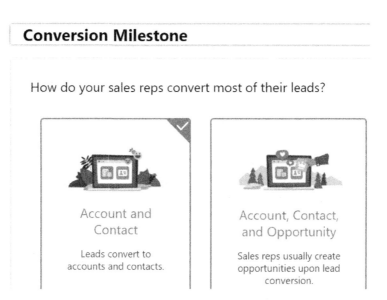

Figure 2.13 – Selecting the lead conversion process

5. The next choice is whether to consider all leads for lead scoring or only a subset. Thinking back to our requirements, we remember that Pickled Plastics Ltd. only wanted to implement the new model for their web leads. Therefore, we select the second option, as shown here:

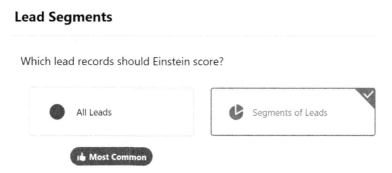

Figure 2.14 – Which leads to score

6. On the next screen, add a row and search for the `Lead Source` field. Make the **Operator** criterion **Equals** and the **Value** criterion **Web**, as illustrated in the following screenshot, and then click **Next**:

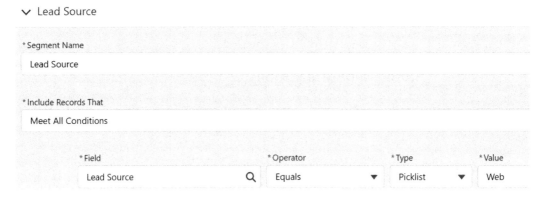

Figure 2.15 – Lead scoring criteria

7. The next part is the most crucial, as this is where we will tell Einstein not to include the **Ready for Conversion** field that would cause data leakage. The recommended option is to include all fields; we will get a warning when selecting to ignore certain fields, but as we know what we're doing, select **Include Fields…**, as illustrated in the following screenshot:

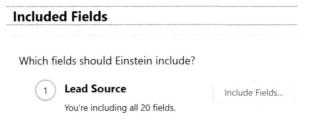

Figure 2.16 – Which fields to consider for scoring

8. On the following screen, search for the **Ready for Conversion** field and deselect it, as illustrated in the following screenshot. Then, click **Apply**:

Figure 2.17 – Deselecting the field that would cause data leakage

9. Congratulations—you are done! Now, all you have to do is wait for the time it takes Einstein to crunch the numbers. Click **Score Leads** to start the process, as illustrated in the following screenshot:

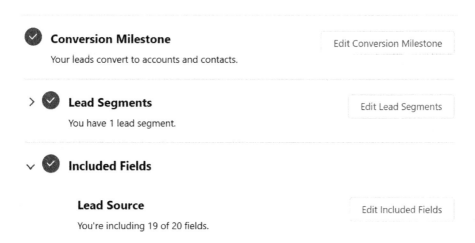

Figure 2.18 – Ready to score

This short example shows the entire configuration flow for Einstein Lead Scoring, and most real-world examples will follow a very similar pattern. Once Einstein is done with the analysis, the score will be available to use on both the record page and list views, and the ScoreIntelligence object will hold the actual numeric score for each lead, which can be used in all the usual locations such as flows, process builders, Apex code, and reports.

Well done! You've built your first Lead Scoring model. We will end this part of the chapter by considering how Opportunity Scoring is subtly different from Lead Scoring.

Opportunity Scoring

If you've followed along this far in the chapter, you are most likely to have a burning question to be answered. We've talked a lot about Lead Scoring, but what about Opportunity Scoring? Wasn't this section meant to be about both? Yes, you are right. But, thankfully, the two are practically indistinguishable from a technical point of view. Between Lead Scoring and Opportunity Scoring, Lead Scoring is by far the more common use case, so it makes sense to focus mostly on that in the run-through. However, in this brief section, we will consider the few areas where Opportunity Scoring is different from Lead Scoring.

The main difference between Opportunity Scoring and Lead Scoring is that the successful event that is tracked by the ML model is different. On an opportunity, it is simply tracked by an opportunity change to its stage in the sales process, to **Closed – Won**. The configuration flow is slightly simpler because you don't need the initial choice of model in this case. The basic requirements are also different. You must have at least 200 closed-won opportunities in the last 24 months, each with a lifespan of at least 2 days. The Opportunity Scoring model also takes a slightly larger dataset into consideration, including the related Account and related Product and Pricebook information. In all other aspects, the user and configuration experience is identical to Einstein Lead Scoring.

This concludes our first main section, looking in detail at one of the Einstein platform features. We started with a big one, so well done for hanging on. We will now look at the perennial problem of generating accurate forecasts—in this case, through the lens of Einstein Forecasting.

Learning about Einstein Forecasting

In the following sections, we will look at the Einstein platform's answer to one of the most vexing business problems around: *How do I generate accurate sales forecasts?* We will look in detail at the feature, its configuration, and the concerns you need to have as an architect when considering using it for a real-world scenario.

The basics of Einstein Forecasting

Forecasting is a central business problem affecting all companies that rely on predictable sales to make money. Turns out, most businesses do the same. The forecasting problem, however, is hard because shifts in demand rarely signal themselves in an easily discoverable way. Not surprisingly, many organizations struggle with producing consistently accurate forecasts.

Einstein Forecasting is Sales Cloud Einstein's contribution toward solving or at least ameliorating this problem. It sits on top of normal Salesforce collaborative, manually updated forecasts, using automated data science to generate predictions based on the data and characteristics of a company's opportunities.

The feature looks at the Opportunity object fields, which not only has a baseline for prediction but also includes related activities and record-change events (for example, how frequently the opportunity is updated) in the mix. It even takes into consideration properties related to the individual sales reps, such as how active they have been on a given opportunity or whether they have a historical tendency to overcommit or undercommit their forecasts. However, you cannot add data from other objects into the mix without replicating it to the Opportunity object, which is a serious limitation in some scenarios. For instance, if you want to take into consideration features from an opportunity's related custom object records, you would have to replicate those features to the opportunity.

To generate predictions, it runs a model tournament behind the scenes to find the best model on a sales team-by-sales team basis. It combines top-down time series-driven forecasting methods such as Holt-Winters and linear regression with feature-driven models such as **gradient boosting machines (GBM)** and bottom-up opportunity field-based predictions. This allows for not only getting a good prediction at the top level but also for analyzing which factors are contributing the most to the forecast outcomes. Predictions are updated several times a day, while the models are updated every month. Unless you have a very fast-moving pipeline, this is unlikely to be a problem.

The predictions generated by Einstein Forecasting are available to sales managers either on the **Forecasts** tab or using the mobile app. The **user experience (UX)** includes both the overall forecasted value set against the committed and achieved forecasts from the traditional forecasting model and also allows extensive drilldown to gain more insight into why a prediction is as it is. Here is how it predicts:

1. First, there is a confidence interval around the main prediction that shows you the range of expected outcomes, given this prediction.

2. Second, you can see how the prediction is constructed from a combination of deals already won in the period—known deals expected to be won, new deals that are expected to come in during the period, and opportunities that will be pulled into the period and thus close down earlier than their present date.

3. Third, you can see the top factors that weigh in positively (for example, this quarter has had a very high win rate) or negatively (for example, there have been low levels of activity for a while), which can help you course-correct if needed.

4. Fourth, you can see trend graphs on both a personal and a team level that show how the prediction will likely materialize over time.

Overall, the features of Einstein Forecasting meet the basic expectations of an AI-enabled forecasting model and are extremely easy to set up and configure. However, while Einstein Forecasting is easy to use, it may or may not be a good fit for your particular requirements.

Let's see which features can be used.

Forecasting use cases

The principal reason to use Einstein Forecasting is to improve forecast accuracy. This is particularly relevant to organizations with low historic accuracy that do not have a substantial in-house data science capability that can build a tailored model. It may be less relevant to organizations with pre-existing detailed analytical forecasting models that have good historical track records.

While forecasting accuracy is indeed the main reason to adopt Einstein Forecasting, this can be done in a complementary way to an existing forecasting process rather than going all in on the ML model. Some organizations may want a second pair of eyes (so to speak) on their pipeline to ferret out blind spots or weaknesses in the overall forecasting process. For these companies, Einstein Forecasting would be valuable as a process improvement tool rather than just for its predictive abilities.

Finally, the insights generated from the bottom-up models that generate the top positive and negative factors can also be used independently of whether the organization is ready to trust the top-level number. Learning that something about this quarter is different from the past, whether positive or negative, can be an important spur to action, even if you retain the traditional forecasting cycle as is.

Now, having considered how to use the Forecasting feature, we will look at its configuration.

Configuring Einstein Forecasting

Configuring Einstein Forecasting is a simple affair once you have confirmed you meet all the prerequisite requirements. However, as there are quite a few of those, the whole process may be less than simple.

Overall, Einstein Forecasting requires the following things to be true:

- Collaborative Forecasts must be enabled and configured. As the old Customizable Forecasting feature has been retired since Summer 2020, this should not be a problem for existing forecasting users, but if you do not have forecasting configured in the org, you must do so prior to configuring Einstein Forecasting. The documentation for doing this can be found at the following link: `https://help.salesforce.com/s/articleView?id=sf.forecasts3_defining_forecasts_settings.htm&type=5`.

- You must use a standard fiscal year; that is to say, it must be a normal 12-month year that follows the Gregorian calendar, although it can start on any day of that year. You can't have custom periods, however.

- You must measure opportunities by opportunity revenue. If you have a custom setup for measuring opportunities, Einstein Forecasting will not work.

- You must have set up a basic forecasting hierarchy, including at least one forecasting-enabled user reporting to a forecast manager.

- You must have been working with opportunities in Salesforce for more than 24 months.

- At least 80% of your opportunities must have the amount populated.

Once all these prerequisites are met, the actual configuration could not be much simpler. You simply activate the feature via Sales Cloud Einstein Assisted Setup, and off you go.

You can see Einstein Forecasting in use in the following screenshot:

Figure 2.19 – Segmentation for Einstein Forecasting

The only real choice you have to make is whether to segment your data to create separate models for new deals versus renewals, as shown in the preceding screenshot. Beyond that, everything runs automatically.

We will now consider the architectural choices around Einstein Forecasting.

Architectural considerations for Einstein Forecasting

All architectural decisions involve a consideration of the goodness of fit. That means not only fitting to requirements but also being fit for the organization's existing system landscape and environment configurations, and not in the least to the culture and processes that are in play in the organization. For Einstein Forecasting, the goodness of fit to the organization is nearly the whole game as far as architectural considerations go.

First, you need to evaluate the extensive prerequisites. If these are not met, it is dubious as to whether Einstein Forecasting will deliver value, as the reengineering effort to fit it in may be extensive. Second, you need to evaluate whether the kind of model you are using with Einstein Forecasting is likely to fit the organization's data. You have little scope for customization, so for instance, if most of the forecast-relevant data lives somewhere else than the Opportunity object, it is probably a no. Third, forecasts are sensitive things, and it can be controversial and dangerous—both internally and toward external investors—to mess too much with a forecasting model. You need to make sure that the organization is ready to adopt, or there will likely be a fallout.

With that said, if you are faced with an organization with low historical forecasting accuracy, good-quality historical data, and a willingness to change, Einstein Forecasting may be a fast way to deliver real value.

Diving into Einstein Activity Capture

Einstein Activity Capture is an automated way of importing messages and calendar events into Salesforce tied to the right contacts in the system. We will go through the basics of this feature and its uses, how to configure it, and what considerations to make as an architect when you are planning to implement it.

Einstein Activity Capture basics

If you have ever interacted with a sales team in a **customer relationship management** (**CRM**)-heavy environment, you will no doubt have heard them complain about the amount of data entry they have to do to keep the CRM up to date. Despite most big organizations having substantial sales operations teams whose job it is (among other things) to keep everything up to date in the CRM, actual salespeople still have to spend time doing basic updates such as logging emails sent to contacts or ensuring that the opportunity status reflects reality.

Enter **Einstein Activity Capture**, a tool designed to automate some of the most uninteresting parts of a sales rep's day job: reconciling contacts, emails, and events from their email client and calendar app to the relevant contacts, accounts, leads, and opportunities in the CRM.

When you install Einstein Activity Capture, which forms a part of several Salesforce licenses—such as Sales Cloud Einstein, Inbox, and High Velocity Sales   and also comes in a Standard version for Sales Cloud with a limited feature set, administrators will be able to create configurations that determine what type of information syncs from users and how that information is mapped into Salesforce, thereby eliminating much of the manual reconciliation sales reps have to do. To be honest, it also means you will have better visibility of activities overall because the data quality in sales CRM objects is nearly always worse than what you would ideally have liked.

The activities are streamed to a separate data repository on **Amazon Web Services** (**AWS**) rather than your main Salesforce org, which has a range of architectural implications. However, from a user perspective, you will see the activities on your normal activity timeline in Salesforce, just as was the case before. However, the activities-related list will no longer work and you won't be able to report on the captured activities using standard reports and dashboards.

Einstein Activity Capture connects exclusively to the main cloud email providers Gmail and Office 365 (on-premises Exchange is also supported under certain conditions), so if you aren't using one of these, you are out of luck.

However, once the connection is established, emails and calendar events up to 6 months back (in the case of Gmail) and 2 years back (in the case of Office 365) will flow into Salesforce and automatically be reconciled to the relevant records in Salesforce. From a user perspective, you will start seeing additional activities synced from your mailbox or calendar on the relevant objects in Salesforce. At present, the Contact, Account, Person Account, Lead, Contract, and Opportunity objects are supported, which will go a long way for organizations that are using more or less standard Sales Cloud to manage their sales process.

Users additionally have control over the sharing of activities. They can be kept private, shared with everyone, or—in a deviation from normal Salesforce sharing practices—shared with a set of up to 20 private or unlisted Chatter groups. Both users and admins can also exclude email addresses or domains from being captured so that sensitive information can be kept out of the system and internal emails can be excluded from the CRM. These two features together help safeguard the inevitable privacy concerns that arise when capturing an email.

The following screenshot shows you how this looks in Salesforce:

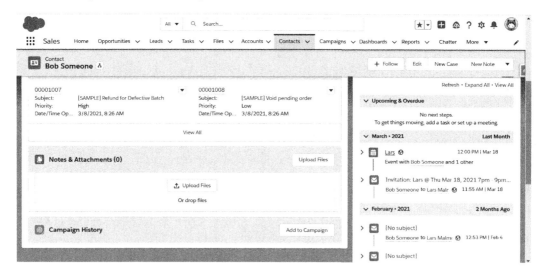

Figure 2.20 – Activity capture in the Salesforce UI

If all this looks and sounds deceptively simple, you are right. So many caveats and considerations need to be taken into account when activating this feature in terms of data privacy, security, and the details of the synchronization. We will cover these elements in the *Configuring Activity Capture* section.

In addition to the user feature discussed earlier, there is also an analytics component to **Einstein Activity Capture**. This includes the **Activity Metrics** feature and the **Activities dashboard**. **Activity Metrics** is a set of fields that can be activated for all users in the org as long as you have a single fully paid **Einstein Activity Capture** license available in the org, whether that comes from High Velocity Sales, Inbox, or Sales Cloud Einstein. These fields summarize important information about the activity related to a Salesforce record such as the last activity date or how long a record has been inactive. These can drive quite sophisticated follow-up processes, so they should be considered valuable in their own regard, not just as an adjunct to **Einstein Activity Capture**. The **Activities dashboard** provides a pre-built Tableau CRM dashboard that goes some way toward compensating for the fact that you can't really report on **Einstein Activity Capture** events. It provides breakdowns of activities by account and activity type, as well as providing trend information on activities over time.

Having understood the basics, let's consider when to use **Einstein Activity Capture**.

Activity Capture use cases

The use case for **Activity Capture** is simply reducing the amount of data entry that needs to be done by sales reps. If you have sales reps that are complaining about the amount of time they spend linking emails and calendar events to records in the CRM, most likely **Activity Capture** will solve this for you. If that is not an issue for you, then it might not be the right fit.

However, there is also an argument to be made for the increased visibility that is generated by using an automated process. A much higher proportion of conversations and events will likely be captured in your CRM, and that information may help kick certain sales processes up a notch because you can now rely more on the history that your company has with a given lead, account, or contact. This may give more flexibility for collaboration across teams and within the sales function.

Also, the **activity metrics** themselves are useful enough that you could make a case for buying a single full **Einstein Activity Capture** license for your org, just to be able to have these fields available to all users. Most organizations will already have some level of customization performing these kinds of rollups, and moving to an out-of-the-box solution will save effort and reduce maintenance in the long run.

Configuring Activity Capture

Einstein **Activity Capture** works based on configurations that define how data from your users' email and calendar synchronizes to Salesforce. Users must be assigned the relevant permission set license and also a separate permission set to access the **Activities** dashboard. The first major choice you will have to make is how to connect your Salesforce org to your email and calendaring application. If you use the Google suite, your choice is simple. The only mechanism that is supported is user-level authentication, which will ask each user to authorize **Einstein Activity Capture** via an **Open Authorization (OAuth)** 2.0 flow. This mechanism is also available with Exchange, but you have two additional options that allow you to configure the connection on an org-to-org level rather than requiring user-by-user authorization.

The org-level connection works by connecting to Office 365 with a company-wide account that uses OAuth 2.0 to connect and access the information on behalf of users. The service account connection works similarly but requires configuring a service account on Office 365 that can impersonate requests on behalf of users. The advantage of these two methods is that you can connect a server-to-server-style connection so that the users won't have to go through the OAuth flow themselves. They will still have to accept the terms of service, however, before they can use the feature.

Creating a configuration is a relatively simple process that requires the admin to name and activate the configuration and then configure which elements from **Email**, **Events**, and **Contacts** to synchronize, their directionality (one-way or two-way), and any exclusion filters for the data to be synced. The admin also needs to configure the default sharing level for activities to select whether newly synced activities are shared by default or not. Refer to the following screenshot for an overview of this:

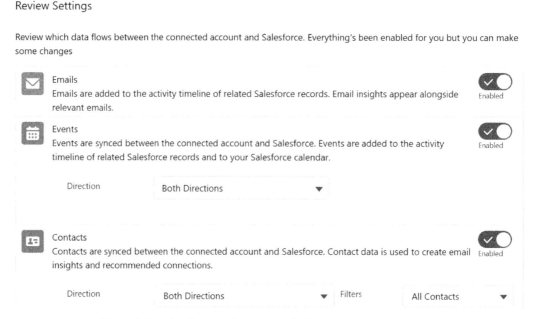

Figure 2.21 – Synchronization options for Einstein Activity Capture

When **Einstein Activity Capture** is activated, a parallel org is created automatically on AWS to hold the information captured from the user's email and calendaring application. It is important to know that you have no control over this environment and will only be able to see the reflection of the data in Salesforce, which is brought in via an **application programming interface** (**API**). This also means that things you might be expecting to be able to do with these activities, such as accessing via automation or in a report, simply cannot be done.

The configuration options are not simple but neither are the architectural choices involved, as we will now consider in the next section.

Architectural considerations for Activity Capture

Einstein Activity Capture is a very powerful tool, but there are at least three important considerations that need to be kept in mind before adopting at scale, outlined as follows:

- **Einstein Activity Capture** involves your org in a three-way integration with bidirectional synchronization across each link.

- **Einstein Activity Capture** uses a separate AWS org to hold the captured activity data.

- Email and calendar data are always a compliance and privacy headache.

Let's go through these in turn.

Three-way, bidirectional integration

When you install **Einstein Activity Capture**, you at the same time install integrations between Salesforce and your email and calendaring application (G Suite or Microsoft Exchange) and Salesforce and AWS—that is to say, your Salesforce org becomes the hub for a bidirectional three-way integration. The following diagram shows the architecture of **Einstein Activity Capture** taken from the relevant security guide (`https://resources.docs.salesforce.com/latest/latest/en-us/sfdc/pdf/sales_activity_capture_security.pdf`):

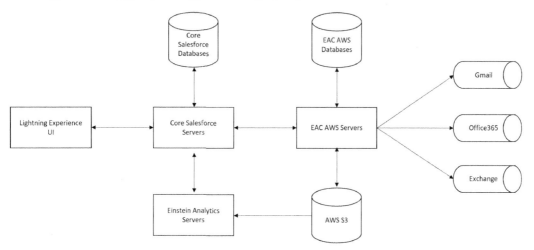

Figure 2.22 – Einstein Activity Capture architecture

In most cases, we trust Salesforce to keep everything running smoothly, and we can probably make the same assumption for **Einstein Activity Capture**. However, in most large organizations, allowing this kind of setup will necessitate getting your infrastructure, security, and compliance teams involved to sign off on the solution before any production deployment.

Separate AWS org

The fact that your data for **Einstein Activity Capture** lives in a separate AWS org means that you have to live with quite a few limitations around what you can do with it.

Specifically, you cannot do the following:

- Use it in dashboards and reports.

- Use it in flows or process builders.

- Customize activities in the way you can for standard activities.

- Use it in Apex code or via an API.

- Control sharing via mechanisms other than non-standard sharing to Chatter groups.

Whether this matters to you will depend on your setup, and of course, you can keep doing all of these things for activities not captured by **Einstein Activity Capture**.

Privacy and compliance

Emails and calendar entries often contain **personally identifiable information** (**PII**) and are frequently of a sensitive kind. What is worse, because of the unstructured components of this data, we can rarely guarantee where such information may appear. Given the non-standard architecture for this feature, you are unlikely to be fully covered by your existing compliance provisions. This, in most cases, means designing and signing off a separate compliance mechanism for **Einstein Activity Capture** when you do the implementation. That isn't a show-stopper in most cases as the compliance features are good and Salesforce has published a security whitepaper on the topic. However, it is an effort that needs to be included in any estimate for implementing this feature in any organization that deals with any kind of sensitive data.

We have now considered **Einstein Activity Capture** in some detail and are now ready to move onto the final feature we need to consider in this chapter, **Einstein Conversation Insights**.

Examining Einstein Conversation Insights

Einstein Conversation Insights is a feature that enables better visibility of what's going on in the sales organization through an analysis of the content of captured sales calls. We will look at the details of this feature, why you would want to use it, and what you need to consider in the following sections.

Einstein Conversation Insights basics

Einstein Conversation Insights is a part of the High Velocity Sales license that also includes a range of other sales-related features and aims to improve sales coaching by allowing managers to zoom in on the parts of sales calls that provide the most impactful or coachable material without having to listen through the entire recording for every call. It does this by scanning transcriptions of recorded sales calls for keywords that are either predefined (for example, words related to price or pricing), related to products or competitors of your company, or that you have defined as custom keywords during the setup of the feature.

Einstein Conversation Insights does not itself record conversations. Instead, it relies on an external recording provider to furnish a recording that is then analyzed by Conversation Insights and stored directly in Salesforce in the Voice Call object. At the time of writing, the supported providers for audio recordings are Salesforce Dialer, Tenfold, and Red Box, and Zoom is supported for video recordings.

Once you have connected a recording provider to Einstein Conversation Insights, the recording is transcribed using a specialized language model. Salesforce AI has published a model card describing this model, so in this case, we can give some details. The model transforms a sequence of phonemes taken from an acoustic model and uses this to transcribe the audio file using the most likely sequence of words.

The model has been trained originally on the Fisher English Training Speech, a language corpus that is a 2003 database of recorded conversations created by the **Linguistic Data Consortium** (**LDC**) for the express purposes of developing automated speech recognition systems. In initial training, it had pilot precision of 89% and recall of 83%, which if you are not an ML expert means that Conversation Insights is right 89% of the time about the keywords it recognizes and catches 83% of the keywords that were there to recognize. It is, however, continuously updated with more data from Salesforce users, so it is expected to have improved since its initial bootstrapping. Nonetheless, Salesforce is only committing to 80% precision and 40% recall.

Salesforce exposes the outputs of this analysis to users in an elegant web UI that shows the entire conversation and allows you to navigate the conversation by the mention of specific keywords, which defines key moments of the conversation. You can also see who is speaking directly in the conversation overview and details about the call, such as the talk/listen-to ratio.

You can see an overview of the Conversation Insights UI in the following screenshot:

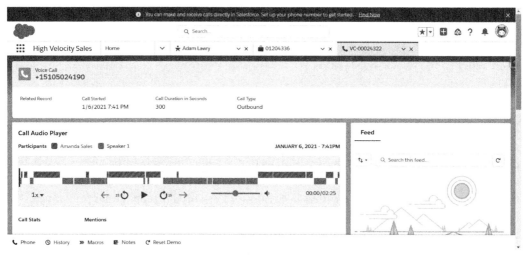

Figure 2.23 – Conversation Insights UI

There is also a strong analytics component to Conversation Insights, where managers can drill into keyword mentions across conversations. For instance, you might discover that a given product is receiving a lot fewer mentions than it used to or that a given competitor is coming up a lot more often.

Finally, managers also receive a daily email highlighting conversations that might be particularly interesting for them from new ones that have arrived, which—depending on your work style—might be a killer feature or extremely annoying.

Conversation Insights use cases

The primary use case for Einstein Conversation Insights is sales coaching. That can come with different emphasis, however. Some organizations will want to use the feature to cover a larger number of conversations by only reviewing moments related to particular keywords that sales managers by experience know will be particularly challenging to reps. However, you can also use it to target more specifically, for instance, particular common objections or what to do when a particular competitor is brought up as part of a conversation. That way, Conversation Insights can be used both as part of the day-to-day improvement and training process, but also to create targeted interventions around problem areas.

The analytical use case for Conversation Insights is also fairly strong. In a nutshell, you get data on what your reps are talking to customers about and what your customers' key interests are at any point in time. Most sales managers will have a pretty strong gut feel for these things, but having data is a nice complement. In particular, it may provide a forward warning about upcoming competitors or a shift in market interest relating to products and services. These will show quicker in the sales conversation than they will on the bottom line.

We will now look at the configuration of Conversation Insights.

Configuring Conversation Insights

Given the sophistication of the feature, it is surprisingly easy to set up. This feat is achieved by outsourcing the complexities of actually getting the recordings from the phone system and into Salesforce for analysis to the recording provider. Currently, there are four recording providers available, three for audio and one for video. For audio, you can go with the Sales Dialer or AppExchange products from Tenfold or Red Box. For video, only Zoom is supported. You can see a current list of products on the Salesforce AppExchange website. Each product defines its own way to configure the recording provider, so there is no general answer to how this is done. The following screenshot shows **Call Coaching Integration Solutions** (Call Coaching was the previous name for Conversational Insights):

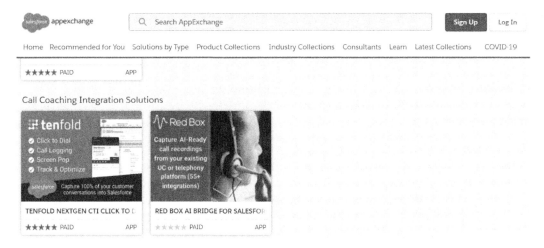

Figure 2.24 – Available solution providers for Conversation Insights

Once the recording provider has been connected, the rest of the configuration process effectively consists of typing in keywords. You need to enter keywords in both predefined categories for **Products and Competitors** in a predetermined configuration screen, as well as any custom keywords that you want to track for your own use. That, however, is it as far as setup goes. Based on your configuration, the recordings will start to transfer in and be analyzed for use within your Salesforce environment.

Having managed to get your calls into Salesforce for analysis, we'll look at the architectural choices involved in implementing this feature.

Architectural considerations for Conversation Insights

The main thing to consider about Einstein Conversation Insights is that it has quite a North American slant. The language model is optimized for American English, as well as the recording providers, and also, the way Salesforce uses the recordings is focused on complying principally with US law. This means that if you are an international company that principally holds sales conversations in languages other than English, you are out of luck at this point. The same goes if you are a company that has to comply with stricter privacy and compliance regimes, such as those found within the **European Union** (**EU**). However, if you are working for a **United States** (**US**) company and are focused on US consumers or businesses, this product will likely be a good fit.

You do, however, in any case, need to vary which keywords you configure within the feature. For instance, any tracking of PII is strictly off limits and you shouldn't try to circumvent this— for instance, by entering a key stakeholder's name as a custom keyword. Also, because the feature is keyword-based, you can get misrecognition in cases where the keywords you're searching for are not easily distinguishable from everyday words. You should pay careful attention to the keywords you provide to maximize the value you get from the feature.

The low configurability of the feature is less of a concern in this case, as very few companies will have the capability to build something like this under their own steam. However, because it comes bundled with the High Velocity Sales package, architects should in most cases carefully consider its placement within a complete High Velocity Sales implementation rather than in isolation.

Now that we've covered the main features of Sales Cloud Einstein, we are ready to move on to the next topic. But first, let's spend a moment summarizing what we've learned.

Summary

In this chapter, we have looked at some of the key parts of the Salesforce Einstein platform, including elements from the Sales Cloud Einstein and High Velocity Sales offerings. We started by learning about Lead Scoring and Opportunity Scoring, which deliver an easy-to-deploy ML-based model for judging the quality of leads and opportunities. We saw in detail how to configure this feature, which is a good representation of the typical flow for configuring out-of-the-box Einstein features.

Then, we reviewed Einstein Forecasting, an automated ML-based forecasting model, which uses your historical opportunity data to generate a prediction of whether your current sales efforts are on track.

We then devoted considerable time to exploring Einstein Activity Capture, a nifty feature that can save sales reps a lot of time entering data into the CRM by automatically matching email, contact, and event data from users' emails and calendars to the relevant records in Salesforce.

Finally, we had a look at Einstein Conversation Insights, a feature that takes sales coaching to the next level by transcribing and analyzing conversations between sales reps and potential customers based on an advanced language model that can identify key moments in a conversation.

For all of these features, we looked at what the features can and can't accomplish, how to configure them, and what you should take into consideration to decide whether they are right for your use case.

This concludes our first look at the features of the Einstein platform. You have learned a lot, so pat yourself on the back. However, this is no time to rest on our laurels. Sales is just one area where Salesforce AI features can deliver value. In the next chapter, we will look at the other classic area of Salesforce functionality and zoom in on AI for service.

Questions

1. What feature would you use if you wanted to know the likelihood that a lead will convert to an opportunity?

2. Which external cloud provider is used by some Salesforce AI services such as Einstein Activity Capture?

3. For what geographical region is Einstein Conversational Insights particularly well suited?

3
Salesforce AI for Service

This chapter will cover the core service-related AI options in Salesforce. We will systematically look at Einstein Bots, Einstein Case Classification, Einstein Article Recommendations, and Einstein Reply Recommendations. As we do, we will cover the main features and configuration options available. For each topic, we will also discuss the pros and cons and what things an architect has to think about when evaluating the feature. We will also extend our Pickled Plastics scenario by building a bot that answers reseller questions.

In this chapter, we're going to cover the following main topics:

- Introducing Service Cloud Einstein
- Deploying Einstein Bots
- Optimizing support with Einstein Article Recommendations
- Speeding up chat with Einstein Reply Recommendations
- Alleviating manual data entry with Einstein Case Classification

After completing this chapter, you will know how to architect solutions using Service Cloud Einstein.

Technical requirements

To follow along with the hands-on parts of this chapter, you will need to register for an org with Einstein Bots enabled, which includes a standard Salesforce developer org. This must also include the Sales Cloud Einstein Dev Org, which you may have created in the previous chapter. If you need a new one, you can sign up for one here: `https://developer.salesforce.com/signup`.

The Code in Action (CiA) video for the chapter can be found at `https://bit.ly/2WJhqbJ`.

Introducing Service Cloud Einstein

Service Cloud Einstein is the customer service offering of the Einstein Platform. It consists of four core offerings:

- **Einstein Bots**, a complete framework for building and deploying bots across multiple channels while leveraging Salesforce's outstanding NLP capabilities

- **Einstein Article Recommendations**, a pre-built machine learning model that makes suggestions for relevant articles based on the text in a case and past case article attachments

- **Einstein Reply Recommendations**, another pre-built model that is applied on top of your historical chat transcripts to generate suggested replies based on the context of a chat conversation

- **Einstein Case Classification**, a model that is built on top of your case history and generates suggestions

As can be surmised from these features, the primary purpose of Service Cloud Einstein is to make your customer service agents more efficient and accurate. By deploying bots, you can free up agent time by collecting information in advance, answer frequent questions, or solve simple cases. The two recommendation offerings save agents time by making in-context suggestions, saving them the time to search for articles or to formulate a common reply in a chat. Case Classification, depending on the level of automation you are willing to go for, can save substantial amounts of back-office processing time by auto-filling fields on your cases.

In contrast to Sales Cloud Einstein, the Service Cloud version does not make high demands on your process. If you are using the standard Case object and standard Salesforce Chat, it will work. It does, however, make relatively high demands of your dataset. In an ideal world, you'd have at least 10,000 cases and 1,000 chat transcripts ready to use in your org. You can make do with fewer cases, but the quality of the models will not be optimal. That being said, if you have a large Service Cloud deployment and you are looking to make efficiencies, Service Cloud Einstein is worth more than a casual look.

In the rest of this chapter, we will go through these features and cover the details of their functionality, configuration, and requirements, as well as the key points of architectural concern that should be taken into consideration when selecting the feature for a project. For Einstein Bots, we will also apply ourselves hands-on to configure some of Pickled Plastics Ltd.'s requirements.

Deploying Einstein Bots

Einstein Bots is a framework for creating chatbots directly on the Salesforce platform. In the following sections, we will explore how and why we should do this.

Einstein Bots basics

A chatbot or bot, at the most basic level of understanding, is a piece of software that conducts a conversation either in text or in speech. Odds are you have interacted with a bot recently. Maybe you use Siri for voice search or have Alexa read you the news. Or, you might have encountered one when reaching out to customer service or when trying to book a ticket for some upcoming event. It is fair to say that conversational user interfaces are growing faster than any other type of human-computer interaction at present.

More and more companies are jumping on the bot bandwagon and for good reason. Deployed skillfully, they can be powerful allies in the quest to improve customer service without going bust. In particular, they can reduce the length of time your customer service agents need to spend on chats with customers by handling routine inquiries, screening and routing the call to the right agent, and gathering the initial information needed to complete a request before it is handed over to a human for finalization.

Einstein Bots is the Salesforce version of this increasingly popular category of artificial agents and it contains a complete on-platform framework for developing, testing, and deploying chatbots across a variety of channels. As always, the key advantage you get relative to other bot frameworks is the direct access to platform data, the absence of any third-party integrations, and the ability to manage and monitor the process end to end directly from within Salesforce. For many brands, this will be a winning proposition for simple bot deployments, although, in all honesty, there are stronger performing technical platforms out there for training custom chatbots if you have aspirations of being at the bleeding edge.

The general guidance for Einstein Bots is to never think of them as replacements for human agents. They can't handle long or complex conversations, get confused quite easily, and need to stick to a very tightly defined domain to be successful. On the other hand, if you can define routine conversations within a tightly scoped domain, you get fast, simple to deploy, and always-on resources to help your customer service team get the job done.

Einstein Bots is built on top of Salesforce's world-leading research into **Natural Language Programming** (**NLP**). It leverages this learning capability alongside the automation capabilities of the Salesforce platform to provide a rich model for building and deploying bots. In contrast to many other NLP platforms, it supports a variety of major languages, rather than just English. It can also be deployed both on the web, mobile, Facebook, and WhatsApp for greater reach. The feature set that will appeal most to existing Salesforce customers, however, is the ability of bots to query CRM data directly and do things on the platform using Flows or Apex actions. This allows quite complex operations to be automated if the right conversational flow can be configured on the frontend.

We will now look at the ways bots can enhance various areas within a CRM.

Bots use cases

You can group bot use cases into three broad categories: qualification, deflection, and routing. In the following sections, we will review each of these in turn.

Qualification

Qualification use cases focus on collecting the necessary information that will enable a customer service agent to quickly resolve an issue once the chat has been transferred to a human being. This will usually include information that identifies the customer and allows the information about that customer to be presented immediately to the agent at the point of transfer. In addition, there will be questions specific to the context of the individual bot. For a customer service bot, you might ask questions about the type of problem the customer is experiencing, and then have them type in a qualitative description that the agent can read to get the basic lay of the land. For a sales bot, in contrast, you may collect information regarding what product categories or preferences the potential customer is looking to discuss.

The qualification process is not only about gathering information that will help the agent at the point of transfer. It also serves the highly useful functions of keeping the customer engaged during the waiting time for an agent to become available and thereby reduce the rate of dropped calls. You may even want to overprovision the options for the bot conversation, with the view of keeping the customer engaged during their wait.

Deflection

Deflection use cases are what most people intuitively think of when they need to come up with options for what a bot might do. A deflection use case is a conversation that happens with a bot so that a human won't need to do it themselves. It includes cases such as answering questions about products and services, giving a status on an order or service request, or looking up articles in the knowledge base based on the customer's query.

It also includes routine transactions, such as a customer reordering a past order, booking a simple appointment, or submitting some additional documentation that has been requested as part of a verification process. The boundaries between what counts as a routine transaction and what needs human interaction are fluid and will be very company-specific. As a general rule, if you have a long history of doing something and it happens the same way more than 80% of the time, you may want to include it as an option in a bot. If not, you may not have as good results. In any case, gracefully handling errors in bot understanding and seamlessly transferring to a human agent when it is required are both indispensable best practices for deploying a bot, especially when you are dealing with a deflection use case.

Routing

Routing use cases resemble qualification use cases in terms of collecting information from the user before a transfer. However, rather than focusing on keeping the user engaged and gathering information to pass on to the agent, the focus in a routing use case is on redirecting the call to the right agent. Routing use cases are particularly relevant in complex organizations, where finding the right expert to talk to might take some digging around.

It is also relevant to organizations that have highly specialized support teams, in which case the bot effectively takes the place of the ubiquitous **Interactive Voice Response (IVR)** solution found in so many call centers. Finally, routing use cases are essential in complex bot setups, where many bots have been deployed to deal with specific use cases – remember that bots need to be highly specialized to perform well. In such architectures, a routing bot will gather the necessary information to hand you on to the specialized bot that will be able to help you with your particular request.

With an understanding of the various bot use cases in hand, we will now proceed to look at how to configure Einstein Bots.

Configuring Bots

The options for configuring Bots are vast and we won't be able to cover everything in this chapter. However, whatever your bot will be doing and how you will achieve that goal, it all starts with some basic setup. The basic way to create a bot is to launch the guided setup flow from the main Einstein Bots interface.

You will have the option of creating a new bot from scratch or creating it from a template (in Beta, at the time of writing). The wizard will take you through steps to configure your bot's greetings, the menu items you would like available as part of the opening dialog, and the chat deployment that you will link this bot to. As we mentioned previously, there is no way you can have bots without configuring the chat and chat deployments. This is true even if you don't ever intend to deploy your bot to a chat channel, but will use a channel such as WhatsApp or Messenger instead. The most important step is the last one because the wizard will set up several basic system dialogs on your behalf that you would otherwise have to deal with yourself.

Once you have configured your basic bot, it is time to make it do things. You'll need to master the following four key concepts to accomplish this:

- Dialogs
- Entities
- Variables
- Intents

Together, these form the building blocks you have available in the bot builder to manage the bot's conversational interface and the actions it takes based on the conversation. Let's go through each of these in turn.

Dialogs are the basic units of control in your conversational interface. They are snippets of conversations around a particular customer intent that moves the bot toward accomplishing a goal. For instance, for an Order bot, you might start with a Welcome dialog, then move on to an Order Status dialog based on the customers' selection, then move to a dialog asking for any further questions, before ending with a finishing dialog saying goodbye to the customer. Effectively, the flow of dialogs making up a conversation is the conversational equivalent of a graphical user interface in a traditional visual system.

Dialogs are made up of a sequence of elements. There are four basic elements available in Einstein Bots:

- **Message**: Displays a configurable message to the user. This can be predefined or based on variables you configure.

- **Question**: Asks the user a question. You can configure fixed choices for the user to select or you can have them type in an answer in free text.

- **Action**: Have the bot do something. In practice, this usually means calling an Apex Action or a Flow to take some action on the platform, but you can also call a range of standard actions, for instance, to send an email without needing to configure it yourself.

- **Rule**: A rule action fires when a configurable condition is met at a point in the dialog. It can do things such as call another dialog to get more information, redirect the user to another dialog, or transfer a user to a human agent.

It can be quite complicated to design a conversational flow that works well across a range of scenarios, and most companies will find that they need extensive testing and optimization of their bot dialogs both before launch and on an ongoing basis to ensure that the user has a good experience.

The second key concept is that of an **entity**. An entity represents a data type that you intend to collect from a customer. While you can create custom entities as you see fit, Salesforce provides system entities corresponding to standard data types: **Text, DateTime, Date, Money, Number, Person, Location, Organization, Percent, Boolean**, and **Object** (standard Salesforce or custom). The principal place where you use entities is within question elements of dialogs. Don't let that fool you into thinking they aren't crucially important. Entities are the way you get input from the user and have to be considered carefully.

When a customer answers a query from the bot, the answer is parsed based on the expected entity and put into a variable you specify. If it can't match the customer's answer to a valid value for the expected entity, you will enter the domain of conversation repair, where you will elicit the information from the customer once more, but rephrase or add more context to enable them to answer more closely to what you were expecting.

You can create custom entities using two different methods, depending on the complexity of your need. The first way is to provide a value list. With this option, you simply list all the answers you consider acceptable in an, often quite long, list. The answer given by the customer will be considered adequate if – and only if – it matches exactly one of the elements on that list. You group the underlying values by providing synonyms so that many synonyms can map to the same value that you will use in your logic.

Variables are familiar territory and they work in the bot context, as they do in just about any other context. In Einstein Bots, they come in three variants: **System**, **Context**, and **Custom**. System variables hold system-level information and are currently limited to the Referer Bot ID for bot-to-bot transfers and the last string of text input by the customer. Context variables let you maintain contextual relationships, even in the case of transfers between channels. For instance, the Salesforce contact ID of the customer the bot is talking to is a context variable. Custom variables are what you use for your logic. There is a fairly standard set of variable types available for custom variables: **Text**, **Number**, **Boolean**, **Object**, **Date**, **DateTime**, **Currency**, and **Id**. You specify these as needed and they are available for feeding into Flows or Actions, which will do things on the bot's behalf.

The final crucial configuration elements for Einstein Bots are **intents**. Intents use the NLP capabilities of the Einstein platform to derive the customer's intention from the words they use in natural language. Most companies, when they are starting with bots, will tend to select an interface that is heavily driven by menus and fixed choices, somewhat like a glorified IVR. However, as they get more comfortable with bots and have more data to work with, moving toward a more natural conversation flow is the *natural* next step. Intents are effectively trained by providing example data. These are called **Intent Sets** and consist of example **Utterances** that exemplify what the bot should be listening for to activate an NLP-driven dialog based on user input. The better your training data, the better the performance of your bot in a dialog, so this is a critical element. Ideally, you need at least 50 examples for each intent you intend to use.

The configuration of most bots will tend to start with a simple menu-driven approach, move toward a hybrid approach as you replace a few well-defined dialogs with intent-driven ones, and then move toward a more pure-play NLP-based interface when you reach full maturity.

With these four key elements, you will be able to configure very advanced bots that can, in theory, accomplish just about whatever you want. But there is also plenty of scope for things to go wrong, and a measured implementation approach is advisable when adopting bots, rather than an all-in approach. You can see an overview of these elements in the following diagram:

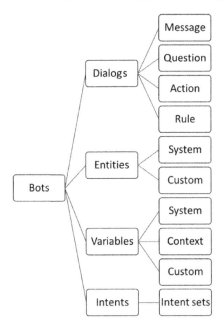

Figure 3.1 – Bot concept map

Having looked at the configuration of bots, we will now consider the architectural decisions that introducing them involves.

Architecture considerations for Bots

The architectural considerations for Bots revolve heavily around their status as conversational agents that introduce a new type of user interface into your organization, but also act on your behalf as agents of the company with a degree of predictability that isn't always perfect. We will also need to consider the architectural consequences of having potentially large populations of bots that interact as part of the overall architecture, and also look at how bots can be monitored and managed over time.

We will start by looking at conversational design.

Conversational design

Conversation is the UX of bots. The way you design the conversational flow makes the difference between a great and a terrible user experience. You can't get around this. And unfortunately, while Salesforce gives us a good baseline for our graphical user interfaces, the same is not true for bots. You are left with only bare rudiments predefined and the bulk of the work is up to you. As an architect, that means you may have to think a lot more about user interaction when you are designing bots than you would in a GUI-based project.

Thankfully, Salesforce has provided some best practices for designing conversational flows. We will cover the main points here, but you may refer to this link for more information: `https://trailhead.salesforce.com/content/learn/modules/conversation-design`.

The following are must-have conversational elements:

- Greeting the customer
- Having the bot introduce itself as a bot
- Giving a clear statement of what the bot can help with; for instance, by providing initial menu options
- Using appropriate conversational turn-taking with the customer
- Leaving enough time for the user to read any messages before sending the next one
- Providing a way to follow up on a conversation if an agent isn't available for a transfer and there is an issue
- Exhibiting basic politeness, such as saying *Thank you* or *You're welcome* when appropriate
- Closing the conversation clearly
- Drawing attention to the available options at each stage of the conversation; for instance, by stating the options

The following are a few nice-to-have conversational elements:

- Calling the customer by their name
- Allowing the customer to finish typing before sending the next message
- Using menus to give the customer well-defined options
- Giving the customer quick reply options, such as yes/no buttons when appropriate
- Escalating to a human when there is trouble in the conversation
- Maintaining a consistent tone of voice in line with your company's brand
- No shouting (such as using ALL CAPS)
- Using emojis where appropriate
- Asking the customer for feedback on the conversation

This guidance, however, is very high-level and you can easily follow all of these points and still build a bad bot. If you are serious about bots, consulting a dedicated resource on conversational design is a great way to invest your time.

Bots, however, are also agents that do work on your behalf. What that entails will be the focus of our next section.

Bots as agents

Bots are agents that work on your company's behalf and are driven by customer conversation. They have profiles for security purposes and interact across well-defined channels and scenarios. However, they are less predictable than classically logic-driven automation, especially as you move toward more pure-play NLP-type bots. That means you have to think hard about security, predictability, and error correction when it comes to bots. If you overshoot the mark, it is possible to think of scenarios where a mistyped or misrecognized user input and an overly general piece of Apex code creates major havoc on your CRM data.

It is best to set strict limits on your bot's actions and have extra checks to ensure you are along the expected path. When there is confusion or uncertainty, trying to recover automatically is laudable, but if it continues, usually the best approach is to redirect to a human being. It comes back to the basic point that you shouldn't try to think of bots as replacements for people, but as supplements. Stepping too far across that line may subject your org to unforeseen consequences as bot complexity grows beyond a manageable size.

As your bot estate grows, you will also need to consider the interaction between bots. That will be our next topic.

Multi-bot architecture

Bots need to be specialized to work well. This is a basic tenet of bot design. The more you can specialize the domain and functionality of your bot, the more likely you are to be able to provide a great experience for your customers. But then what do you do when you have many bots doing many different things? As the number of bots grows, there may be gray zones in terms of which should be handling what query, it may get cumbersome to have separate configurations for each bot, or you may simply want to present all of your bots in a single interface to help the customer.

Multi-bot architecture is a complex topic and we cannot cover it adequately here. However, a good starting point is usually building a routing bot that forwards the customer to the right endpoint based on the information it collects. This is one of the major use cases for routing bots. That way, you can have a single point of entry into your bot population without losing the ability to have deeply specialized domain bots responding to queries. It also helps in separating development across teams if you have several projects going on at once.

Bots, once deployed, will need ongoing monitoring. We will explore this topic next.

Monitoring bots

Building bots is an incremental process. You start with assumptions about what users are likely to say and how they say it and then you continuously refine that over time to accurately reflect what happened as opposed to what you assumed. This cycle is crucial to a successful bot deployment and you have to plan for it in your initial implementation plan and overall design.

Salesforce provides a range of tools to help you do this, including an AppExchange package with common bot metrics, a model management page to track the performance of your intents, and the ability to include bot-related data in both standard reports and Tableau CRM. In other words, there is no scarcity of tool support in this area, but you will still have to plan for what and why to measure specifically for your bots.

Now that we've covered the basic theory of Einstein Bots, we will look at a hands-on example.

Einstein Bots at Pickled Plastics Ltd.

Pickled Plastics Ltd. has a large community of resellers across countries. Many of these resellers are small stores that do not have considerable IT infrastructure or skills available. To serve these customers, Pickled Plastics is looking to introduce bots to handle common reseller transactions via a variety of channels, including web chat, Facebook Messenger, and WhatsApp. One of the most common queries that is found across countries and resellers is an inventory check on a particular **Stock Keeping Unit** (**SKU**). Resellers will call to check the stock level of items when planning for restocking orders or when they have a major order of something in the pipeline, but don't have the local inventory to fulfill it. The **Chief Information Officer** (**CIO**) has mandated that this query be used as a **Proof-of-Concept** (**PoC**) for Einstein Bots, and in the following section, we will be implementing a simple bot to demonstrate the viability of answering this query automatically. We will start by covering the prerequisite of setting up a **Chat Deployment** in the Org.

Setting up a Chat Deployment

To set up a Chat Deployment, perform the following steps:

1. Log in to your org and go to **Service Setup Home**, where you can access the relevant configuration wizard, as shown in the following screenshot:

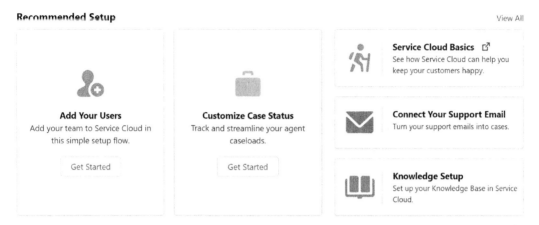

Figure 3.2 – Service Setup Home screen

2. Click **View all** and select **Chat with Customers** to start the configuration, as shown here:

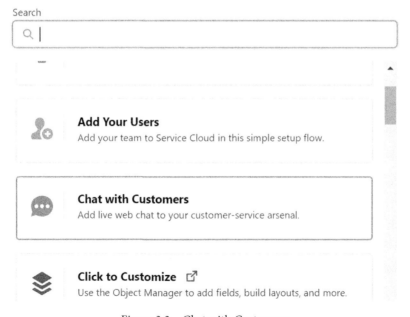

Figure 3.3 – Chat with Customers

3. Click **Start** to start the process.

Chat with customers instantly
Connect with your customers wherever they are with live, web-based chat. With a click of a button (literally), your customers can get stellar support.
Start

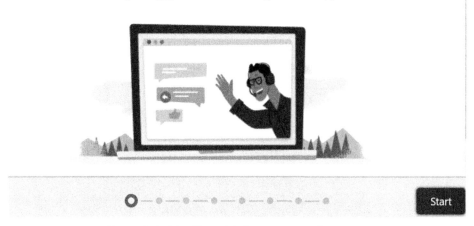

Figure 3.4 – The Chat with Customers configuration

4. In the next step, you will configure a chat queue. Here, you can enter any name you like. Also, select yourself as a user to assign the right licenses and add yourself as a member to the queue, as shown in the following screenshot:

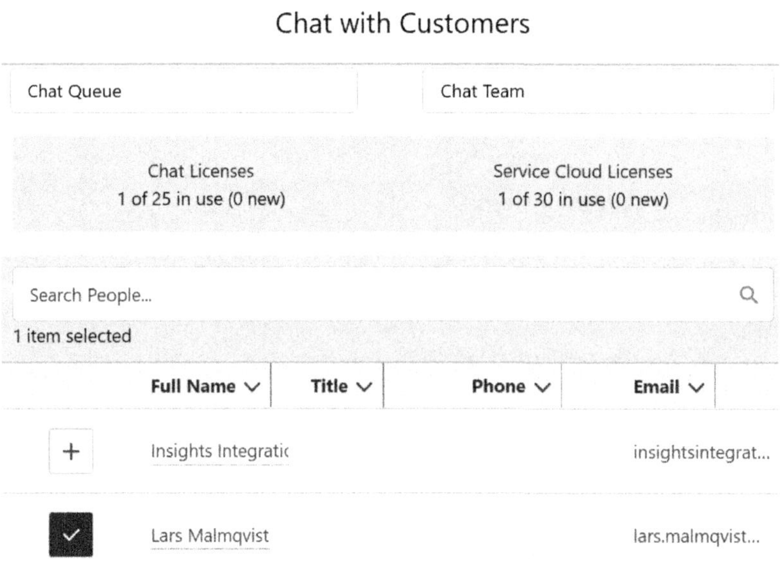

Chat with Customers
Chat Queue
Chat Team
Chat Licenses
1 of 25 in use (0 new)
Service Cloud Licenses
1 of 30 in use (0 new)
Search People...
1 item selected
Full Name
Title
Phone
Email
Insights Integratic
insightsintegrat...
Lars Malmqvist
lars.malmqvist...

Figure 3.5 – Creating a chat queue

5. The next step allows us to set a priority for the chat queue. Leave this as **1**.

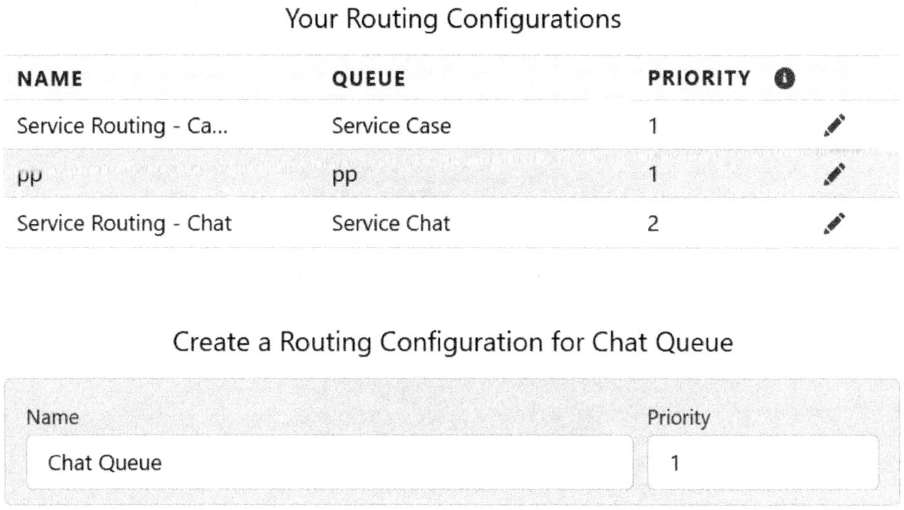

Your Routing Configurations

NAME	QUEUE	PRIORITY ⓘ	
Service Routing - Ca...	Service Case	1	✏
pp	pp	1	✏
Service Routing - Chat	Service Chat	2	✏

Create a Routing Configuration for Chat Queue

Name	Priority
Chat Queue	1

Figure 3.6 – Prioritizing chats with your other work

6. Now, you can adjust the chat workload for the agents using this chat deployment. You can leave the settings as-is.

7. The following screen is used to configure the deployment of your chat on your website. For **Website URL**, type in `*.force.com`. The domain name needs to be unique, but beyond that requirement, you can select anything you like.

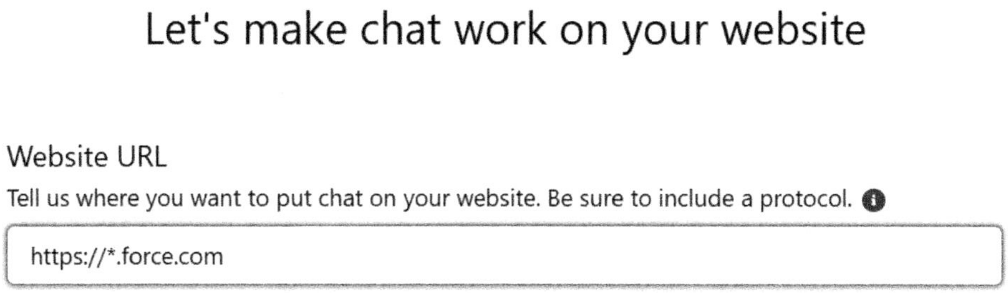

Let's make chat work on your website

Website URL

Tell us where you want to put chat on your website. Be sure to include a protocol. ⓘ

```
https://*.force.com
```

Figure 3.7 – Deploying a chat to your website

8. Then, you need to select the type of chat deployment you are dealing with. For Einstein Bots, you should select the **Service** type, as shown here:

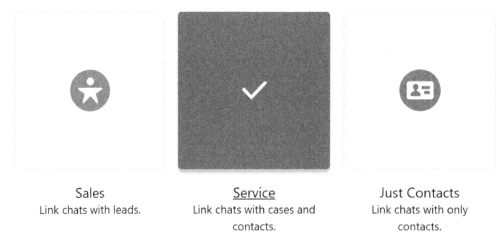

Figure 3.8 – Type selection

9. The next step will ask you to select whether you want to enable offline support. In this case, you can leave it off.

Figure 3.9 – Offline support

10. The configurator will now show you the code snippet you will use to embed your chat into your website. You can copy/paste it now or get back to it later. Refer to the following screenshot:

Chat Code Snippet

Paste this code immediately before the closing body tag for each page in https://*.force.com where you want to make chat available.

```
<style type='text/css'>
    .embeddedServiceHelpButton .helpButton .uiButton {
        background-color: #005290;
        font-family: "Arial", sans-serif;
    }
    .embeddedServiceHelpButton .helpButton .uiButton:focus {
        outline: 1px solid #005290;
    }
```

Figure 3.10 – Code snippet for your website

11. The chat is now set up and you can start creating your bot, as indicated in the following screenshot:

You're ready to chat

You just added web chat to your customer service channels. You're all set to chat with customers in the service console!

Figure 3.11– Completed chat setup

With the chat setup complete, the prerequisites are now complete for creating your bot.

Creating the Bot

To create your bot, follow these steps:

1. The next step is to create the bot by using the configurator. First, however, you need to enable Einstein Bots. To do so, search for `Einstein Bots`, go to the link, and click **On**, as shown here:

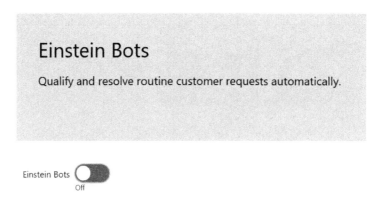

Figure 3.12 – Enabling Einstein Bots

2. Leave the settings for **Bot Options Menu** as-is and go on to create your bot by clicking **New**.

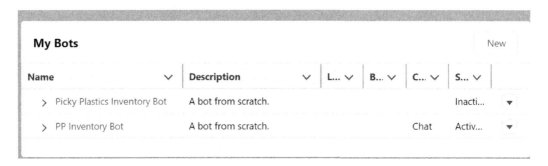

Figure 3.13 – Bot Options Menu

3. We'll be creating a bot from scratch, so please select that option rather than creating from a template.

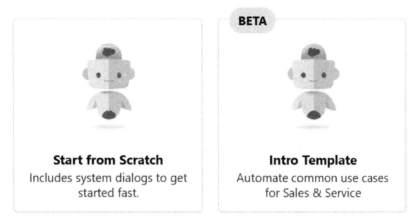

Figure 3.14 – Selecting a Bot type

4. Next, give your bot a name, such as `Pickled Plastics Inventory Bot`. You should leave the language as **English** for our example.

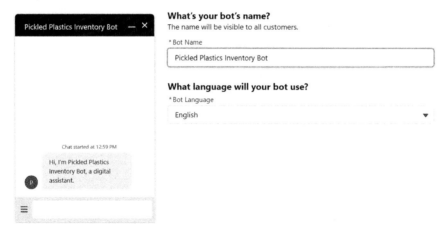

Figure 3.15 – Personalize your bot

5. The next step defines the top-level menu items that will greet the user, along with the options that the bot can help them with. For the PoC, you only need one option; that is, **Check Inventory for Product**.

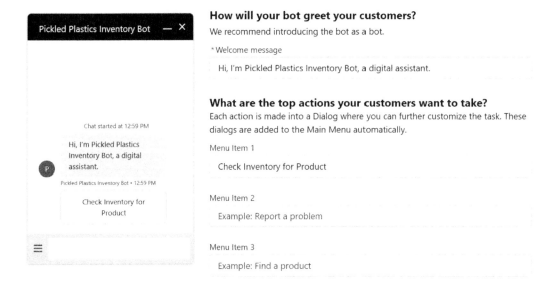

Figure 3.16 – Bot greeting

6. Now, link the bot to the chat deployment you set up in the previous section. Pick the name you gave your chat deployment in the lookup.

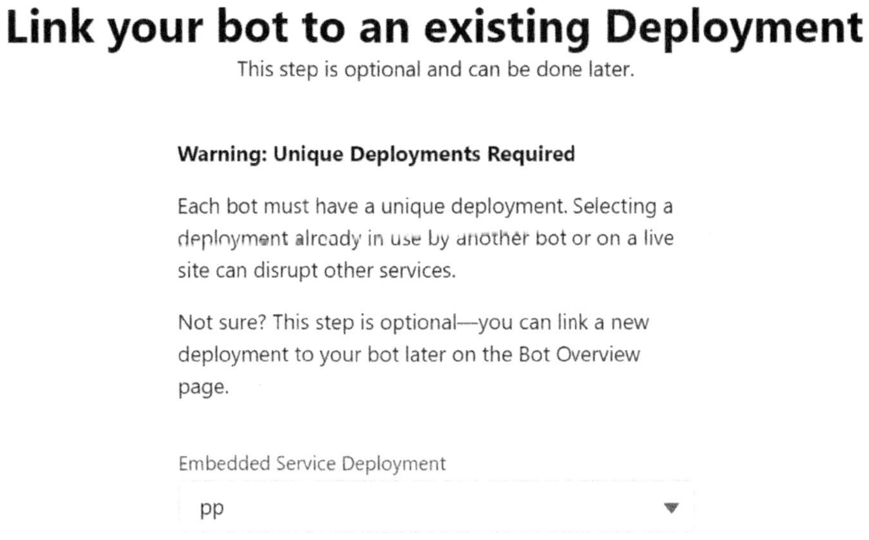

Link your bot to an existing Deployment

This step is optional and can be done later.

Warning: Unique Deployments Required

Each bot must have a unique deployment. Selecting a deployment already in use by another bot or on a live site can disrupt other services.

Not sure? This step is optional—you can link a new deployment to your bot later on the Bot Overview page.

Embedded Service Deployment

pp ▼

Figure 3.17 – Link to chat deployment

7. The final step is the most important because this step is where all the basic bot configuration is generated. Once this step completes, you will have a functional skeleton that you can build your unique bot on top of:

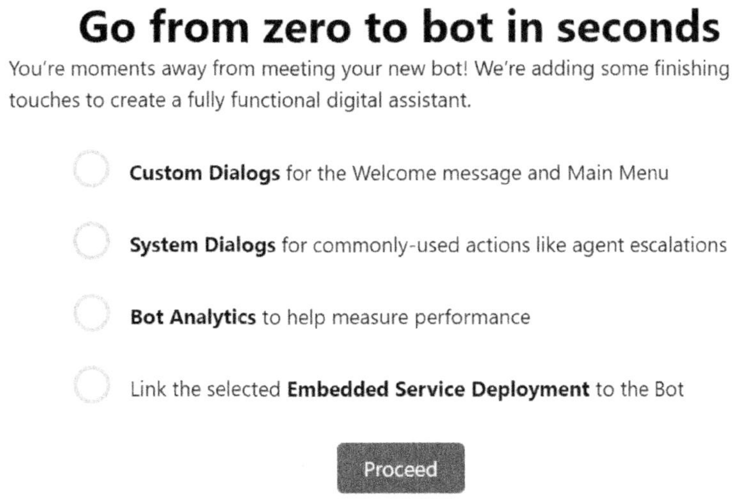

Go from zero to bot in seconds

You're moments away from meeting your new bot! We're adding some finishing touches to create a fully functional digital assistant.

○ **Custom Dialogs** for the Welcome message and Main Menu

○ **System Dialogs** for commonly-used actions like agent escalations

○ **Bot Analytics** to help measure performance

○ Link the selected **Embedded Service Deployment** to the Bot

Proceed

Figure 3.18 – Finish Bot configurator

Your bot has now been set up, but it doesn't do much yet. We will remedy this in the next section.

Configuring the dialog

To make your bot function as per requirements, follow these steps:

1. Once you have completed the configurator, you will enter **Bot Builder**, where you will build your PoC Bot. You will already have a dialog called **Check Inventory Status** created in your menu settings in the configurator.

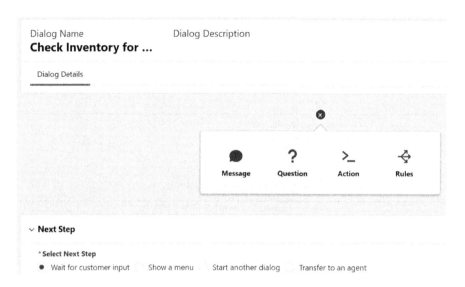

Figure 3.19 – Check Inventory Status dialog

2. Now, configure this initial step by adding a question element. Under **Bot Asks**, type What is the Product ID? and select **[System] Text (Text)** in the **Entity Name** field.

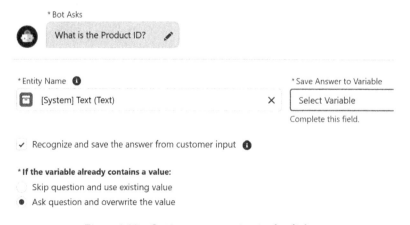

Figure 3.20 – Setting up a question in the dialog

3. Create a new variable to hold the answer and call it `Product ID`.

VARIABLE DETAILS
Stores a specific piece of data collected from the customer or output from Salesforce.

* Type

Custom   ▼

* Name   * API Name

Product ID   Product_ID

* Data Type

Text   ▼

☐ Contains a List

Figure 3.21 – New variable definition

4. In the same way, create another variable that will hold the quantity of the answer and call it `Product Quantity`.

5. Open the **Conversation Repair** section, add a **Repair Attempt**, and enter some text for the repair such as `I'm sorry that doesn't seem to be a number I recognize. Can you try again?`, as shown in the following screenshot:

∨ **Conversation Repair**

While the variable is not filled, the bot will reprompt with these message variations. We recommend providing additional context in the message, such as format requirements. ⓘ

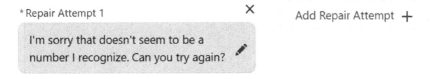

* Repair Attempt 1   ✕   Add Repair Attempt ✛

I'm sorry that doesn't seem to be a
number I recognize. Can you try again? ✏

What should the bot do next?

● Repeat the repair attempts until variable is filled (Default)

◌ Move on to next dialog step (Variable may not be filled)

Figure 3.22 – Repair conversation text

6. Expand **Next Step** and select **Start another dialog** at the bottom of the same screen.

7. Now, create a new dialog from the lookup. Call it `Get the Product Inventory`. This will contain the lookup logic for the inventory. You could have put all of this in the initial menu item, but to keep a separation between the menu and the business logic, we have created this new step.

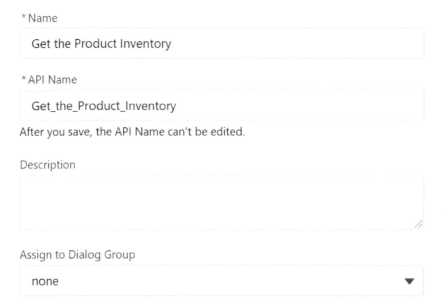

Figure 3.23 – Creating a dialog

8. Before we can configure this step, we will need to create some logic for the bot to go and get the inventory. To start this process, we will add a **Quantity on Hand** field to the product record that will hold the number of products in the current inventory. To do this, go to **Setup**. Then, under **Object Manager**, find the **Product** object, select **Fields & Relationships**, and select **New**.

9. Select **Number** for the type, call it `Quantity at Hand`, and give it 0 decimal places. Then, select the default options for the remaining steps.

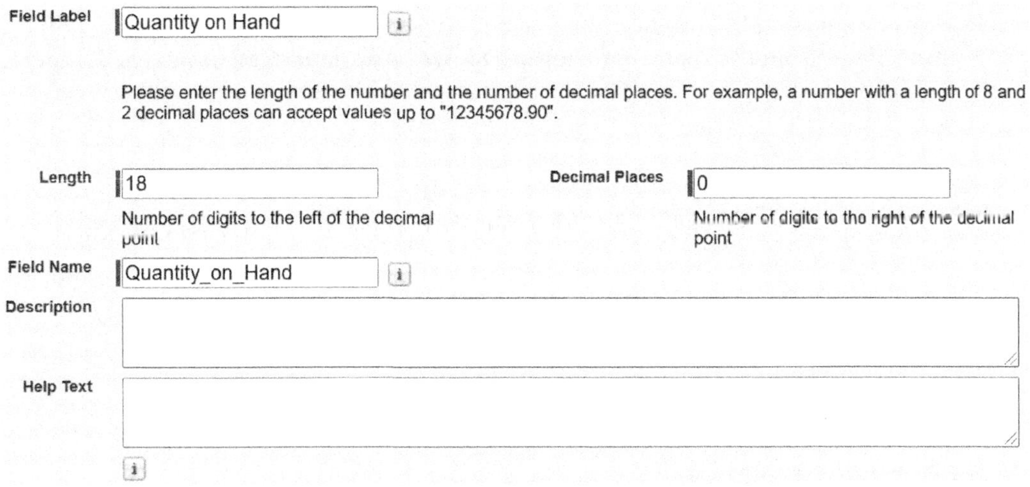

Field Label   Quantity on Hand   [i]

Please enter the length of the number and the number of decimal places. For example, a number with a length of 8 and 2 decimal places can accept values up to "12345678.90".

Length   18   Decimal Places   0

Number of digits to the left of the decimal point   Number of digits to the right of the decimal point

Field Name   Quantity_on_Hand   [i]

Description

Help Text

[i]

Figure 3.24 – Adding a field for the quantity at hand

10. Go to the main **Product** list view and create a product to use to test your bot, as follows:

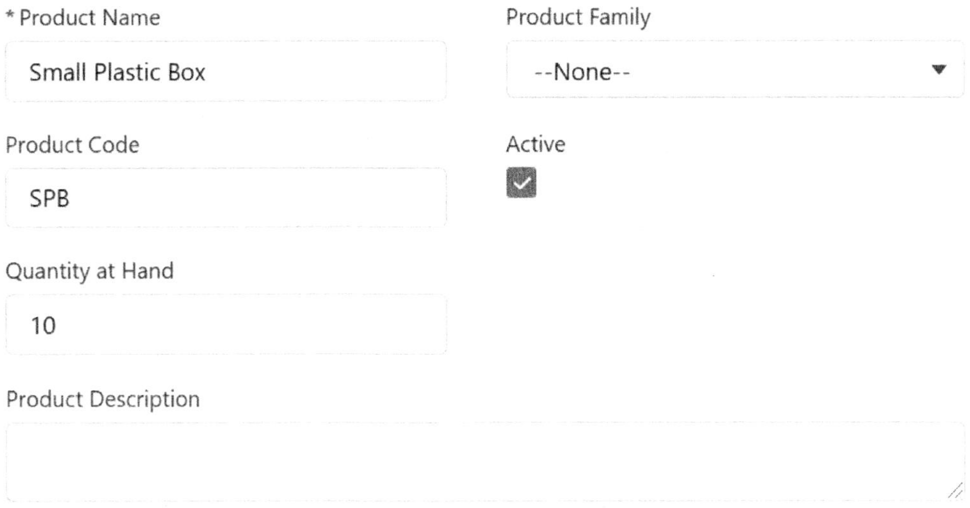

* Product Name

Small Plastic Box

Product Family

--None--

Product Code

SPB

Active

✓

Quantity at Hand

10

Product Description

Figure 3.25 – Adding a product to the database

11. Now, you need to create a new flow that queries the quantity at hand based on the user's input from the chat. Go to **Setup | Flows | Autolaunched Flow (No Trigger)** to create a new flow.

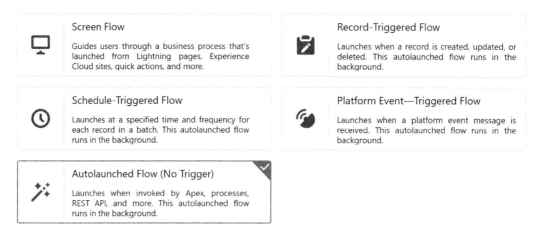

Figure 3.26 – Creating a new flow

12. Under **Manager**, create a new **Resource Type** called `Variable` whose **Data Type** is **Text** named `Product_Name`. Ensure that the **Available for input** box is checked.

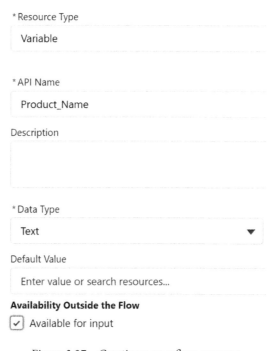

Figure 3.27 – Creating a new flow resource

13. Then, again, under **Manager**, create a new resource of the `Variable` type with **Data Type** set to **Number**, named `Product_Quantity`, and select **Available for output**, as shown in the following screenshot:

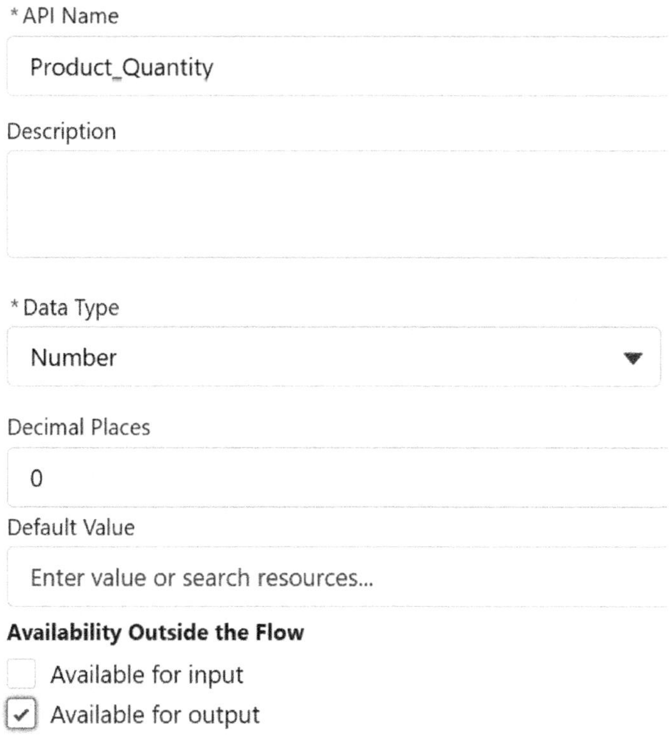

* API Name

Product_Quantity

Description

* Data Type

Number ▼

Decimal Places

0

Default Value

Enter value or search resources...

Availability Outside the Flow

☐ Available for input
☑ Available for output

Figure 3.28 – Creating a variable for the flow

14. Now, create a new **Flow** step of the **Get Records** type, call it **Get Product Quantity**, set **Object** to **Product**, and add a **Name** filter equal to the `Product_Name` variable you created earlier.

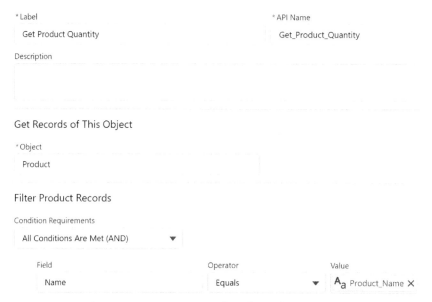

Figure 3.29 – Getting records with product quantity

15. Continue by selecting to only store the first record. Select **Choose fields and assign variables (advanced)**, choose **In separate variables**, and map the `Quantity_at_Hand__c` field to `Product_Quantity`, which you created earlier.

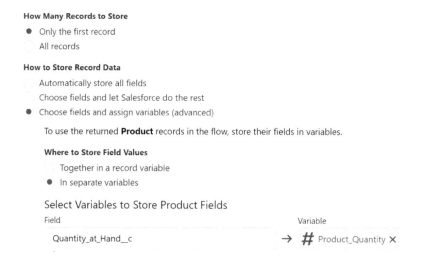

Figure 3.30 – Getting records with flow activity

16. **Flow** is now ready to use, so save it and activate it, as follows:

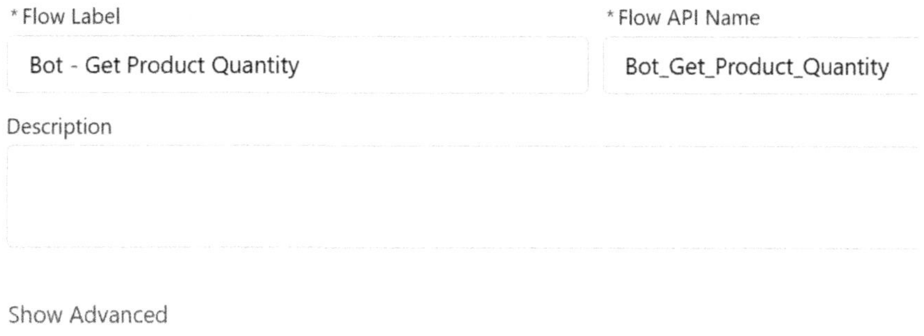

* Flow Label

Bot - Get Product Quantity

* Flow API Name

Bot_Get_Product_Quantity

Description

Show Advanced

Figure 3.31 – Saving the flow

17. Now, go back to your bot and continue configuring the **Get the Product Inventory** dialog by adding an action. Set **Action Type** to **Flow**, select the flow you just created, and configure the **Input** and **Output** variables by mapping them to the corresponding variables in the Bot.

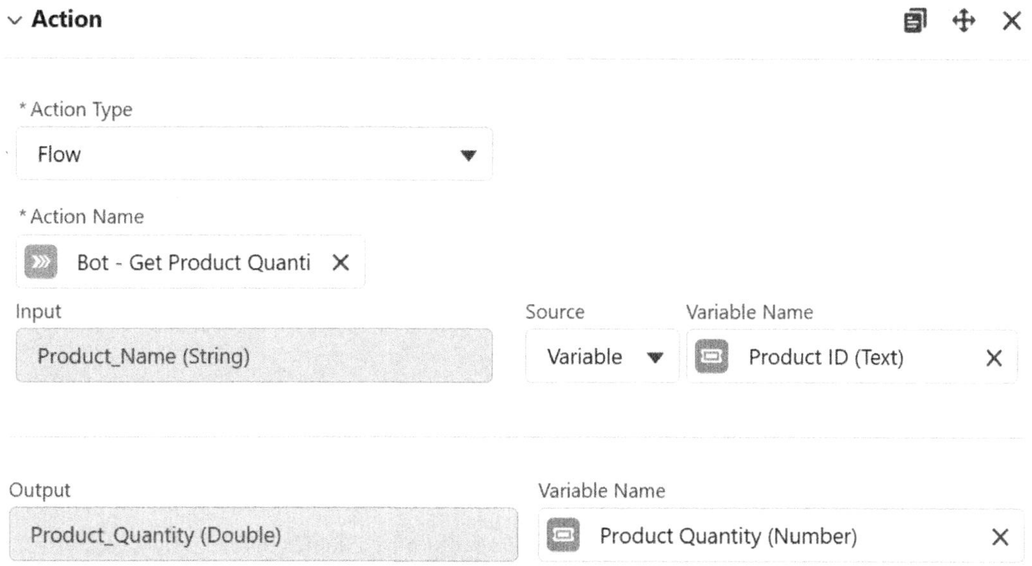

⌄ **Action**   ▤ ✛ ✕

* Action Type

Flow   ▼

* Action Name

≫ Bot - Get Product Quanti ✕

Input	Source	Variable Name
Product_Name (String)	Variable ▼	▣ Product ID (Text) ✕

Output		Variable Name
Product_Quantity (Double)		▣ Product Quantity (Number) ✕

Figure 3.32 – Getting the product inventory dialog

18. Now, add a **Message** element and enter some text stating **We have {!Product_ Quantity} {!Product_ID} at hand.** This will merge the variables into the text. To finish, select **Start another dialog** as the next step and then select the **End Chat** dialog. Refer to the following screenshot:

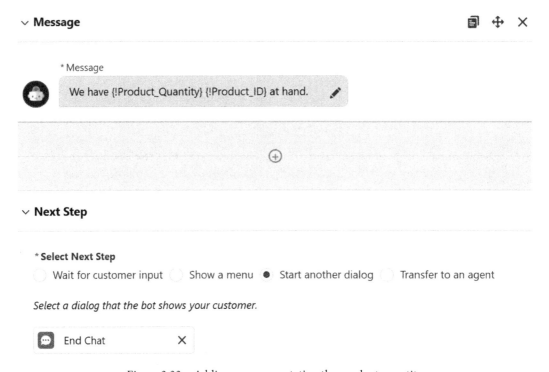

Figure 3.33 – Adding a message stating the product quantity

With that, we have configured the basic bot functionality. Now, we can start testing it by previewing it.

Previewing your Bot

To test your bot before deployment, follow these steps:

1. Your bot is now ready to try out, so after saving it by clicking **Save**, activate it by clicking the **Activate** button and selecting the bot deployment you created previously.

2. By clicking **Preview**, you can now test the dialog you just created, so go ahead and try to ask for the product you created previously:

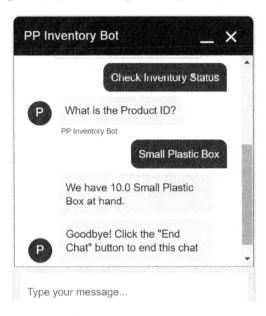

Figure 3.34 – Bot preview

Congratulations on creating your first Einstein Bot! Now, we will look at the other Service Cloud Einstein features.

Optimizing support with Einstein Article Recommendations is a feature that allows you to improve article suggestions from your knowledge base using machine learning. We'll explore how in the following sections.

Einstein Article Recommendations basics

Einstein Article Recommendations automatically suggests content for your customer service agents to link to customer cases. It does so based on a machine learning model that analyzes past cases and the articles in your Salesforce Knowledge article repository, which speeds up the resolution time and improves customer service. Fundamentally, it works by examining new cases as they come in, identifying keywords from the text fields within the case while taking the case's language into account, and feeding those keywords to a model for matching. The model then predicts what articles might be relevant and shows these to the agents in the console.

The only hard prerequisite for installing Einstein Article Recommendations, other than the requisite licensing, is to have a minimum of three knowledge articles published. Salesforce, however, strongly recommends that you have at least 1,000 cases and 500 case article assignments in your org. As always, the better the quality of your historical data, the better the quality of the recommendations you will receive. Note that you will need three articles and, ideally, commensurate cases and case article attachments for each language you are planning to get recommendations in.

Article Recommendations are generated by an NLP model that retrains itself on the data in your org continuously. Based on overlaps in case and article data, it ranks articles in your knowledge base by relevance and recommends the top few ranking articles for consideration by the agent. The relevance ranking considers several factors, including language, overlap in textual content, similar attachments in the past, past dismissals of the article as irrelevant, the term span of certain key terms, and the longest common subsequence between the knowledge article and the case. You can only affect what text is fed to the model, which still gives you a fair bit of leverage in terms of the configuration since much of the relevance ranking is based on various measures of textual similarity.

From an agent's point of view, the experience of using Einstein Article Recommendations is near-identical to traditional search-based suggestions. You see the suggested articles in the knowledge sidebar and from there, you can attach them to the case. You do, however, get a new relevance ranking score and the opportunity to mark an article as **Not helpful**, which will be fed back to the machine learning model. This is both a blessing and a curse, as we'll discuss in the *Architectural considerations for Reply Recommendations* section.

The maturity of your knowledge management implementation and the impact of changing to an automated recommendation engine needs to be considered as part of this implementation. If you don't have robust processes in place to keep knowledge articles fresh, introducing article recommendations may not add long-lasting value to your environment.

We will now consider how Article Recommendations can be used.

Article Recommendations use cases

The basic functionality of Article Recommendations is simple, but it has a few different use cases. First, it can help identify knowledge articles that can help the customer service agent service the customer better. In this scenario, the *use case* would be less about the ability to attach content to cases and more about the ability to automatically search the knowledge base. That will often be the most high-value proposition for companies with large product ranges or complex configurations, where helping a customer with their problem can require much searching.

On the flip side, for companies that have smaller knowledge bases and less complex configurations of products, the higher value proposition may just be the ability to quickly and near-automatically attach relevant knowledge articles that can be shared with a customer to enable them to resolve their problem. Here, Article Recommendations are used to reduce the processing time of customer service requests and free up agent time.

Configuring Article Recommendations will be our next item to cover.

Configuring Article Recommendations

The configuration of Einstein Article Recommendations is a simple affair, assuming you already have Lightning Knowledge set up and have added the Knowledge component to your Lightning Console. If not, you will have to do that as a prerequisite and you will also need to wait a bit until you have sufficient data to work with.

To set up Article Recommendations, you must enable the feature, follow the steps to select the languages and fields that you want to include, and then activate and build your model. The available languages include Dutch, English, French, German, Italian, Portuguese, and Spanish. The only step that requires substantial thought is what fields to include and in what order to put them as this will determine the input to your model and also give the model a hint of the importance you assign to these fields. You will also need to distinguish between a primary field (usually, this is the case subject) and other supporting fields. By default, all users will get access to the new recommendations if they have access to the Lightning Knowledge component, but you can restrict this if needed.

Now, we will cover the architectural concerns for Article Recommendations.

Architecture considerations for Article Recommendations

The first important consideration for implementing Article Recommendations is whether you have sufficient historical data to implement reasonably. If you don't have lots of local data, the model will still run but will be less accurate and not customized to your environment, which might give a bad user experience. There is also a risk that once you introduce a feature like this, some imperfect choices may become popular and therefore self-reinforcing. This may mean that other, better content is crowded out from the model over time because the imperfect choices have been used so much that they have become the default recommendations. Therefore, you need to be careful with your timing when implementing this feature.

Second, there is a subtle change management challenge to consider when rolling out this feature because it is so similar to standard suggestions from a UX perspective. Therefore, finding ways of communicating and highlighting the new way the recommendations are generated, why they are going to be better, and why agent feedback is so useful, will help make rolling out this feature much more successful than just turning on the technical bits.

Third, the ability to choose what text is fed to the model is a powerful tool for customizing the recommendations engine. You should think carefully about which fields are included and how they are structured. For additional control, you could think about introducing new fields that aggregate the information you want to feed the model from other fields; for instance, if you want to separate the text that is fed by record type or the language of the case. In general, more is more with this type of model, but you may still have exceptions. Also, think carefully about how you order the fields as your ranking is a cue for the model. Finally, don't forget to build a monitoring step into your processes after your initial deployment. Salesforce provides a handy scorecard that will give you a good view of the accuracy and quality of your model to help you develop it further.

Article Recommendations is a useful feature, especially if you have the required historical data. Next, we will see how to speed up chats with another Einstein feature.

Speeding up chat with Einstein Reply Recommendations

Einstein Reply Recommendations gives AI-powered suggested replies to agents using Salesforce Chat. In the following sections, you will learn how this works and what you need to adopt it successfully.

Einstein Reply Recommendations basics

Einstein Reply Recommendations is a way for you to leverage your old chat transcripts to generate suggested replies to common customer queries using a machine learning model. It works similarly to standard Quick Text, which you would write manually in so far as the agent is concerned, but the actual text is generated from historical conversations. Before you start getting concerned about inappropriate suggestions surfacing from some quirk of the AI compromising your customer conversations, it is worth noting that only suggestions that you have reviewed and approved will be suggested.

When you turn on this feature, Salesforce will build a model for leveraging your historical chat transcripts, as stored in Salesforce, and generate a list of candidate suggestions. These are extracted from the historical data based on the underlying NLP model. You have very little control over the model's operation, but that matters less than in other cases because you will have to review and possibly edit the suggestions before publishing them. From an agent's perspective, they will see an **Einstein Replies** component in their Lightning Console, which will allow them to either post or edit the suggested reply.

You need a minimum of 1,000 closed English chat transcripts in your org, in addition to the required licensing, before activating this feature. For now, English is the only supported language. One particular consideration with Reply Recommendations is that it is one of the few features that is recommended to test out directly in production. This is because of the data requirements and the impossibility of migrating a model between sandbox and production. Salesforce recommends assigning the license to a few expert agents who can evaluate the suitability of the model as a starting point.

Next, we will look at how to use Reply Recommendations.

Reply Recommendations use cases

The use case for Reply Recommendations is two-fold. On the one hand, you get a speedup in agent replies because they can use template content to communicate with the customer. On the other hand, you can increase the consistency of communication by having approved content recommended that is relevant to the conversation that's in progress.

This means that Reply Recommendations can be used both for increasing efficiency and for improving the consistency of the company's tone of voice across channels. Both of these use cases will require appropriate training for the agent so that they understand when to use the template answers and when to make a custom reply.

Next, we will cover the configuration process for Reply Recommendations.

Configuring Reply Recommendations

The process for configuring Einstein Reply Recommendations starts with you activating the feature and building the model. No choices need to be made here – it all happens behind the scenes. If you don't meet the data requirements, the model won't be able to build. Otherwise, after a suitable amount of time (up to 48 hours), you will be able to go on to the next step and review the generated replies. The candidate replies will be visible in a list view that lets you review all of the candidates and select which to publish.

The publication process, which in this case means publishing the replies as Quick Text, is the major part of the configuration as this is where you have the opportunity to categorize and edit the generated replies. When you publish, you will have the ability to specify the publication folder, message name, message text, category, channels, and activation status for the Quick Texts. This editing is manual but gives you complete control over which parts of the model you use where. For instance, you may find that some replies that are appropriate in a WhatsApp conversation may not be in a web chat.

The final step is to make the feature available for agents, which means assigning the relevant permission set, giving them access to the Quick Text Folder where you have published the replies, and adding the Einstein Replies Lightning component to the **Messaging** and **Chat** pages where you want it available.

Finally, we will look at the architectural concerns involved in Reply Recommendations.

Architecture considerations for Reply Recommendations

A particular weakness of Reply Recommendations is that you can't effectively develop the model in a sandbox. The same is true for Article Recommendations and Case Classification, but the data requirements of Reply Recommendations make it more problematic. This is because you can more readily experiment in a sandbox with the other two features before doing a final build in production.

This breaks normal architectural guidance, so you need to carefully plan the deployment if you're using this feature. Here, you should architect a canary deployment where only a few users get access to the feature initially, allowing you to resolve any issues before it is rolled out to a larger audience.

Another weakness that you need to plan around is the fact that the model, in contrast to most Einstein Platform offerings, is not continuously updated. The model is built once when you turn on the feature and one more time when you hit 10,000 chat transcripts. Therefore, the ongoing value of this feature may diminish considerably.

Reply Recommendations is a feature that can add value to your support agents by giving them good options for common responses if you have the data that's required. We will finish looking at Service Cloud Einstein by looking at Einstein Case Classification.

Alleviating manual data entry with Einstein Case Classification

Einstein Case Classification is a powerful feature that lets you automate routine tasks based on historical data. In the following sections, we will explore when and how to include this feature in a Salesforce project.

Case Classification basics

Einstein Case Classification is a handy feature that predicts the values of checkboxes, lookups, and drop-down lists on your new case records based on the historical data present in old cases. In contrast to many other Einstein features, Case Classification lets you configure both what fields to predict and what historical dataset to learn from, allowing you to segment your data. This gives you enhanced control over the process, but also means you need to be extra diligent when planning for the feature deployment.

You also have field-level control over what to do with the prediction that the Case Classification model makes. The lowest level of automation that's supported, which is also the default, is for the model to suggest the top three choices for the agent to select. If you're more confident in your model, you can go to having the best value already selected and filled into the record for the agent simply to confirm. The highest level of automation is to save the best-predicted value without agent review. If you select this highest level of automation, you also have the option of using Einstein Case Routing to automatically apply assignment rules or skills-based routing.

Case Classification use cases

Case Classification has the following two principal use cases:

- It can improve efficiency by automating, or partly automating, the process of filling in Case fields. If your business process has a lot of back-office processing steps to do on incoming cases to make sure they are processed correctly, then this can be a major time saver. Typically, this helps when you can generate enough confidence in the machine learning model to let it assign values on its own.

- However, even if you are not quite ready to take this step, Case Classification is useful to ensure consistency and data quality by suggesting the most likely values to agents. This can reduce manual processing errors substantially by limiting the field of selection for the fields covered in the model. In a call center setting, where you often have high staff turnover, this can be very useful.

Now, let's take a look at configuring Case Classification.

Configuring Case classification

As always, you will start the configuration journey by enabling this feature. Once this feature has been enabled, you will create a predictive model. You can have up to five of these to serve different segments. Segmentation is done based on conditions defined against Case fields. You have the standard range of conditions available to define these. Segments define the types of Cases that the model will predict for, as well as those that it will learn from. If you only want to restrict what cases are learned from, for instance, to only use recent cases, then you can use another option called **Example Cases**. These two options can also be combined, although there is rarely a good reason to do so. In general, the model learns from the last 6 months of data, unless you restrict it further.

Once you have defined segmentation and example cases, you need to select the fields that you want to predict. You can select fields of the picklist, lookup, or checkbox type and you can select up to 10 fields to predict. The quality of the predictions will depend a lot on how many historical cases have data for the field. As a rule of thumb, you should have at least 400 instances to include a field; 400 – 1,000 gives low-quality predictions, 1,000 – 10,000 cases gives medium quality predictions, and more than 10,000 gives high-quality predictions.

Once you have defined your model, you have to build it, which will take a little while. Once it has been built, you need to define what Einstein Case Classification should do with the predicted value for each field. The default will be to show the top three predicted options, but you can define confidence thresholds for **Select Best Value** and **Automate Value** that will determine the use of those features. For instance, you could have a rule that says that if the model is 90% confident in its prediction, it's fine to automatically save the value in the field, whereas at 80% confidence, it can put in the value automatically for the agent to approve. Once you have completed this for all the fields, your model will be ready to use. Your agents will be able to use it once you have added the Einstein Field Recommendations Lightning component to the relevant Case pages.

Having looked at the configuration side of Case Classification, let's examine some of the architectural decisions involved when implementing it.

Architectural considerations for Case classification

The most substantial architectural decisions you need to make when designing a feature deployment for Einstein Case Classification surround fields and segmentation. Starting with segmentation, you need to consider what the relevant limits are to your Case data. These can be limits of type, geography, or timing. You may, for instance, not want to learn from cases in a country you no longer serve or may realize that cases beyond a certain age are likely to have overly poor data quality to give good results.

When it comes to the fields, the scope, both in terms of the number of fields to include for prediction and the degree of automation you aim for, are key concerns. Going for fuller automation will bring greater rewards, but also greater risks of misclassification. You need to balance the cost of rework and negative consequences on customers when things go wrong versus the very real efficiency gains. This may require a good deal of experimentation to get right and given the difficulties of doing this exploration work in a sandbox, you have to plan it carefully, such as by deploying the feature to a full copy sandbox for experimentation, although this will probably be against your normal practice for development and release.

Einstein Case Classification can be a real time saver for your customer service agents if you allow it to work automatically. However, you need to trust the automated process, which will require both trial and error and analysis. We will now summarize what we have learned in this chapter to help improve your service processes with AI.

Summary

In this chapter, we looked at the four parts of the Service Cloud Einstein offering: Einstein Bots, Einstein Article Recommendations, Einstein Reply recommendations, and Einstein Case Classification. We spent the most time and energy on Einstein Bots, learning how to design and configure conversational agents. Introducing bots can transform an enterprise and spending the time to deeply understand how and why will pay dividends in years to come.

We then moved on to Article Recommendations, a handy way to aid your agents in locating knowledge base articles. If you have a big article database on Salesforce and are using it to resolve cases regularly, this is the offering for you. We learned that Reply Recommendations is probably the weakest of the Service Cloud Einstein pack because while it seems highly useful to be able to generate replies based on past conversations, the fact that this does not happen continuously makes the feature likely to be time-limited. Finally, we saw how Einstein Case Classification can be used to speed up case processing times by automating data entry tasks based on historical information. If you have the data and the confidence to go with a high degree of automation, this feature can be a quick and major win. All in all, you now know how to improve the efficiency of your Service processes in Salesforce using the built-in AI options.

Well done – you have covered a lot of ground in the last two chapters, along with this one! In the next chapter, we will transition out of the core Salesforce Clouds to look at the AI offerings in the Marketing and Commerce Clouds.

Questions

1. What feature could you use to optimize your knowledge management workflow?

2. What are the four key elements you use to define a dialog in Einstein Bots?

3. When are Einstein Reply Recommendations refreshed?

4
Salesforce AI for Marketing and Commerce

This chapter will cover the Einstein features that are available in the Salesforce Marketing and Commerce Clouds. First, we will examine how these clouds are different from the core clouds we've looked at so far and what that means for Einstein features. We will then survey the features in Marketing Cloud and Commerce Cloud from a high-level point of view to allow you to judge whether they might be right for your organization.

In this chapter, we're going to cover the following main topics:

- Introducing Einstein for marketing and commerce
- Using Marketing Cloud Einstein
- Implementing Commerce Cloud Einstein

After completing this chapter, you will have gained an understanding of how to personalize customer journeys across marketing and e-commerce activities using Einstein Platform features.

Technical requirements

There are no technical requirements for this chapter as, unfortunately, the features under discussion are not generally available for trial use. If you have access to a Marketing Cloud test instance or a Commerce Cloud sandbox, you can follow the descriptions provided.

Introducing Einstein for marketing and commerce

Marketing and eCommerce are some of the biggest areas in the current tech landscape. This includes the AI space, where options to customize and personalize marketing and promotional activities attract many players.

Unsurprisingly, Salesforce also has offerings in both these areas: Marketing Cloud and Commerce Cloud. However, these two products are significantly different from the clouds we've been dealing with so far. Neither of these two products was originally developed by Salesforce; instead, they were brought in-house via acquisitions. Marketing Cloud came from ExactTarget and Commerce Cloud came from Demandware.

Both of these companies were leaders in their space when acquired by Salesforce and they have only improved since their acquisition. However, they are built on substantially different technical architectures and while Salesforce has sprinkled a veneer of consistency over the user interface, they are different products that require different skill sets.

In addition, the scope of AI offerings for these two products is immense. We will be covering 15 features in this chapter versus the 4 or so we've been covering so far. That means we can't go through the Einstein features in quite the same way that we have for the previous chapters. That would require book-length treatments in their own right. However, we will be able to survey the landscape and get a good feel for which might be appropriate for our use cases.

The fundamental purpose of the features in both Marketing Cloud and Commerce Cloud can be summed up as personalization. Almost everything we will be discussing here is aimed at creating a smoother, tailored, personal, and human user experience for the customer or potential customer.

As we will see in the following sections, you can get very far down the road of creating truly personalized experiences by using the features included in the Einstein toolkits for marketing and commerce. We will start by looking at Marketing Cloud.

Using Marketing Cloud Einstein

Marketing Cloud Einstein arguably has the most advanced standard offerings in the Salesforce Einstein platform. Just take a look at the following screenshot, which shows an overview dashboard that contains a multitude of features:

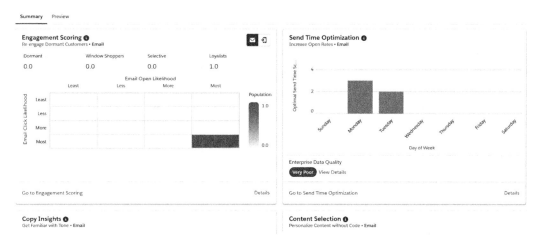

Figure 4.1 – Marketing Cloud Einstein dashboard

The marketing space is also an area where Salesforce continuously fuels its in-house capabilities with new acquisitions, such as the recent acquisitions of Evergage or Datorama. The fundamental purpose of these offerings is to be able to deeply personalize the communications that are made to customers and potential customers. We will see how to do this in the following sections.

Einstein Engagement Scoring

It's no secret that some people are more likely to open messages and engage with your content than others. Nor is it hard to see how having a good metric for that likelihood to engage could help your marketing efforts. For instance, you could base an audience on the properties that are shared by your best-performing subscribers, which allows you to effectively tailor your communication to both new and existing subscribers based on their predicted likelihood to engage. You could also look at less well-performing segments and try to find new ways to better engage them with your communications.

Einstein Engagement Scoring is the best way to accomplish this kind of targeting in Marketing Cloud. Based on historical data, it calculates a predicted score for subscribers to engage with your content. Currently, it calculates separate scores for email engagement and mobile push engagement, so long as you are using these in your Marketing Cloud setup. The scores are stored in standard Data Extensions, which allow them to be used across pretty much all standard Marketing Cloud features.

The model for Engagement Scoring doesn't allow you to do any customization or configuration. You simply turn on the feature and that's it. As we've seen many times already, you do need adequate historical data to be able to use the feature. You need a minimum of 1,000 subscriber events registered for the last 90 days to be able to use the feature, but as always, more is better. There is a current limitation of only being able to use this feature for up to 250 business units, but that should be adequate for most organizations.

Once you've activated the feature, you have the option of customizing the scoring thresholds that are used for grading contacts based on their likelihood to engage. Engagement Scoring uses the following scheme to score subscribers:

- Excellent: Most likely to engage
- Good: More likely to engage
- Fair: Less likely to engage
- Poor: Least likely to engage

The default values for each category are based on the industry averages for key KPIs such as *open rate*, *click rate*, *purchase rate*, and *retention*. However, if you have your own internal benchmarks that are supported by the necessary data, you can configure Engagement Scoring to use those instead.

Of course, generating the score is just the first step: you will need to use it with other features for it to generate value. First, you get a set of out-of-the-box engagement dashboards, which will allow you to track your engagement metrics day by day and take corrective action if you see that they are not as you want them to be. An example dashboard is shown in the following screenshot:

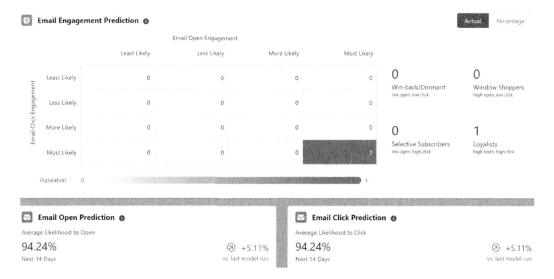

Figure 4.2 – Einstein Engagement Scoring dashboard

For mobile engagement data, Marketing Cloud Einstein will also generate a Data Quality Score to help you assess the state of your engagement data.

However, you can also operationalize the score directly in a variety of ways. Einstein Engagement Scoring assigns a persona to each contact based on their propensity to engage, which can be used with **Journey Builder**, the Marketing Cloud tool used to create custom user journeys, to create a personalized user journey for different engagement levels. If you are using Audience Builder, you can also use this score as the basis for new audiences, either by directly segmenting on this value or by using the subscriber properties associated with the different engagement levels.

The following screenshot shows how this looks when constructing a new journey in Journey Builder:

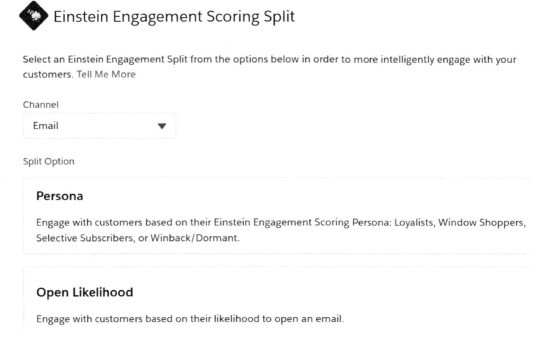

Figure 4.3 – Adding an Einstein Engagement Scoring Split

Having covered the powerful tools available with Einstein Engagement Scoring, we will now move on to its close cousin, Einstein Engagement Frequency.

Einstein Engagement Frequency

Have you ever experienced email fatigue from a brand sending you too many messages? You're not alone if you have. You might even like the brand and its messages, but if they don't get the sending cadence right, there's a good chance you will unsubscribe, despite any initial goodwill you might have had.

Einstein Engagement Frequency is the AI answer to this problem. Based on data from the last 28 days of event data, it calculates a score for each subscriber that indicates the optimal number of messages to send to a subscriber over this period. At least five emails need to have been sent over that period for the model to have enough data to work with, so it will only work well for frequently communicative brands.

Einstein Engagement Frequency is another model that is simply turned on globally and then available without any options for configuration or customization. It has a dependency on Journey Builder and this must be provisioned in your Marketing Cloud account if you wish to activate this feature.

The following steps explain how to activate Einstein Engagement Frequency:

1. First, go to **Setup** and find **Einstein Engagement Frequency** in the menu under **Einstein**. This will take you to a screen with a button saying **Activate**, as shown here:

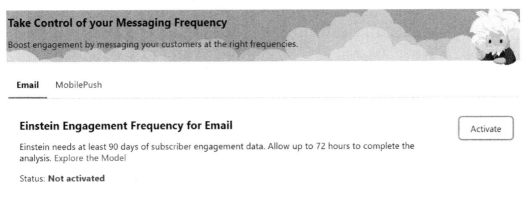

Figure 4.4 – Activating Einstein Engagement Frequency

2. When you click this button, the model will start building, which will take up to 72 hours. Its status will be shown, as shown in the following screenshot:

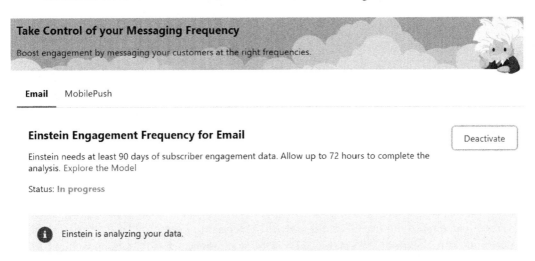

Figure 4.5 – Einstein Engagement Frequency model status

This process is indicative of how you activate most Einstein features in Marketing Cloud.

The feature comes with a saturation dashboard that marketers can use to judge the saturation levels of their subscriber base when it comes to email sends. This can be used to optimize the future send schedule. If you want to activate this data directly, it is on you to devise a mechanism or process to suppress email sends to saturated subscribers. Einstein Engagement Frequency does not provide features out of the box for this purpose.

Einstein Engagement Frequency is a small feature with a very singular but useful purpose. In the next section, we will shift gears and look at Einstein Messaging Insights, a powerful AI-based analytics feature.

Einstein Messaging Insights

One of the simultaneously most irritating and most interesting things about digital marketing is that the second you think you've worked out the formula for engaging your audience, the ground is likely to shift from under your feet. Having the ability to proactively find and react to such shifts is crucial to retain engagement with your audiences in the long term.

Einstein Messaging Insights helps marketers with this problem by detecting and highlighting unusual events related to your email sends, such as an unusually high or low open rate for emails in a particular customer journey. Einstein Messaging Insights is an anomaly detection model that uses historical data to detect metric values outside the expected band, coupled with a list of contributing factors that may help explain the anomaly.

As with so many of the Marketing Cloud Einstein features, there is no real configuration involved. You simply turn on the feature for a given business unit and then the model will be generated and the insights will start to appear. In contrast to other features, you don't need pre-existing data for the feature to work as it will monitor the data over some time and only then start flagging anomalies. In particular, Einstein Messaging Insights pays attention to open rate, click rate, and unsubscribe rate.

The way that Einstein Messaging Insights evaluates and flags email sends is different between batch sends, which are email sends that are sent out to a particular audience in a big batch, and journey sends, which are email sends that are sent to an audience based on a particular customer journey.

For batch sends, Einstein Messaging Insights uses a group of similar email sends from the last 90 days as the baseline for comparison. The variables it uses for determining similarity aren't fully disclosed but include send size and several other factors. Based on the baseline performance, the feature generates a 95% confidence interval and flags an anomaly for any value falling outside this bound, which will lead to generating *insight*. It also produces a list of top contributing factors that the model indicates are likely to have had an impact on the anomalous outcome.

For journey-based insights, Einstein Messaging Insights takes all the email sends that occur as part of that journey when generating insights into account. It uses up to 90 days of historical data for comparison and evaluates the rates based on a 95% confidence interval for expected values. If a value falls outside this range, insight is generated. Unfortunately, the top contributing factors that are shown for batch data aren't available for journey sends.

Einstein Messaging Insights allows marketers to be proactive about responding to the shifting sands of digital marketing. In the next section, we will look at Einstein Copy Insights to help guide marketers in selecting the right subject line for their email sends.

Einstein Copy Insights

The subject line of an email is one of the most important factors in determining whether subscribers are likely to open your email. Many digital marketers will obsess for untold hours over the exact wording of their subject lines. This too, however, is an area where Marketing Cloud Einstein can help them out.

Einstein Copy Insights uses Salesforce's cutting-edge capabilities in **Natural Language Processing** (**NLP**) and text analytics to generate insights about the language in your subject lines, providing helpful guidance to marketers wanting to increase their reach and engagement.

This is another model that you just turn on and then it runs on its own. It is turned on globally rather than at the business unit level, and everyone will have access once you turn it on. The model analyzes 90 days of data on a rolling basis to determine what linguistic features in subject lines contribute to successful email sends.

Fundamentally, the NLP model extracts language features from the subject line and uses those features to analyze historical email send performance. It then applies the same model to predict the language features likely to contribute to successful sends in the future, which a marketer can use as input to craft better subject lines.

You can drill into the factors driving top-performing subject lines using a pre-built dashboard. This includes the ability to see the following elements:

- A view of top-performing subject lines from your historical sends, as well as your most frequently used subject lines.
- Language Factor Insights based on the model's linguistic features, which give you a view of what elements are having an impact.
- Emotional Tone Insights provides a view of the model's take on the tone of your subject lines.
- Top performing and frequently used phrases from across subject lines, along with their performance metrics.

Einstein Copy Insights is another useful but limited scope feature that helps marketers with one particular problem. Einstein Splits, on the other hand, has the flexibility to help orchestrate a large number of different use cases. We will look at this in the next section.

Einstein Splits

Personalized customer journeys are the bread and butter of digital marketing. The more personalized the content, timing, and context of a message, the more likely it will resonate with the recipient. Einstein Splits is a broad-based feature with several variations that allows you to use AI models as part of building your customer journeys, thereby improving their impact.

Einstein Splits are implemented as Journey Builder activities, which means they are activated directly when you're constructing your customer journeys. The split types are based on the data that's generated from other models, such as Einstein Engagement Scoring, but by using them as activities directly in Journey Builder, it is possible to activate these machine learning models concretely as part of a marketer's day job.

Einstein Splits comes in the following variants:

- **Persona split**: This splits a customer journey based on the Einstein Engagement Scoring Persona of the subscriber. There is a path for each of the personas – Loyalist, Window Shopper, Selective Shopper, and Winback/Dormant. You can use these to provide a unique experience based on the subscriber's engagement level.

- **Web Conversion Likelihood split**: This is similar to the Persona split but is based entirely on the user's likelihood to convert on a web action. This requires you to have web tracking installed, but if you do, you can split based on the same four likelihood categories that apply to Einstein Engagement Scoring, from Least Likely to Most Likely.

- **Click Likelihood split**: This is very similar to the Web Conversion Likelihood split, but rather than splitting on the subscriber's propensity to convert on a web action, it looks at the likelihood that they will click on a message in your email send.

- **Subscription Retention Likelihood split**: This uses the same scale as the previous two splits, but it creates paths based on the user's likelihood to remain subscribed to your mailing list.

- **Open Likelihood split**: I bet you can guess this one: it creates paths based on the usual likelihood classifications but based on the subscriber's propensity to open your email.

By combining these split types with the regular activities in Journey Builder, you can generate advanced scenarios for personalization based on how a user falls within these categories.

The following steps show how to add an Engagement Scoring Split:

1. Go to **Journey Builder** and click on **Create New Journey**, as shown in the following screenshot:

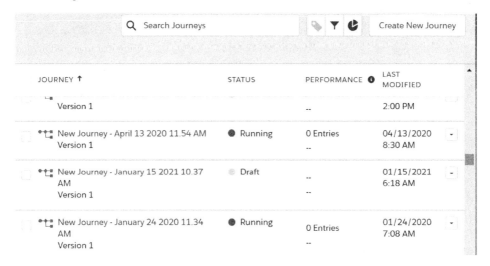

Figure 4.6 – Create New Journey button

2. Select **Multi-Step Journey**, as shown here:

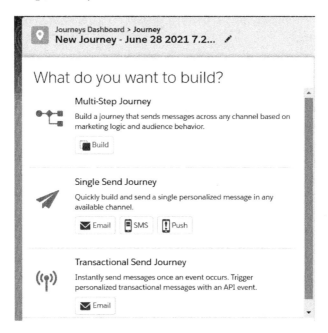

Figure 4.7 – Selecting a journey type

3. On **Journey Builder Canvas**, add a **Data Extension** component and then a **Scoring Split** activity by dragging from left to right. The following screenshot shows what this should look like:

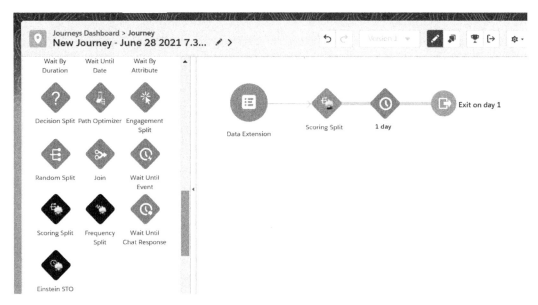

Figure 4.8 – Journey Builder Canvas

4. Now, click the **Scoring Split** activity and click on a persona to bring up the following screen:

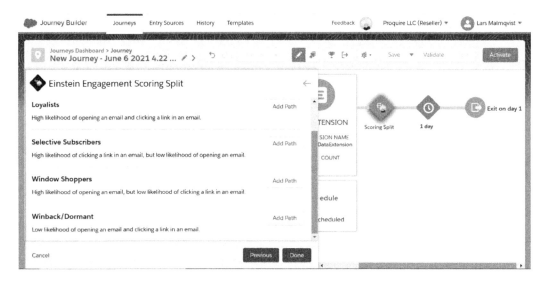

Figure 4.9 – Einstein Split with different persona types

5. From this screen, you can add separate paths for each persona or only for some. In this case, just click on **Add Path** for **Loyalists** and click **Done**. This will create two branches – one for **Loyalist** and one for **Remainder**. This can be seen in the following screenshot:

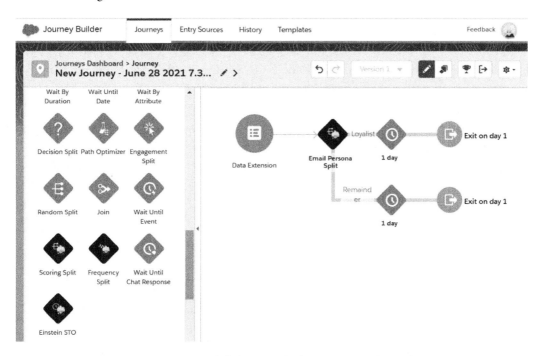

Figure 4.10 – Journey with different paths for Loyalists and other personas

From here, you can customize the journeys as you wish, perhaps by sending special offers to your best customers.

Imagine, for instance, that you want to target customers that are likely to open your emails by providing them with a complimentary voucher for products they are likely to buy.

You could achieve this scenario using a combination of a Subscription Retention Likelihood split, followed by an Open Likelihood split, followed by an *email sent* that contains a voucher code for a discount on your products.

Einstein Splits is an important part of your marketing personalization toolkit and an excellent way to activate some of the models that Marketing Cloud Einstein can generate for you out of the box. In the next section, we will look at another powerful feature that allows you to perfectly time your email sends, known as Einstein Send Time Optimization.

Einstein Send Time Optimization

If you spend any time on blogs dedicated to digital marketing, you will inevitably run into a discussion of when the best time to send a message to your audience is. There are many points of view and great differences between the analyses that people have made over time. It is also constantly changing, so the heuristics that worked today won't necessarily make the cut tomorrow. That being said, send time is important regarding whether a recipient engages with your email. This is also a problem that allows quantitative analysis to be performed to provide ongoing optimization of send times. Enter Einstein Send Time Optimization.

Einstein Send Time Optimization is a double threat consisting of a machine learning model that generates optimal send times for subscribers based on historical data and a Journey Builder activity, which uses the predicted time from the model to time individual email sends as part of customer journeys.

This is one of the more sophisticated models in the Marketing Cloud Einstein portfolio, although as usual, it allows for no configuration or customization. However, based on your last 90 days of data, the model crunches about 20 factors relevant to predicting the best time of day to send to individual subscribers. Then, it creates a model by combining these factors with relative weights to form a complete prediction. The output is a likelihood score for each of the 168 hours of the week for each subscriber in your dataset, at least for the subscribers where sufficient past data is available to predict with confidence.

In particular, the model considers engagement behavior such as the number of sends, click rate, open rate, unsubscribes per send, and spam complaints during the period in question. Then, it combines that with factors derived from data and metadata about sending patterns and campaign execution.

Once the model is running and predictions have been generated, these are used with the Einstein Send Time Optimization activity in Journey Builder. A simple flow is shown in the following screenshot:

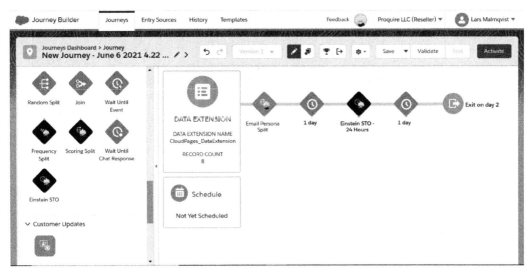

Figure 4.11 – Example customer journey for STO

When such an activity is encountered in a flow for a user with a personalized score, the system will randomly select one of the top three send times within the next period, as selected in the following screenshot, and use that to send whatever message the customer journey calls for.

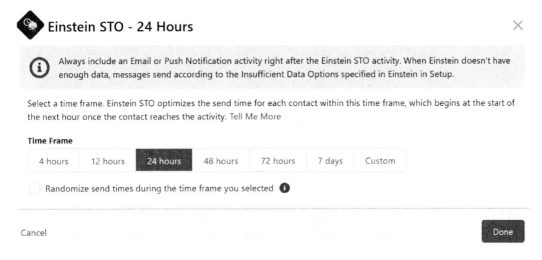

Figure 4.12 – Send Time Optimization activity

If there isn't enough data for a subscriber, a default model will be applied instead.

You can analyze the operation of **Einstein Send Time Optimization** in the dashboard view, as shown in the following screenshot:

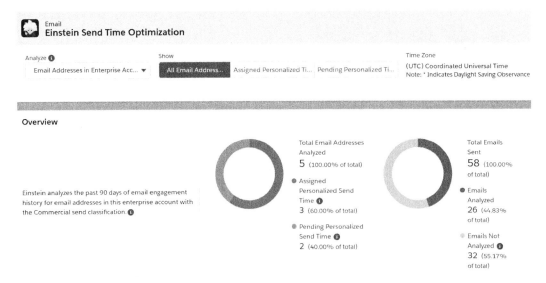

Figure 4.13 – Einstein Send Time Optimization dashboard

The combination of the machine learning model, which is continuously updated, and the Send Time Optimization activity, which sends emails based on that model, can help you ensure that even when optimal timings change, your setup is still sending emails at optimal intervals. We will now look at a different type of recommendation mechanism as we consider Einstein Content Selection.

Einstein Content Selection

Most brands today have a lot of content. Catalogs of assets sitting around in content management systems of various stripes and are often selected for use based on the whim of a marketer or designer. However, with the rise in data-driven marketing, there is a drive toward using smarter methods for picking the right personalized content assets to send to subscribers.

Einstein Content Selection is a sophisticated mechanism for automatically selecting the most engaging content on a subscriber-by-subscriber basis to optimize their engagement with your email sends. It continuously analyzes the click-to-open rate for content assets that you have uploaded, leveraging A/B testing automatically in the background to select the most appropriate piece of content to insert into your email.

The details of the model are not disclosed and as always, we have no configuration options on that front, but in contrast to some of the features we have been discussing, Einstein Content Selection has a fairly wide range of configuration options available in terms of how it is deployed in your specific instance.

To begin with, however, you need an asset catalog. The asset catalog, which contains the URL and metadata for each image you want to be able to use in your marketing materials, is the foundation for Einstein **Content Selection**. Once this is in place, you can start to use the feature, although the other features we'll discuss shortly can all significantly help improve its value.

You create the asset catalog by filling out a CSV template file with metadata about your assets. This will most likely need to be generated from an existing content management system and mapped to the Salesforce format. This asset information includes the basics, but also an asset class that you can use to group your different types of marketing assets. Once you have generated this file and imported it into Marketing Cloud, you have covered the basics of the feature.

Einstein Content Selection is deployed via a content block that you can include in your email templates. You don't need to specify anything else if you want to use the basic functionality of the model. The feature will start experimenting with different assets in the corresponding location and optimize which is used based on the click-to-open rate observed for each asset.

Several additional features allow you to improve and enrich the functionality of Einstein Content Selection. The most important of these is being able to synchronize your customer profile information to enable Einstein Content Selection to take profile information into account when making content choices, thereby enabling real personalization. You can also map profile information to asset classes to specify what types of assets are relevant to different kinds of users.

You can enable this feature by going to Einstein's **Content Selection Settings** and selecting the sendable **Data Extension** that contains the profile information you want to be used for personalization. You can then manage which profile attributes are considered by Einstein Content Selection.

To give Einstein **Content Selection** guidance about which content to select in different circumstances, you can use **Content Selection Rules**. These are business rules that you specify to avoid common pitfalls that can happen when content is selected by an automated process.

Content Selection Rules come in the following three forms:

- **Fatigue rules**: These rules are created to avoid assets being selected too frequently, resulting in subscribers tiring from seeing the same material over and over again. You can define these based on days since the last selection, days since the last click, and the maximum number of selections.

- **Exclusion rules**: These rules exclude certain assets from being shown to certain audiences. You define them in terms of asset attributes and consumer attributes. For instance, if you have an asset class that includes sports images and a customer profile attribute that indicates interest in sports, you could exclude this asset class from the customers who are not interested in the topic.

- **Variety rules**: Variety rules prevent the same image from being selected multiple times for the same message. You simply specify an asset attribute. Then, assets with that attribute are prevented from recurring more than once in a given message.

With **Content Selection** rules, you have good control over how your content is shown to subscribers, avoiding common issues that can occur in automated systems.

There is also a considerable analytics component that comes out of the box with Einstein **Content Selection**. Using Performance Analytics, you can drill into why particular assets were selected for particular subscribers. This gives you a detailed understanding of how content selection is working in your case. You can also drill into how different asset classes and asset attributes are performing by using the built-in dashboard. The following screenshot shows the basic dashboard for **Content Selection**:

Figure 4.14 – Einstein Content Selection dashboard

Einstein **Content Selection** is an advanced and comprehensive feature that allows you to easily get started with content personalization for your email sends.

The next feature that we will discuss is also content-related but helps you organize and keep track of your assets by automatically tagging them using computer vision.

Einstein Content Tagging

Computer vision is a rich field with many applications to CRM. Einstein Content Tagging is one such application that applies Google Vision capabilities to the JPEG and PNG files in your Marketing Cloud account. It works by automatically scanning through your files once every 24 hours and applying up to 25 tags, as suggested by the computer vision model, to the new image files in your account. This allows you to find the images you need for your content faster. However, only files that are less than 10 MB are tagged.

When you enable Einstein **Content Tagging**, you need to select a few different configuration options:

- **The maximum number of tags per image**: This can be any number between 1 and 25.

- **Tag prefix**: This is a prefix such as `Einstein__` that will be appended to each tag to help you distinguish between manually and automatically assigned tags.

- **Confidence level**: How confident the vision model needs to be about a given tag for it to be applied. The scale goes from 0.5, just as likely to be right as not, to 1.0, absolutely certain.

Once you have configured the feature, you also have the option of changing the tagging location and language that the tag is generated in.

The following screenshot shows how to configure **Einstein Content Tagging**:

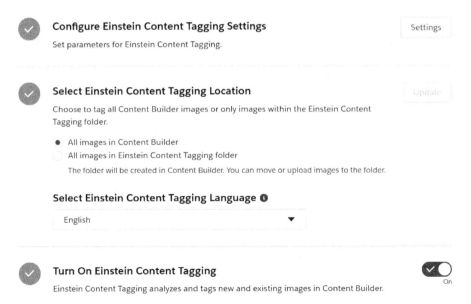

Figure 4.15 – Einstein Content Tagging configuration

Einstein Content Tagging is a small feature that helps by improving the findability of content in your Marketing Cloud account. What's even better is that it is available in more than 100 languages. We will now move on to one of the biggest features in the Marketing Cloud Einstein arsenal, Einstein Recommendations.

Einstein Recommendations

Einstein Recommendations is the AI-powered product and content recommendation engine for Marketing Cloud. It comes in two variants: one for email and one for the web.

In the following two sections, we will cover both of these. First, however, we will cover the commonalities and provide an overview of setting up the recommendation engine to serve recommendations.

Einstein Recommendations overview

A good recommendation engine is often the difference between a customer who converts and one who doesn't. Think about it – how many times have you followed a recommended product on an eCommerce website and ended up buying something? Einstein Recommendations leverages the Einstein Platform's AI capabilities to deliver this capacity to your Marketing Cloud account. The model combines behavioral data with machine learning and business rules that you can define to create personalized recommendations across web and email channels.

The way it works in practice is by algorithmically filtering a catalog based on the attributes of assets in those catalogs. Hence, it stands to reason that the first thing you need to set up to use Einstein Recommendations is a catalog. There are three types of catalog supported by Einstein Recommendations:

- **Product**: A catalog of products available for purchase.
- **Content**: These are content assets such as blog posts or videos that can be viewed by your customers.
- **Banner**: Graphics that can be included in your emails or websites, such as a call to action.

Each type of catalog has different fields to fill out, and you can upload them to your Marketing Cloud environment either through flat-file upload or by streaming updates orchestrated via JavaScript.

The following screenshot shows an overview of the process of importing a catalog:

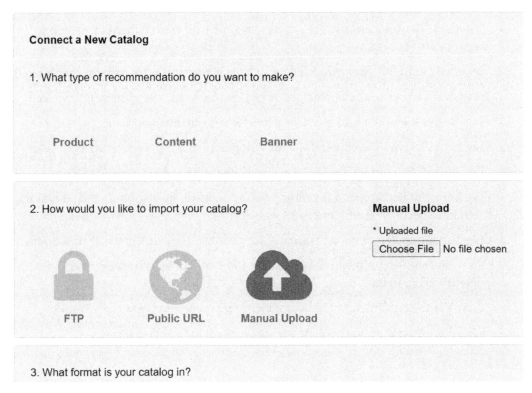

Figure 4.16 – Importing a catalog

The second prerequisite for using Einstein Recommendations is installing the **Collect Tracking Code**. This is a snippet of code that you install on your website to capture visitor behavior, which is necessary to generate good and contextually relevant recommendations. How this is done is a bit outside the scope of this book, but generally, it is done by your web administrator by including a code snippet provided by Salesforce in the relevant templates on your websites and storefronts.

Einstein Recommendations recommends assets based on recommendation scenarios. There are 30 pre-configured scenarios you can use as a starting point, grouped into three different sections. The following lists give a brief overview of all of them:

Reference Item Scenarios:

- **Bought Bought**: Recommend what other people who bought this item also bought.
- **Bought Bought Merge**: Same as Bought Bought, but for an entire basket.
- **Click Bought**: Recommend what other people who clicked the same link also bought.

- **Category Bought**: Recommend what other people who viewed items in the same category bought.

- **Category View**: Recommend what other people who viewed items in the same category also viewed.

- **Search Bought**: Recommend what other people who made the same search bought.

- **Search View**: Recommend what other people who made the same search viewed.

- **Tag**: Recommend the most popular items for a given attribute value.

- **Tag Intersection**: Recommend the most popular items for a set of attribute values.

- **Tag Recent**: Recommend recently available items for a given attribute value.

- **Tag Enjoyed**: Recommend the most popular items for an attribute value, measured both in terms of view and purchases.

- **Tag Top Rated**: Recommend the most highly rated item for a given attribute value.

- **View Bought**: Recommend the items that were bought by other customers who viewed a given item.

- **View View**: Recommend items also viewed by people who viewed a given item.

- **View View Merge**: Same as View View, but for all the items in a cart.

User Data Scenarios:

- **Bought Bought Last Cart**: Recommend items that were also bought by other users that also bought the last item a user added to his/her cart.

- **Bought Bought Last Purchase**: Recommend items that were also bought by other users that bought the same last item the user has bought.

- **Favorite Tag**: Recommend the most popular items that are in the categories and most interesting to the user based on their affinity profile.

- **Last Views Merge**: Recommend items also viewed by other users that viewed any of the last seven items viewed by a given customer.

- **Recently Viewed**: Recommend any of the last seven items viewed by the customer.

- **User Affinities**: Return recommendations that match the top five affinities that a user has on his/her profile.

- **View Bought Last Cart**: Recommend items that were also bought by other users that also viewed the last item a user added to his/her cart.

- **View Bought Last Purchase**: Recommend items that were also bought by other users that viewed the last item a customer bought.

- **View View Last Cart**: Recommend items that were also viewed by other users that also viewed the last item a user added to his/her cart.

- **View View Last Purchase**: Recommend items that were also viewed by other users that also viewed the last item a user bought.

Site Data Scenarios:

- **New Releases**: Recommend up to 100 items added over the last 14 days.

- **Top Enjoyed**: Recommend the most popular items across the site.

- **Top Grossing**: Recommend the products that have generated the most revenue across the site.

- **Top Sellers**: Recommend the best-selling items from across the site.

- **Top Views**: Recommend some of the 100 most viewed items from across the site.

The following screenshot shows how these are used as part of an email recommendation:

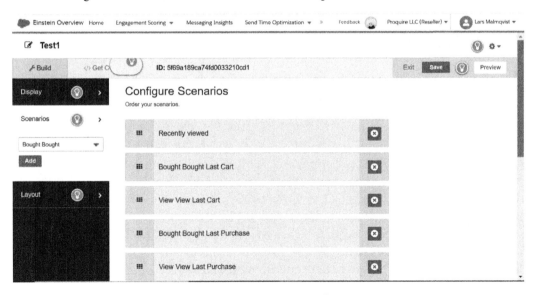

Figure 4.17 – Configuring recommendation scenarios

If none of these options fit your scenario, you also have the option of building recommendation scenarios using **Rule Manager**. This allows you to specify rules based on asset attributes and then specify actions to take, given those attributes. For instance, you could specify a rule that if an asset is classified as a dog-related product, do not show any recommendations related to cats on the same page. You can be as creative as you like in these specifications, although in many (if not most) cases, the out-of-the-box scenarios will work well.

The following screenshot shows the interface for configuring rules:

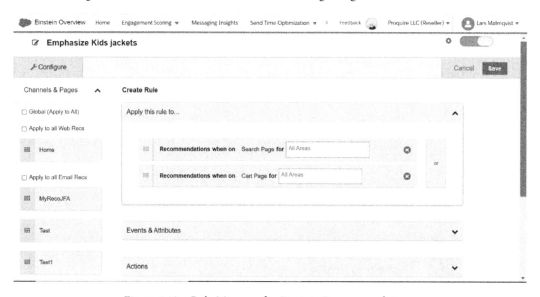

Figure 4.18 – Rule Manager for Einstein Recommendations

Recommendations can be generated with a feature called **waterfall predictions** or without it. If you don't turn waterfall predictions on, then Einstein Recommendations will return results from the first recommendation algorithm (scenario) that returns the full number of requested recommendations. For instance, let's assume you have decided you want five recommendations. Your top scenario is **View View Last Cart** but that only gives you four recommendations. That is less than five, so this algorithm will be ignored and the next one in line will be tried. This will continue until a single algorithm produces all five recommendations. On the other hand, if you turn waterfall predictions on, Einstein Recommendations will aggregate recommendations from different scenarios in order of priority. So, in the previous example, it would take the first four and then take one recommendation from the next most preferred scenario, making up the total five.

We will now look at the first of the two ways recommendations can be activated for customers: **Email Recommendations**.

Einstein Email Recommendations

Email Recommendations embed Einstein Recommendations within Marketing Cloud email templates. With Email Recommendations, you include snippets of HTML code in your email template that correspond to the number of recommendations you want to see in the template where you want the recommendations to appear.

An image tag references a script that will generate the recommendation image shown to the user, and an anchor tag tracks the click on the recommendation. Recommendations are always shown as images, which may have some consequences for the mobile responsiveness of your email design.

You can manage the recommendations that are available via a pre-configured dashboard, as shown in the following screenshot:

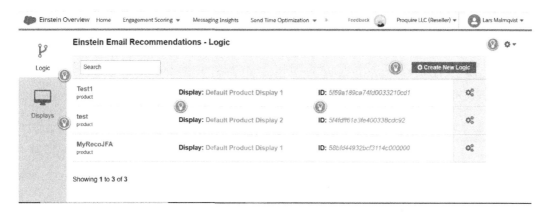

Figure 4.19 – Einstein Email Recommendations dashboard

Here, you can create, edit, and monitor recommendations, as well as see the embedding code needed to use them in templates. For each recommendation, you can customize the logic, layout, content, and scenarios used.

For instance, as shown in the following screenshot, we can change the layout of
the recommendation:

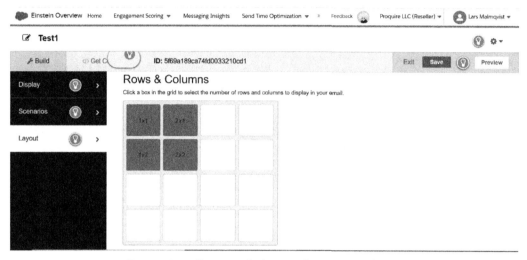

Figure 4.20 – Changing the layout of a recommendation

This means you can adapt what is shown in the image and what scenarios, like the ones
described in the previous section, are used to drive this particular recommendation.

In the following screenshot, we can see how the display can be changed:

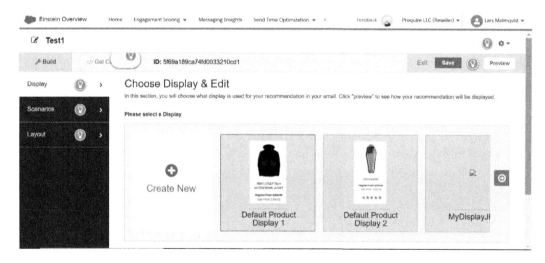

Figure 4.21 – Choosing a display for recommendations

Email Recommendations is a powerful tool, but it's even more powerful when it's
combined with the second type of recommendation, **Einstein Web Recommendations**.

Einstein Web Recommendations

To use **Einstein Recommendations** on your website, you must follow the same format that you did for email but using a different user interface.

The following screenshot shows the introductory dashboard for **Web Recommendations**:

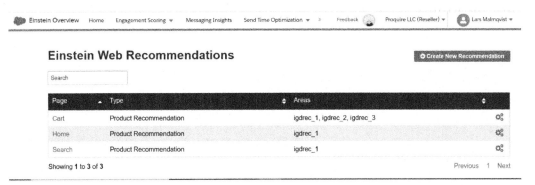

Figure 4.22 – Web Recommendations overview

You need to configure the type and location of the recommendation, along with the display format and scenarios that the recommendation should use to generate options.

These scenarios can be configured with both a strategy and a user-friendly string to be displayed on the page, as shown here:

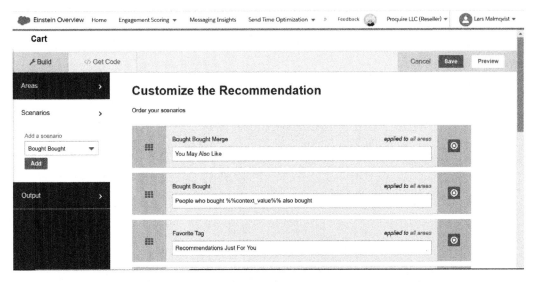

Figure 4.23 – Customizing Web Recommendations strategies

In addition, you need to configure a content area with the name and number of recommendations to generate for each recommendations area you will be providing on a given page, as shown in the following screenshot:

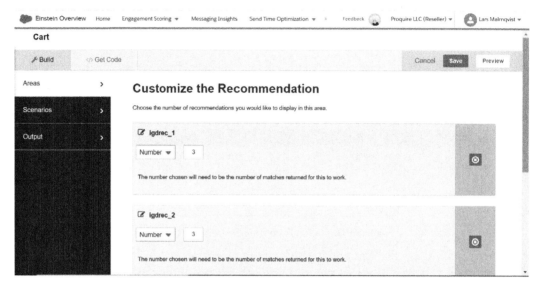

Figure 4.24 – Customizing the content area

You need to configure one recommendation per page that you want to use the recommendations on. These recommendations are delivered via an API call to Marketing Cloud, which is accomplished via a client-side call.

You can get the recommendations in either JSON format or as HTML/JavaScript. The recommendation is to work straight with the JSON you receive from the API call if you have the technical capabilities in-house.

Once everything has been configured, you can get the code to render the documentation from the recommendations dashboard and get your web administrator to facilitate its inclusion on the relevant pages on your website. You can see an example of this in the following screenshot:

Install Recommendation on your Site

Below you will see code for your web recommendations. You or a web developer will need to style the rendered HTML to match your website's style.

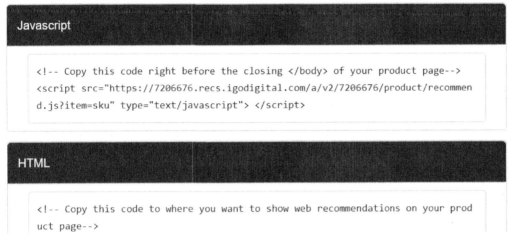

```
Javascript

<!-- Copy this code right before the closing </body> of your product page-->
<script src="https://7206676.recs.igodigital.com/a/v2/7206676/product/recommen
d.js?item=sku" type="text/javascript"> </script>
```

```
HTML

<!-- Copy this code to where you want to show web recommendations on your prod
uct page-->
```

Figure 4.25 – Code for installing recommendations on your site

Einstein Recommendations is a powerful and incredibly flexible recommendations engine for both email and web use cases. We will now shift gears again as we look at the social media insights provided by Einstein Social Insights.

Einstein Social Insights

Einstein Social Insights brings the power of sentiment analysis, the AI subdiscipline that builds models to infer the mood or emotional content of the text, to social listening in Marketing Cloud.

Social Insights monitors conversations and posts on social media and classifies their tone into positive, neutral, or negative sentiments. This information then becomes available to reports and dashboards for analysis and provides insight into the kinds of conversations customers are having about your brand.

The sentiment model that's used by Einstein Social Insights is unusual in so far as you can provide direct input to train it. This happens through the keyword scoring mechanism, which can be accessed via the **Manage Model** option in **Social Studio**. Here, you can see the precision and recall of your current model and then provide input to the sentiment model by scoring the positivity or negativity of keywords and phrases.

You can then add keywords, along with a value to indicate how positive or negative they are. The model will reevaluate its precision and recall based on these manual changes and also calculate an agreement score between the model and the manually scored keywords and phrases. Salesforce recommends getting a sentiment agreement score of 79%, which will likely mean manually labeling hundreds if not thousands of phrases.

Social Insights can help brands that prioritize social listening as a way to engage with their customers better. This helps them respond to and leverage trends in the conversations their customers are having about the brand. The final feature we will look at in this section, **Einstein Vision for Social Studio**, enhances social listening even further by applying computer vision to images posted by consumers.

Einstein Vision for Social Studio

Einstein Vision for Social Studio applies pre-trained image classifiers to help scan incoming social posts for information relevant to marketers. It also enriches the images with information that contains the judgment made by those classifiers.

For instance, the classifiers might find that an image has your brand's logo present, a cup of coffee, and is set in a kitchen. You can probably imagine the kinds of scenarios that this would be useful for. For instance, you might find that your brand is being posted in particular kinds of locations or along with certain types of objects, which may help you respond effectively with messages that target these kinds of scenarios.

The four classifiers that **Einstein Vision for Social Studio** can apply are as follows:

- **Logo**: Recognizes about 2 million different logos and is the most accurate of the classifiers available.

- **Scene**: Can distinguish 60 different kinds of scenes, such as a beach or a kitchen.

- **Food**: Recognizes 200 different kinds of food.

- **Object**: Recognizes 1,000 different kinds of objects.

You can use any subset of these classifiers if some are not relevant to you.

Enabling **Einstein Vision for Social Studio** requires reaching out to your account executive, as well as Marketing Cloud support, so at the time of writing, it's not what you'd consider a standard feature. However, for brands that are heavily invested in social listening, this feature is another good addition.

We have now seen the extensive and varied features that Marketing Cloud Einstein puts at an architect's disposal. We will now move on and have a look at Commerce Cloud Einstein.

Implementing Commerce Cloud Einstein

Commerce Cloud Einstein is Salesforce's AI offering for B2C storefronts built on Commerce Cloud. It is focused on providing easy out-of-the-box offerings that drive fast value. It does so by saving time and effort in setting up the features while providing a great user experience to customers. We will start with the biggest and most important feature: Einstein Product Recommendations.

Einstein Product Recommendations

We have already met the powerful recommendations engine driving Einstein Recommendations in Marketing Cloud. Einstein Product Recommendations is the native Commerce Cloud option for providing recommendations for other products in the catalog. In contrast to the general-purpose Einstein Recommendations, Einstein Product Recommendations is focused entirely on providing good product recommendations as part of an e-commerce website. Therefore, the two are complementary, although they overlap in some functionality.

The configuration of Einstein Product Recommendations is complex and requires specialist knowledge as well as communications with Salesforce support to enable and configure certain elements. Therefore, we will not be able to go into the full detail here, but we will cover enough that you can get a high-level view of whether this might fit your organization.

Einstein Product Recommendations works based on product and catalog feeds that have been set up against your production Commerce Cloud instance. It combines these with live behavioral data from the website to generate recommendations for shoppers as they browse your storefront.

You use Einstein Configurator to configure Einstein Product Recommendations for your requirements. You configure recommenders using a combination of recommender types, strategies, and actions.

The recommender types are used to generate recommendations based on some input. The available recommender types are as follows:

- **Product to Product**: Generate recommendations based on products similar to the current one.

- **Products in All categories**: Generate recommendations globally across categories.

- **Products in a Category**: Generate recommendations within a category.

- **Recently Viewed**: Generate recommendations based on the products a user has recently viewed.

- **Complete the Set**: Generate recommendations based on items complementary to the shopper's current selection.

The recommender types define what is used as input to the recommendation engine, but strategies are the elements that define how recommendations are generated. You can choose between the following strategies:

- **A customer recently viewed items**: Based on the products a user has recently viewed.

- **Customers who bought also bought**: Based on the products bought by customers who bought the current item.

- **Customers who viewed also viewed**: Based on the products viewed by customers who viewed the current item.

- **Customers who viewed ultimately bought**: Based on the product bought by customers who viewed the current item.

- **Product Affinity**: This calculates product-to-product similarity and uses for the recommendation.

- **Real-Time Personalized Recommendations**: Based on the shopper's past purchases and browsing behavior.

- **Recent Most-Viewed Products**: Based on items complementary to the shopper's current selection.

- **Recent Top-Selling Products**: Based on recently top-selling products.

- **Complete the Set**: Based on items complementary to the shopper's current selection.

You can define multiple strategies for each recommender and Einstein will use each, in turn, to generate recommendations up to the required number.

Recommendations can also be refined with rule actions that show, hide, promote, or demote items that match certain criteria. This could, for instance, be used to give preference to certain brands or hide options that are irrelevant in a particular context.

These recommendations can be activated on the storefront by including content slots in your templates that are reserved as placeholders for recommendations. This is something that requires both administrators and developers to implement successfully, but it does let you tailor the deployment so that it fits your exact brand requirements.

Einstein Product Recommendations is a must-have for heavy users of Commerce Cloud, but it is also specific to this product and requires considerable configuration and development to get up and running. On the other hand, it has immense flexibility in how you can configure and embed it, which makes it commensurately powerful.

We will now look at a much simpler feature in the Commerce Cloud Einstein repertoire: Einstein Predictive Sort.

Einstein Predictive Sort

The position of a sort order can matter immensely for results. Just ask the thousands of SEO specialists who dedicate their lives to getting websites onto the first couple of slots in the Google search result ranking. In Commerce Cloud, you can configure complex sorting arrangements for search results, dropdowns, and other ordered user interface elements. Historically, this is done manually, but with **Einstein Predictive Sort**, you get to leverage machine learning to improve the ordering of your results.

Einstein Predictive Sort is fundamentally a machine learning model that uses data about individual shoppers to customize the ordering of their search results. It correlates information from product catalogs with the shopper's order history and their current web behavior to calculate their affinity toward different products. This is done in real time as they browse, and their affinities are saved to a cookie to allow it to be used immediately by the storefront pages to customize the search order.

The configuration of **Einstein Predictive Sort** happens during the normal setup of sorting rules within Commerce Cloud. This is a complex topic in its own right and we don't have time to cover it here. However, in a nutshell, an administrator will set up a dynamic sorting rule in the backend that's used for site configuration and include predictive sort as an attribute.

Very little is said about how the predictive mechanism that powers **Einstein Predictive Sort** works in practice. This means your results may vary considerably based on different ways of configuring your sorting rules. If you want to adopt this feature, some level of trial and error will likely be necessary to get to a good level of functionality. That being said, the promise of greater real-time personalization for shoppers is a proposition many brands won't want to dismiss immediately.

We will now continue our discussion of Commerce Cloud Einstein by looking at Einstein Search Dictionaries.

Einstein Search Dictionaries

Maintaining a good search engine on a website is no small feat of engineering, especially these days, where Google is so ubiquitous as to have become a verb. One key part of providing a good search experience is for the search engine to understand variations in how the user might express themselves.

Some examples include the following:

- **Synonymy**: The user might use a different word that means the same or roughly the same thing.

- **Hypernymy or Hyponymy**: The user might use a less specific word – a hypernym, or more specifically, a hyponym – with the same search intention in mind. For instance, a user looking for a smartphone might just search for a phone, which is a hypernym, or for iPhone, which is a hyponym.

- **Common phrases**: Things that go together in a search, such as **Einstein Search Dictionaries**.

This is by no means is a comprehensive list, but you hopefully get the point that having a good search dictionary is essential to a good search.

Einstein Search Dictionaries takes at least some of the manual drudgery out of creating and maintaining such dictionaries by updating them based on live searches, not just on your storefront, but across all the Commerce Cloud customers that are using the feature and consent to sharing anonymized search data.

Einstein Search Dictionaries is one of the few Einstein features that are enabled by default and doesn't require activation. However, if you want to partake in the data from the wider network of Commerce Cloud users, you will have to accept the Einstein Data Privacy Agreement.

The recommendations appear in a special dictionary under the general interface, which is used for managing search dictionaries in Commerce Cloud. From there, the process is simple. The recommendations are created automatically and the administrator simply decides whether to reject or approve them.

While some of the basic administration of your search dictionaries will remain, even when using **Einstein Search Dictionaries**, it is a hard feature to disparage since it alleviates administrative work, improves the user experience, and comes turned on automatically.

We will now continue our exploration of Commerce Cloud Einstein by looking at Einstein Commerce Insights.

Einstein Commerce Insights

Market basket analysis is a classic application of machine learning that's been in use for more than a decade by both online and offline retailers. It works by identifying commonly bought item sets – that is, items that are frequently bought together – to enable promotions and cross-sell opportunities on closely related products.

For instance, if someone buys diapers, you may want to show them a promotion for wet wipes, whereas if they buy beer, you may want to show them a promotion for potato chips. Some of these correlations will be well known to marketers, but the power of this approach is that you can quantitatively discover the relationships that do exist in your data without any preconceived notions, and you can also get a sense of the strength of the relationship.

Historically, this type of analysis has been fairly heavyweight and therefore stayed in the domain of large retailers, but with **Einstein Commerce Insights**, this type of functionality is brought to users of Commerce Cloud.

Commerce Cloud Einstein uses the product and order feeds exposed by Commerce Cloud to perform the analysis. This is done weekly and takes 30 days of historical data into account. Therefore, you are somewhat limited with the analysis and will have to review it on an ongoing basis to get value.

This functionality is exposed as a pre-baked reporting interface that allows you to group and drill into the data with a variety of dimensions such as period or category. For each product in the analysis, you will see a list of other products that the given product was purchased with, as well as the proportion of baskets for which that was true. For instance, you might find that wet wipes were bought with diapers 60% of the time. Other views may show aggregated information about sales and baskets, but the analysis of common baskets will likely be of most interest to most users.

With that, we have concluded our discussion of Commerce Cloud Einstein and also the content for this chapter. Take a deep breath – we've gone through a lot of material.

Summary

In this chapter, we have examined the AI features present in the Marketing and Commerce Clouds. This was a high-paced exploration of a multitude of features that help personalize the customer journey across both email and the web, and you may be feeling slightly dizzy from the experience. Well done for hanging on.

In the *Using Einstein Marketing Cloud* section, we looked at features such as Einstein Splits and Send Time Optimization, which can help you target the right people at the right time with your email messages. We also looked at Einstein Recommendations and Content Selection, which can tailor the content of messages to individual users. Overall, we saw a deep level of capability, perhaps deeper than anywhere else in the Einstein Platform, that can be deployed in a range of common scenarios with little configuration required.

For Commerce Cloud, we looked at specialized AI capabilities that focus on personalizing the shopping experience. This included recommending products using a variety of strategies, such as using **Einstein Product Recommendations**, tailoring the order of search results using **Einstein Predictive Sort**, and improving the overall search experience using **Einstein Search Dictionaries**. In general, the features in Commerce Cloud have a deeper level of configurability, but also require much greater technical skill on behalf of the organization that needs to deploy them.

Now that we know how to create unique and personalized experiences for our users, let's learn how Salesforce Einstein can be tailored to specific industry requirements as we look at industry clouds in the next chapter.

Questions

1. Why would you use Einstein Send Time Optimization?
2. Where do you activate the personas generated by Einstein Engagement Scoring?
3. What classic AI application does Einstein Commerce Insights use?

5
Salesforce AI for Industry Clouds

This chapter will cover how Einstein has been brought into Salesforce's various industry clouds, including the Health, Financial Services, Manufacturing, Consumer Goods, and Nonprofit Clouds. As most of these features have been created using other elements rather than being unique, this is more of a showcase for how Einstein features can be used than a discussion of new technical material.

In this chapter, we're going to cover the following main topics:

- Introducing Einstein for Industry Clouds
- Using Health Cloud Einstein
- Implementing Financial Services Cloud Einstein
- Working with Manufacturing Cloud Einstein
- Optimizing with Consumer Goods Cloud Einstein
- Analyzing with Non-profit Cloud Einstein

After completing this chapter, you will have gained an understanding of how to use Salesforce AI solutions within industry-specific solutions.

Technical requirements

There are no technical requirements for this chapter as, unfortunately, the features under discussion are not generally available for trial use. If you have access to the industry clouds discussed, you can follow the descriptions provided.

Introducing Einstein for Industry Clouds

For Salesforce, industry, clouds are a strategic priority at the moment. Both through the work they have been doing on their industry-specific cloud offerings and through their recent acquisition of **Vlocity**, they have made it clear that they see the fastest time to value for their enterprise customers by adopting industry clouds on top of the core clouds that are already in use.

As part of this development, each industry cloud has also been getting upgrades related to the Einstein Platform. It now makes sense to talk about a Health Cloud Einstein and a Financial Services Cloud Einstein much in the same way as we previously talked about Sales Cloud Einstein.

These features are often much more specific and, to some extent, more complex and difficult to use than many we have looked at so far. This is not surprising as the problems being addressed are much more specific, and the number of customers for each feature is smaller.

That being said, for the organizations that fit the bill, these features can be extraordinarily powerful. In the following sections, we will go through the Einstein offerings for the major industry clouds in the Salesforce portfolio and see how they might be able to help.

Using Health Cloud Einstein

Health Cloud is Salesforce's offering for healthcare and life sciences customers. It contains a complex data model and associated functionality that caters to the needs of providers of healthcare services such as hospitals and health insurance companies, and pharmaceutical companies and medical device manufacturers. From an Einstein perspective, it focuses on analytical applications that give greater insight into common issues faced by these types of organizations. We will see how in the following sections.

Analytics for Healthcare

Analytics for Healthcare is a predefined set of dashboards and Einstein Discovery Stories built on top of Tableau CRM that enable customers to drill into several relevant dimensions for different types of Health and Life Sciences organizations. There are separate dashboards for analyzing care performance, patient referrals, utilization, patient segmentation, social determinants, visit and team insights, and emergency response. In addition, Health Cloud customers get access to a subset of Manufacturing Cloud Einstein, but we will cover that in the *Working with Manufacturing Cloud Einstein* section. The dashboards come in both an analytics app, which gives a full overview of the process, and embedded dashboards, which show relevant information on record pages.

The app comes licensed with Health Cloud but still requires a considerable amount of setup. First, it is a requirement that both Tableau CRM and Health Cloud are already configured and ready to use within your environment. Second, you need to assign the right permissions to administrators, end users, and the integration user that is used for data transfer. Several of the subcomponents, including referral management and utilization management, have extensive prerequisites of their own that are too complex to cover here. Just know that you will need to do specific setup and installation tasks for each of the various dashboard components you want to make use of in your environment. In addition, there is a limitation on Analytics for Healthcare, which means that Sales Cloud Einstein features and Salesforce Inbox are not supported.

Having met all these prerequisites, you can create the app in Tableau CRM using the predefined template. Once the app has confirmed that you have completed all the prerequisite tasks, you can pick which elements to install. As Health Cloud has different ways of modeling patients, you will also need to specify the relevant record types within your org. The app will take some time to create, but once the setup is completed, you can share it with the relevant users in your organization. Once you've completed the app's setup, you still need to configure the synchronization schedule for the data needed by the app, and then embed the relevant dashboard components on the record pages within your org. At this point, you can start looking at the functionality.

The Analytics for Healthcare app contains the following functionalities, at least if you install everything:

- **Care performance**: These dashboards focus on letting care coordinators know how well members are adhering to their defined care plans and enabling proactive action to prevent members from going too far off track, thereby helping to manage patient risk. There are prebuilt views that show overall adherence to the plan across the whole patient population, but this can also be broken down by patient risk. Care coordinators can also drill into the details and see members with care plans that are overdue or at risk of becoming so. This part of the app also includes an Einstein Discovery Story, which is a predefined analytical machine learning model that analyzes underlying factors such as age or type of care, which might help predict adherence to a care plan. There is also an associated embedded dashboard that allows care personnel to see any upcoming or overdue care plans for patients, as well as any outstanding care requests.

- **Referral analytics**: Referrals, which are typically from other parts of the healthcare system, are the way many healthcare and life sciences companies get new customers. Therefore, these companies need to deliver a great new patient experience to referrals so that they become great customers and advocates of the relevant products and services. Referral analytics enables this by delivering a set of dashboards that help uncover bottlenecks and inefficiencies in the referral process, and they also understand what the top sources of referrals are for the company. This includes a view of referrals by age, which can be used to prevent anyone from getting stuck in the process.

  There is also a view of referral efficiency, which couples the process of converting a referral into a patient while taking the efficiency of the care being provided to those patients into account. In addition, there is a dashboard showing metrics related to the top-performing sources of referrals. Like the care performance area, referral analytics also includes a predefined Einstein Discovery Story that is focused on predicting the likelihood of referrals converting into a patient, which allows care staff to take appropriate action, should it be required. Perhaps the most interesting part of the referral analytics area is the embedded dashboard, which can be used on a patient record to get an immediate view of how the appointment bookings for this particular patient compare to the norm. For instance, we can see whether their care is following a normal pattern and whether they are being paid enough attention by care personnel. This allows for the kind of personalized care that drives great patient experiences.

- **Utilization analytics**: This area focuses on the care request process. Specifically, it provides an overview of whether timely care is being provided to patients. The focus is more traditionally analytical than the first two areas we covered. There are no Einstein Discovery Stories or embedded analytics here. Instead, we find detailed dashboards on care requests and their status against SLAs, how they are segmented, which care requests are denied and reopened, what open care requests are present in the system, what services are the most frequently requested, and how care requests are distributed across providers.

- **Patient segmentation**: This is a single dashboard that can be used to segment your patient population by common dimensions such as age, conditions, and, most importantly, risk. It is useful for getting a good high-level view of the patient population for a given company.

- **Social determinants**: This is another single dashboard that focuses on letting you explore the social determinants of health in your patient population. That way, you can understand the barriers that exist between your patients and a good health outcome.

- **Visit and team insights**: These are dashboards for medical device companies that rely on visits with healthcare providers to sell their products. They let your sales reps plan for visits better by ensuring that the right merchandise is in stock, as well as by flagging opportunities for potential additional sales in the accounts to be visited. It also provides traditional sales analytics for your reps and accounts.

- **Emergency response**: These dashboards are a subset of a wider Emergency Response offering that Salesforce has made available for Health Cloud customers. It focuses on managing the emergency intake of patients and identifying any hotspots for patient intake.

Overall, Analytics for Healthcare provides a very detailed analytical picture that helps Health Cloud users manage their businesses. There is a smattering of AI capabilities in the pre-built Einstein Discovery Stories, but in general, the offering mainly consists of traditional analytics. Analytics for Healthcare, however, has been joined by a specialized offering on Risk Stratification that extends these capabilities. We will cover this next.

Analytics for Healthcare – Risk Stratification

The **Analytics for Healthcare: Risk Stratification** module focuses on identifying high-risk patients. This means patients that are likely to consume extraordinary amounts of care resources in the future, as well as those who may benefit from preventative interventions to reduce their risk of developing future conditions.

Installing the risk stratification module is complex. It contains all the steps that were mentioned for the general Analytics for Healthcare app, but it adds substantial additional complexity:

1. It requires a separately managed package to be installed and configured in addition to the core Health Cloud package.

2. You need to manually configure several elements such as XMD, layouts, and picklist values, both in Tableau CRM and in the core Salesforce module.

3. You need to manually schedule an Apex job to calculate and recalculate the risk scores.

The bottom line is that you need a highly technically qualified resource to install and manage this feature.

The risk scoring flow works by combining data from care programs with patient information and, on that basis, calculating a risk score that is mapped to the **CMS Hierarchical Condition Category** (**HCC**), a common risk adjustment model that is used within the US healthcare system. Based on that mapping and the combined information, the risk scoring algorithm calculates the risk for the patient and generates a summary result. This flow is shown in the following diagram:

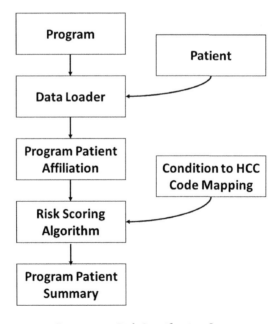

Figure 5.1 – Risk Stratification flow

You have an array of tools available to manage the mappings and data that is used for the calculation. This is configured using standard Health Cloud tools.

The output of this process is a unique Program Patient Summary for each patient that can be accessed using Tableau CRM dashboards. This summary contains the calculated risk score, along with demographic, clinical, and insurance information related to the patient.

Note that the calculation and information are based on US healthcare requirements, so they may be of little utility in other parts of the world, although it may provide immediately actionable insights for those that are US-based. We will now move on to the last Health Cloud Einstein component, explained in the next section.

Einstein Discovery for Appointment Management

Einstein Discovery for Appointment Management seeks to reduce no-shows at health appointments by using machine learning to calculate the appointment times specific users are most likely to show up for. It does this using a predefined Tableau CRM analytics app, which is configured in a similar way to the modules under Analytics for Healthcare.

The central feature in this app is **Einstein Discovery Story**, which analyzes attendance in your patient population and generates a predictive model based on the story. This predicts a patient's likelihood to show up for a given appointment. This prediction is used by the appointment scheduling feature alongside a configurable threshold to pick the best appointment slots for a given patient.

For instance, you could configure a threshold of 80% to only book slots where the model is 80% sure that the patient will show up based on their particular characteristics. Unsurprisingly, this is another feature where having ample historical data will lead to superior results.

It's worth noting that users with access to Einstein Discovery for Appointment Management will have access to Personal Health Information for all patients in your system. Therefore, any rollout should be very selective. Salesforce deactivates this feature by default for Health Cloud users for this very reason.

With that, we have covered the main features of Health Cloud Einstein and will proceed to the next major industry cloud in the Salesforce portfolio: Financial Services Cloud.

Implementing Financial Services Cloud Einstein

Financial Services Cloud is Salesforce's offering for the wider financial services market, including retail and consumer banking, insurance, and wealth management. Given the great disparity between the operating procedures of these fields, it is a wide and comprehensive industry offering. This applies to the Einstein offering as well. While there are some common features across the industry segments, there are also specific templates for each segment in its own right. We will go through the main analytical offerings in the next section and then look at the other non-analytical features included in Financial Services Cloud Einstein.

Tableau CRM for Financial Services

Tableau CRM, which contains a range of pre-built dashboards, and Einstein Discovery Stories are the mainstays of the Financial Services Einstein suite. As we saw with Health Cloud Einstein, enabling and configuring these features is anything but trivial. In general, you need to follow the steps of enabling Tableau CRM, assigning the right permission sets and permissions both from a security and a licensing perspective, setting up data synchronization between your Salesforce core org and Tableau CRM, and then creating, sharing, and configuring the specific apps you are looking to use within your Financial Services Cloud environment. Bear in mind that these features all have specific detailed configurations that must be accomplished. Again, you may want to consider bringing in specialist help if you are looking to use these features in practice.

The Financial Services Einstein suite contains a range of apps, each of which has functionality tailored to particular segments within the wider financial services industry. We will go through each of these in turn in the following subsections.

Analytics for Wealth Management

The **Analytics for Wealth Management** app provides comprehensive and actionable intelligence to financial advisors about their current and potential customers. It consists of a combination of dashboards, both overview and embedded, as well as Einstein Discovery Stories, which predict churn and propensity to add assets. **Client Acquisition** dashboard is used to target the most promising leads within your current pipeline by showing you different views of your pipeline and what factors tend to facilitate a conversion. **Client Interactions** dashboard, in contrast, focuses on current customers and flags any clients that might need an advisor's attention. **Events and Seminars** dashboard, as you'd expect, tracks the performance of events and seminars. There is then a sequence of dashboards for **My Book of Business**, **My Clients**, and **My Households** that gives a detailed advisor-level view of the current status. Finally, **Sales Performance** dashboard drills into the current performance of sales activities, both on an individual and an aggregate level.

Next to Analytics for Wealth Management, there are two complementary apps: **Predict Client Churn Risk for Wealth Management Analytics** and **Predict Likelihood to Add Assets for Wealth Management Analytics**. These each contain an Einstein Discovery Story that shows the likelihood of account churn on the one hand and of adding assets on the other. These must be installed and configured separately but are part of the overall offering on wealth management analytics contained in the Financial Services Cloud. Finally, there is a wealth of embedded dashboards that provide context information on clients, leads, financial accounts, and their progress toward certain goals. This means much of the information discussed in this section can be made actionable in the context of individual records, substantially increasing the overall value of the offering.

Analytics for Insurance

The insurance offering in **Financial Services Einstein** is parallel to the one for Wealth Management in that it contains pre-packaged dashboards and a sophisticated Einstein Discovery Story focused on predicting policy renewal. This offering focuses both on the needs of individual insurance agents and on the managers in charge of the overall pipeline, which is reflected in the structure of the dashboards. It is a highly sales-oriented solution that will appeal to many organizations within this space. The agent-focused dashboard centrally contains a view of the agent's customers and their policies, along with related information. This includes high-level KPIs around customers and policies, along with trend information and a view of earnings and fees related to those policies. There are also breakdowns of customers by attractiveness and demographics. This provides the agents with a greater understanding of their segmentation, as well as a metric-based view of how the agent has been interacting with customers over time.

In addition, we will find these additional sections:

- Policies up for renewal

- Claims against the agent's policies

- Product analysis, along with the associated metrics, to help the agent understand what to sell to whom

- Traditional sales analytics surrounding sales performance, customer acquisition, and cross/upsell opportunities

The manager's view of this data is not substantially different from the agent's view of their individual sales performance. It simply aggregates the information across the team. That way, the sales manager can view the complete book of business for their team, along with sales performance and customer acquisition metrics. Similar to the Wealth Management Analytics offering, there is a range of embedded dashboards that can embed the information we've discussed into individual record pages, although perhaps not quite to the same extent. Finally, the add-on app, known as **Einstein Discovery for Insurance Analytics**, can be installed separately and provides both an overview and embedded dashboards for showing the likelihood that a policy will be renewed. This gives the insurance agent a heads-up on any policies that may require extra attention.

Analytics for Retail Banking

This is a fairly classic analytics app focused on the needs of retail banks. It contains a summary KPI dashboard with totals related to clients, fees and charges, and activities. In addition, it has a breakdown of customers indicating which may be at risk and require attention, as well more traditional demographic breakdowns. There are also analyses of activities and fees and charges that answer top-level questions regarding what you are spending your time on or which customers were charged a particular kind of fee.

This app is in line with most of the others we have discussed, and it also has a dashboard focused on client acquisition that helps manage your pipeline activities. Finally, because of the branch-based structure of most retail banks, there is a dedicated **Branch Management** dashboard that provides a comprehensive view of activities at the branch level.

Consumer Banking Starter Analytics

This is a basic analytics offering that intends to help consumer bankers grow their asset base. It is quite simple as it only provides basic views of clients, referrals, opportunities, and activities at an individual and team level. This simplicity stands in contrast to some of the other offerings we've discussed so far in this section, and it stands to reason that for some clients, going all-in on the more complex solutions is a step too far to begin with. Therefore, consider the starter analytics apps for smaller or less mature customers that are adopting **Financial Services Cloud**.

Wealth Starter Analytics

The full-fledged Wealth Management Analytics app is one of the most capable offerings in the Financial Services Einstein suite. However, it is can also be a little overwhelming, simply because of its large scope. Wealth Starter Analytics provides a softer starting point for smaller or less mature organizations to get started. The app is based on a dashboard view of your book of business. From there, you can drill into views of accounts, client interactions, pipeline, cases, and marketing programs. Each of these views provides simple overviews of your data, broken down and ordered in a way to make them easily accessible and actionable.

Client Segmentation

This app breaks down clients to help you prioritize your time and activities toward the most promising clients. It has views for describing activities, client goals, filtering clients by various parameters, and a particularly interesting 80/20 view that shows you revenue against activities on a client basis to discover what clients give the most bang for your buck.

Analytics for Mortgage

This app provides specialist capabilities for managing your lending pipeline. It provides an overview of your loan application pipeline, along with forecasting that can be broken down and analyzed in several different dimensions. It also has additional pipeline management views that you can use to prioritize particular applications and drive them through the process quickly.

Overall, Tableau CRM for Financial Services Einstein has a massive amount of pre-built analytical capabilities. However, any particular customer will only tap into a relatively small subset of this. For wealth management and insurance, it is fair to say that the capabilities are well developed and extensive. The other offerings are more traditional and while they will save you time in setting up analytical dashboards yourself, they are probably not beyond what most banks would already have in-house.

We will now consider the other Einstein features in Financial Services Cloud, starting with Einstein Referral Scoring.

Einstein Referral Scoring

Einstein Referral Scoring is a pre-built predictive model that scores referrals and leads according to their likelihood to become customers. It shares many features of other predictive models we've discussed earlier in this book, such as Einstein Lead Scoring. In fact, like Lead Scoring, it is entirely based on the information in the Lead object. Before you can use this feature, you need to enable it and assign the right permission set licenses to users in your org.

You need a certain minimum number of records in your Lead object to be able to generate predictions. The theoretical minimum is 400, with a minimum of 100 of those being in each outcome category, positive and negative. However, if you want to segment your referrals in any way, for example, web leads versus leads from events, you will need a minimum of 400 records for each segment. In practice, that means a large enough data volume to have had 400 records in your smallest segment. However, even if you don't meet that threshold, you can use global predictions for all the records of a given record type, so long as you meet the minimum of 400 records overall. You just won't be able to create additional segmented predictions until you have sufficient data.

During the process of creating a new prediction, you have several options that you can configure. First, Einstein Referral Scoring for Financial Services Cloud will add several formula fields to your Lead object. This will pull in related account information that is useful to the scoring process, such as the person's annual income. You can deselect any that you don't want to use. You can include and exclude record types and what fields the prediction is based on, and you can even use a custom field as the outcome variable if, for some reason, you aren't using the standard lead conversion process. Finally, you can segment the prediction based on the fields on the lead record.

Once you have generated predictions, you can make them available in the user interface using the Einstein Top Referrals lightning component. This component shows you the top referrals based on the score calculated by the machine learning model. You can refine this list further by filtering on picklist values from the Lead object and the Lead record's creation time.

Einstein Referral Scoring is a flexible and configurable lead scoring model for Financial Services, so it will be of interest to many customers in this segment. Next, we will consider how AI can help deal with forms and documents in financial services.

Intelligent Document Automation and Form Reader

Intelligent Document Automation and Intelligent Form Reader are two offerings within Financial Services Einstein that apply OCR to automatically extract data from financial documents. The key difference between the two is that Intelligent Document Automation simply extracts values from documents when they are uploaded, but doesn't automatically do anything with them. Intelligent Form Reader, in contrast, seeks to map the values from the input document to fields in a Salesforce object.

Intelligent Document Automation is targeted principally at loan officers that need to check a considerable amount of documentation from applicants to process their loan applications. The feature is set up by configuring the relevant document types and giving the required permissions to the loan officers. When this configuration is done, a process will be started whenever a user uploads a document in one of the relevant file types (PDF, JPG, or PNG) to the Financial Services Cloud. This process will extract any recognizable values using OCR and save the result to the OCR Document Scan Result object in Salesforce, where it can be activated using standard Salesforce features.

Intelligent Form Reader is built on top of the Amazon Web Services component known as Textract, which allows you to extract structured data from unstructured input files. Intelligent Form Reader works by mapping between the input document types that you define and fields on a Salesforce object. There are some standard form types you can use, but you can also upload a custom one. Based on the form definition extracted from the input form, you can map the values to Salesforce objects. For Intelligent Document Automation, for example, the process of generating the OCR result and mapping the data across happens automatically upon uploading a relevant document.

The current offering focuses on mortgage applications, but we hope that this highly useful feature is extended more widely. Now, we will consider the final feature within Financial Services Einstein, known as Einstein Bots for Financial Services Cloud.

Einstein Bots for Financial Services Cloud

Einstein Bots for Financial Services Cloud is a set of predefined bot templates that are designed to handle common requests within a financial services context. While you are unlikely to be able to use these unmodified, they give you a head start when implementing bots within a financial services organization. Since we discussed how to set up Einstein Bots in detail in *Chapter 3, Salesforce AI for Service*, in the *Einstein Bots at Pickled Plastics Ltd.* section, we won't discuss the preliminary configuration steps. There is no difference from the general case. The specific bots and accompanying data are installed directly from AppExchange, with no additional configuration.

There are two key transactions included within the package: reporting a lost card and registering an international travel plan. These can be trialed using Embedded Service and a set of sample data provided with the AppExchange package. Both transactions include fairly sophisticated functionality, such as email verification of the customer's identity, so they provide a good demo to take forward internally to make the case for adopting bots as a customer service channel.

Financial Services Einstein contains a full set of analytical capabilities across a range of industry segments. If you happen to be among the segments where the capabilities are fully developed, this can be a real win. However, for other areas, it is not quite as advanced. Now, let's continue our discussion with Manufacturing Cloud Einstein.

Working with Manufacturing Cloud Einstein

Manufacturing Cloud is Salesforce's industry solution for manufacturing companies. It builds on top of its Sales and Service core clouds and extends them with capabilities such as account-based forecasting and sales agreement management, which provide specific capabilities for the industry. Compared to the other industry clouds we have seen so far in this chapter, the Einstein capabilities of Manufacturing Cloud are fairly limited, encompassing an analytical app with a set of preconfigured dashboards and Einstein Discovery Stories. We will explore these in the next section.

Tableau CRM for Manufacturing

The **Tableau CRM for Manufacturing** template is installed in a similar way to what we've seen so far. You need to enable Tableau CRM in your org and assign the right permissions and permission set licenses, field-level security, and data synchronization.

There are, however, several app-specific choices that are unique to manufacturing:

1. You have the choice of what features to include. You can select or de-select Sales Agreement, Sales Target, Account Forecast, and Rebates to include or exclude analytics related to those areas.

2. You have some options around how to make data available at the security level.

3. You can select what Einstein Discovery Stories to include.

4. You can configure how to credit orders to sales targets.

There are overview dashboards related to all of the main areas within the Manufacturing Cloud, including account health and insights, product performance, pricing insights, sales agreements, whitespace analysis, and sales agreements. All of these dashboards are comprehensive and can be broken down by a broad range of parameters, such as account characteristics, product family, or date range. They are, by and large, fairly traditional analytical dashboards that present high-level metrics, as well as the opportunity to drill in to individual records for further detailed investigation.

As we've seen several times already, there are also embedded dashboards that allow you to activate this information in the context of individual records. For instance, you can get an embedded view of the performance of your sales agreements, which allows you to rapidly assess the state of play.

There are also three Einstein Discovery Stories that provide some predictive power on top of the underlying data:

- Maximize Sales Agreement Product Renewals, predicts the likelihood that a given Sales Agreement will be renewed. This enables you to focus your renewal efforts where they are needed.

- Get Price Recommendations for Products and Schedules, gives pricing guidance for the products and schedules attached to sales agreements to improve your pricing performance.

- For users using rebate management, the Rebates Einstein Discovery story helps you increase your revenue by highlighting factors that have an impact on profitability.

The Einstein offering for Manufacturing Cloud is in the same line as those for Health and Financial Services Cloud and provides a full-fledged view of the sales side of a manufacturing business. There are, however, fewer additional features that leverage the underlying AI capabilities of the Einstein Platform. We will continue by exploring Consumer Goods Cloud and its associated Einstein offering.

Optimizing retail compliance with Consumer Goods Cloud Einstein

Consumer Goods Cloud serves companies that provide consumers with their products. It leverages AI to optimize the visits made by field reps so that they can spend less time doing routine inspections and have a greater impact when they make their store visits. The Einstein offering is central to the proposition in Consumer Goods Cloud. We will see how in the following sections.

Analytics for Consumer Goods

As with all the other offerings we have been discussing in this chapter, Consumer Goods Einstein has, at its center, an analytics app with some additional Einstein Discovery Stories for added predictive capacity. The setup for the Analytics for Consumer Goods app follows the same pattern we have seen already, so we will skip it for now.

Once you have installed the analytics app, you will have access to both the overview and embedded dashboards, in line with what we have seen already. But Analytics for Consumer Goods contains an additional category of dashboards specifically for merchandising activities.

The dashboards and embedded dashboards primarily focus on sales performance, again following a pattern we have seen in other industry clouds. You can see performance both at the level of the individual sales rep and at the level of the team. However, to accommodate the retail-centric nature of consumer goods, some views look at store and sales territory performance. At the store level, this performance is tied to retail execution KPIs and related store visits. Some dashboards allow managers to explore product performance and analyze whitespace based on store sales. This information can be embedded in the context of particular stores to give actionable information ahead of further engagement.

There are two pre-configured Einstein Discovery Stories that come with Analytics for Consumer Goods: Maximize Store Product Sales and Minimize Out-of-Stock Occurrences in a Store. The Maximize Store Product Sales story identifies factors that could impact product sales for either an individual store or a group of stores. The Minimize Out-of-Stock Occurrences in a Store predicts what products are likely to run out for stores, allowing your field reps to proactively contact or visit those stores to avoid running out of stock.

Analytics for Consumer Goods follows the general trend for industry clouds of providing a strong analytical app with some added predictive power. However, there is considerably more to the Einstein offering in this cloud, which we will see when we explore Einstein Visit and Visit Task Recommendations next.

Einstein Visit and Visit Task Recommendations

Einstein Visit and Visit Task Recommendations uses a combination of a flow, an Einstein Next Best Action Strategy, and optionally an Apex class to generate recommendations for what stores to visit next. The strategy runs in a flow and generates recommendations based on configurable parameters that you provide. If more advanced processing is required, you can do so in an Apex action. The configuration of this feature shares much with the overall Einstein Next Best Action feature, which we will discuss in *Chapter 6, Declarative Customization Options*.

Einstein Visit Recommendations works in much the same way and is also configured to provide recommendations along the lines of Einstein Next Best Action. What makes these features powerful, however, is that Salesforce has provided templates for both flows and Apex code that you can customize to your need, as well as provide an interface directly in Consumer Goods Cloud to use them. This makes it easier for you to create a genuinely tailored experience for your users.

This means that field reps have easy and contextually relevant access to these recommendations once you have set them up. Given the crucial place of store visits in the Consumer Goods world, this is nothing to sniff at.

We will finish this section by looking at the last Einstein feature in the Consumer Goods cloud, known as Einstein Object Detection.

Einstein Object Detection

Einstein Object Detection is a purpose-built image classifier that works based on your dataset to identify objects in images taken by your field reps. This ensures compliance and improves retail execution. In contrast to most of the Einstein Platform features we have seen so far, this is a custom machine learning model that is built on your dataset.

That is both a blessing and a curse. First, it means you need to provide an annotated dataset of images of a sufficient size and quantity for the model to be able to accurately identify the objects in question. However, it also means that whatever objects are central to your brand, you can include them in the dataset and have them detected in images.

The dataset is the central point in this feature. You need to provide good quality images with accurate bounding box information that identifies the objects you need to identify, and you need to do this while respecting the 10 GB overall size limit, which has a limit of 1 MB per picture. Unless you already have an in-house team working on vision models, generating this will take some time.

The good news is that once you have constructed the dataset, Einstein does the rest. You simply upload the dataset and build the model and then whenever a sales rep uploads an image to a relevant location, the object detection model will run and save the detected objects to a Detected Object object within Salesforce.

Consumer Goods Cloud is a fairly sophisticated user of Einstein features with a focus on improving the experience for the sales reps in the field. We will close our discussion of industry cloud Einstein capabilities by considering Non-profit Cloud Einstein.

Analyzing with Non-profit Cloud Einstein

Salesforce provides strong cloud offerings for both non-profit and education organizations. However, from an Einstein Platform perspective, there is currently not much to dig into. For the Education cloud, no unique features are provided at all, whereas the Non-profit Cloud includes two analytical templates both focused on fundraising, but with little to no AI or machine learning capabilities included. We will consider these next.

Fundraising Analytics and Performance Analytics

Fundraising is one of the central activities of non-profit organizations. Most non-profits that adopt Salesforce do so at least partially to better manage the fundraising process. Therefore, it is not surprising that an analytics offering in this space would make a good complement to the offerings in the industry cloud. It is somewhat more surprising to find that there are two such templates.

The reason for this is similar to what we saw for several offerings under Financial Services Cloud. The Fundraising Analytics template can be used from the word go, while the Performance Analytics template requires 3 years of back data in your core objects to be effective.

The key feature of the Fundraising Analytics template is to bring in donation data from Salesforce and visualize it in pre-built dashboards, which helps you identify your most effective sources of donations. There's a set of pre-built dashboards that visualize different aspects of donation performance and various lenses that can be used for exploratory analysis.

The Fundraising Performance Analytics template is a more structured offering that provides a long list of KPIs across three categories:

- **Donors**: Including totals and details for numbers, donations, retention rates, and types.

- **Giving**: Including totals and growth numbers both by the donor and in currency terms, as well as various breakdowns of this information.

- **Performance**: Focused on net gain/loss over a certain period and providing details on donor churn, participation, and recapture rates.

The Non-profit Cloud is probably the poorest served of the industry clouds we have surveyed in this chapter in terms of Einstein capabilities, but given the tremendous focus Salesforce has on both industry solutions and Einstein, we can only expect this to improve over time. Having finished looking at the industry clouds and their Einstein capabilities, we will quickly recap what we've learned before moving on to the next chapter.

Summary

In this chapter, we looked at a variety of industries and found that there's a high degree of variability in what Einstein features are provided by the industry clouds, as well as how broadly they might be applicable. Common to many of the industry clouds is a focus on analytics rather than machine learning models. This shouldn't surprise us as the journey toward deploying AI is significantly behind the one toward deploying advanced analytics in most industries.

However, we also found several predictive models, either standalone or using Einstein Discovery Stories, that gave an added predictive capability on top of the analytical apps. We also saw some full-fledged and unique models, such as the Intelligent Document Automation in Financial Services Cloud, which ups the game for what is possible within industry clouds.

It is always difficult to make predictions, especially without a model to help, but it seems likely that industry clouds will be a major growth area for AI applications in the future. This is simply because machine learning models often perform best in a narrow context and industry clouds provide that narrow context, where they can shine. So, although there is some way to go from what we have been looking at in this chapter to the full scope of AI capability within the Einstein Platform, this is a space to watch. Now, we will shift gears one more time and begin exploring the Einstein Platform's declarative customization features in the next chapter.

Questions

1. What feature set is found in all industry clouds?
2. What standard Tableau CRM feature is leveraged in several industry clouds to provide predictions?
3. What feature would you use to automatically process financial documents for use in a workflow?

Section 3: Extending and Building AI Features

This section will explain the options an architect has for building on top of existing AI features, building new AI features on the Salesforce platform, and integrating third-party AI services. We will look at the admin features that can be used to customize AI solutions in *Chapter 6, Declarative Customization Options*, and then move on to both native and third-party API-based solutions in the following chapters.

This section comprises the following chapters:

- *Chapter 6, Declarative Customization Options*
- *Chapter 7, Building AI Features with Einstein Platform Services*
- *Chapter 8, Integrating Third-Party AI Services*

6
Declarative Customization Options

This will be a hands-on chapter that shows how you can use generic Einstein declarative features to create your own solutions as well as discussing when that is the right approach. By working through this chapter, you will gain knowledge of how and when to use the declarative features of the Einstein Platform. We will be using our Pickled Plastics Ltd. scenario throughout to ground our examples.

In this chapter, we're going to cover the following main topics:

- Introducing Einstein declarative features
- Giving timely advice with Einstein Next Best Action
- Predicting outcomes with Einstein Prediction Builder
- Generating insights with Einstein Discovery Stories

After completing this chapter, you will have gained an understanding of how to use out-of-the-box features to configure advanced AI solutions on Salesforce, using clicks not code.

Technical requirements

To follow along with the examples in this chapter, please register an analytics-enabled developer org. This can be requested using the form here: `https://developer.salesforce.com/promotions/orgs/analytics-de`.

The Code in Action (CiA) video for the chapter can be found at `https://bit.ly/3iztq7g`.

Introducing Einstein declarative features

In this chapter, we change gears again. So far, we have primarily been looking at features that come out of the box with various Salesforce clouds. We've had to do some configuration, but nothing particularly strenuous. Mostly, things work out of the box.

While that can be a great strength, it also means that when you hit the limits, they are hard. Typically, you can't bend a feature to match requirements, even though, technically, the requirements are quite close to the core functionality.

Once you hit the limit, your next port of call should be to see if you can meet your requirements using some combination of declarative features to avoid the overhead of having to use code and train your own models. Powerful as such solutions might be, they are also more expensive, higher-maintenance, and riskier than declarative solutions.

In this chapter, we will go through three features of the Einstein platform that can help you create custom AI solutions without having to go all the way to a programmatic solution. We will start with Einstein Next Best Action, a way to give timely AI-guided advice to users about the highest impact actions they can take in a given context.

Giving timely advice with Einstein Next Best Action

In this section, we will cover Einstein Next Best Action, which, technically speaking, is a framework for making in-context recommendations for record-related actions in Salesforce. That means based on a strategy and the properties of a record, you can give customized recommendations.

In the next two sections, we will first give an overview of the feature and then move on to a simple hands-on example.

Overview of Einstein Next Best Action

Einstein Next Best Action is best thought of as a framework for providing in-context action recommendations on Salesforce record pages using a highly configurable recommendation engine. Typical use cases include the ability for customer service agents to give special offers, upsell, or cross-sell options to customer's when they have them on the phone, but it can also be used, for instance, to ensure data quality by prompting field inspection or to suggest actions that may lead to the speedier resolution of a support case. The recommendation strategies can be simple and based on manually configured business rules or can deploy advanced AI models to enhance or generate suggestions. It is therefore a very scalable feature that allows you to get started with very little fuss but can stretch to quite advanced scenarios.

Recommendations are shown using a pre-built Lightning component on the relevant record pages and will show recommendations based on the strategies associated with the object you find yourself on. The recommendations work by launching a screen flow whenever a customer service agent accepts a recommendation. Optionally, you can also have the flow launched when a recommendation is rejected, for instance, to call out to an external system to register the rejection. Do keep in mind that in the context of Einstein Next Best Action, the action is always a screen flow notwithstanding the broader meanings of the term in the rest of the Salesforce world. Salesforce orgs get 5,000 recommendations for free each month, but further recommendations must be paid for. In general, pricing is usage-based, but there are also individual SKUs available.

There are four key parts to setting up Einstein Next Best Action:

- Screen flows
- Recommendation records
- Strategies
- The Einstein Next Best Action Lightning component

Screen flows will be familiar territory for most readers of this book, so we won't go into much detail here. What is important to know, however, is that only recommendations associated with an active screen flow will be shown in the UI by Einstein Next Best Action.

Recommendations in the context of Einstein Next Best Action are just records in the Recommendations object. You can create a minimal record by specifying a name, description, object, labels for acceptance and rejection, and the associated screen flow to launch. However, the fact that we are dealing with records means they can be created automatically by other processes such as a flow or Apex code, for instance, to populate recommendation records based on a product catalog or a marketing campaign defined in another system.

By far the most advanced part of Einstein Next Best Action is Strategy Builder. It resembles Flow Builder from a user interface perspective, but it has elements related to loading recommendations, filtering and transforming loaded recommendations, and selecting between branches of recommendations coming from different load steps. We will go through the available elements in the following sections.

Elements for loading recommendations

It has the following elements for recommendations:

- **Load**: Simply load from the Recommendations object based on a set of filters. Note that each *Load* or *Generate* step creates a separate branch that can be selected by the branch selection steps.

- **Generate**: Generate recommendations based on calling an Apex action that returns a list of recommendation records, for instance, by calling a custom machine learning model via an API.

- **Enhance**: Call an Apex action to enhance a recommendation, for instance, by inserting a personalized discount, previously generated by a Load or Generate step.

Elements for filtering and transforming

Here are the elements for when we filter and transform:

- **Filter**: This element filters down the recommendations based on criteria that reference the recommendation record or the polymorphic $Record variable that refers to the object record to which the Recommendation pertains.

- **Limit Reoffers**: This element allows you to limit how many times a user sees a recommendation over a specified period.

- **Map**: This element allows you to transform the incoming recommendation fields, for instance, to merge text from the $Record variable into the description or labels shown to the user.

- **Sort**: This allows you to sort recommendations based on values in the recommendation record.

Elements for branch selection

Here are the elements for selecting a branch:

- **Merge**: Take two branches and merge them into one, for instance, because you want to enhance or filter them in a common way.

- **Selector**: The branch selector element allows you to filter what branches make it through to be shown to the user based on configurable filters that are unique to each branch going into the selector element.

- **First Non-Empty Branch**: This takes the first branch in the order in which they appear on the canvas that has any recommendations coming through at all and only uses those, ignoring recommendations coming from any other branch.

Once you have created your screen flows, recommendation records, and strategies, you surface your recommendations using the highly configurable Einstein Next Best Action Lightning component, which gives you options such as how many recommendations to show and whether to launch the underlying flow on rejection as well as acceptance. There is also a slightly less functional version of the component called Suggested Actions, which can be deployed on community pages.

From an architectural point of view, Einstein Next Best Action is a slightly dangerous feature. The fact that you can extend and transform recommendations nearly infinitely using a variety of code-based methods either by pre-generating recommendation records in the object or using an Apex action at runtime means that you can find a way of solving a plethora of requirements using Next Best Action. It, therefore, has the problem that many good features have of risking overuse, which can also lead to gradual maintainability issues as you start small and then scale. To this comes the predominantly usage-based pricing, which can quickly become expensive if you use it extensively.

That being said, for enhancing customer service and sales efficiency, this feature can be a great fit, since timely advice given in context is always going to beat reminders and notifications. We will now move on to consider how our friends at Pickled Plastics Ltd. might use this feature.

Einstein Next Best Action at Pickled Plastics Ltd.

Pickled Plastics Ltd. is a company that does the majority of its business with a large number of other small businesses such as individual stores. To be proactive about their sales efforts and to be able to effectively collect payments, it is essential to have good contact information for these accounts. A review of the current accounts in their Salesforce system has shown this to be lacking.

As one step to address this problem, Pickled Plastics has decided to proactively gather contact information during customer support cases. They have decided to use Einstein Next Best action to show a recommended action to customer service agents when they are faced with an account without a phone number. As there have been invoicing issues with some companies in the technology sector, they want to show a different action to also collect a billing address for these customers.

To accomplish this goal, we will follow these steps:

1. First, we create two screen flows for the actions to collect a phone number or both a phone number and billing address. If you're wondering, yes, there are ways we could combine these into one, but to keep the example simple in this case, we will go with two.

2. Go to **Setup | Flows**, click **New Flow**, and select **Screen Flow** as shown in the following screenshot. Select **Auto-Layout** when asked.

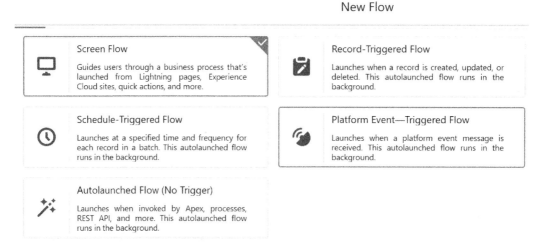

Figure 6.1 – Create a new screen flow

3. Click + to add a screen element as in the following screenshot:

Figure 6.2 – Adding a screen element

4. Under **Screen Properties**, enter the name `Collect Phone` as shown in the next screenshot:

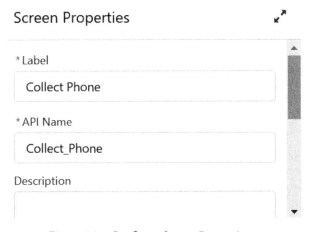

Figure 6.3 – Configure Screen Properties

5.   From **Components**, add a **Phone** component. Give it the API name
     PhoneNumber:

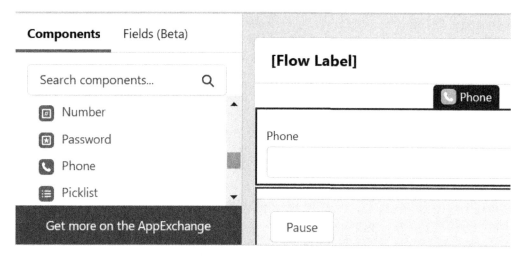

Figure 6.4 – Adding a Phone component

6.   Click on **Done** to exit the screen element or just exit the screen element.

7.   Add a variable called recordId as shown in the following screenshot:

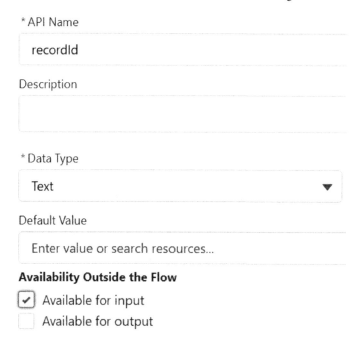

Figure 6.5 – Adding a recordId variable

8. Click + again and add a **Get Records** element:

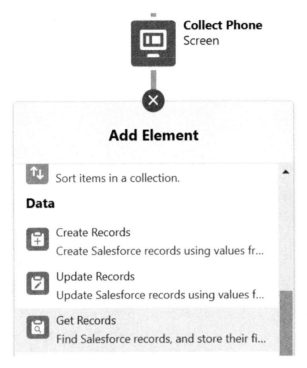

Figure 6.6 – Get Case record

9. Label it Get Case, put the object as Case, and filter as shown in the following screenshot:

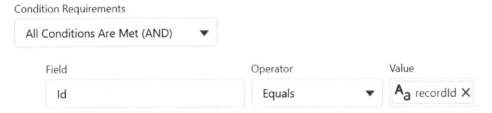

Figure 6.7 – Get Case filter

10. Click + again and add an **Update Records** element:

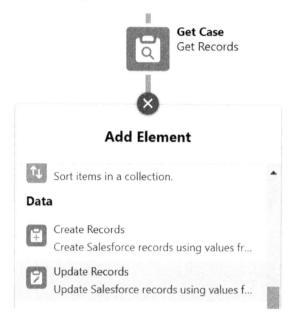

Figure 6.8 – Add element to update the account

11. Label the element as Update Account, click **Specify conditions to identify records, and set fields individually**. Set an object of **Account**, and then set the filter and field values as in the following screenshot:

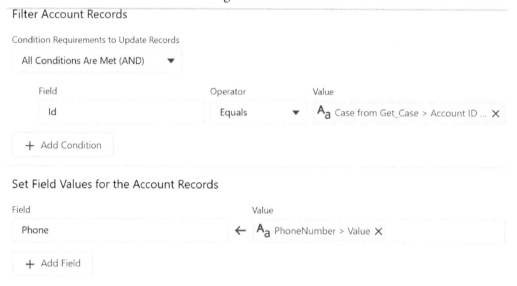

Figure 6.9 – Update Account details

12. Save and activate the flow with the name Update Phone Rec.

13. Now save the flow with the name Update Phone and Billing Rec to clone it for the second version as in the following screenshot:

Figure 6.10 – Clone the flow for the second version

14. Open the **Collect Phone** screen element.

15. Add an **Address** component. Give the API the name Billing Address.

16. Exit the screen element.

17. Open the **Update Account** element.

18. Update the field mapping to capture the different elements from the BillingAddress screen component in **Account Record**. For updating the billing address, add the following to the **Update Account** step:

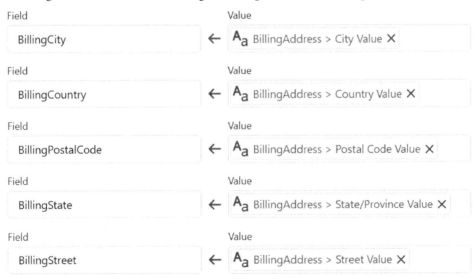

Figure 6.11 – Adding billing fields to update

19. Now save and activate and you're done with the flow part.

Having now prepared your screen flows, we will go on to create our recommendations:

1. Recommendations are simply created as records in the object of the same name, so navigate to this object by opening the App Launcher and selecting the object, create a new record, and set the values as per the following screenshot:

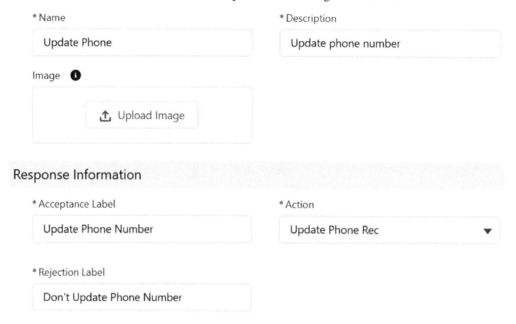

Figure 6.12 – Add a recommendation record

2. Add a second recommendation record, replacing **Phone** with `Phone and Billing` in the record details. Set **Acceptance Label** and **Rejection Label** as shown in the following screenshot:

Figure 6.13 – Phone and Billing recommendation

3. Now you have prepared your flows and recommendations, all that remains is creating your strategy and making the recommendation available on the page layout. To create a strategy, go to **Setup | Next Best Action** and click **New Strategy**. This brings you to the strategy canvas.

4. Call the new strategy `Recs for Contact Info` and set the object to `Case`, as follows:

* Name

| Recs for Contact Info |

* API Name

| Recs_for_Contact_Info |

Description

| |

Object Where Recommendations Display ⓘ

| Case |

☐ Template ⓘ

Figure 6.14 – Create a new strategy

5. Now add a **Load** element from the toolbox and name it `Load Phone Update`. Add a filter as shown in the following screenshot:

Filter Recommendation Records

Condition Requirements

| All Conditions are Met ▼ |

Field	Operator	Value
AcceptanceLabel	Equals ▼	Update Phone Number

Figure 6.15 – Load recommendations

6. Add another load element, but call it `Load Update Phone and Billing` and change the filter value to `Update Phone Number and Billing Info`.

7. Now add a **Filter** element and configure it as shown in the following screenshot:

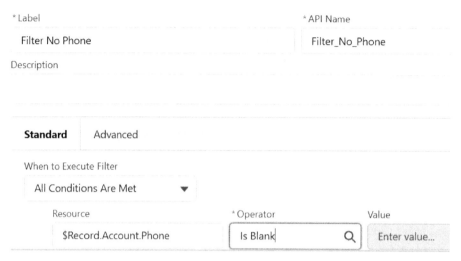

Figure 6.16 – Adding a filter to a strategy

8. Then add another filter with some additional conditions, which you can see in the next screenshot:

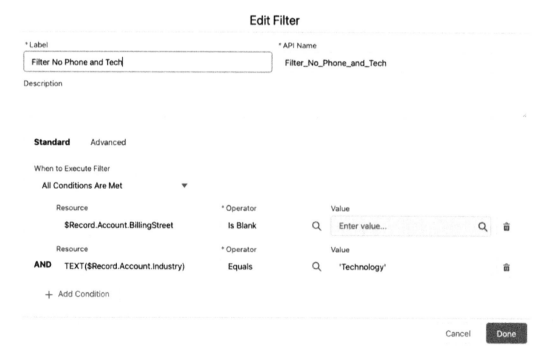

Figure 6.17 – Adding an advanced filter condition

9. Rearrange the elements to look like the following screenshot and save them. You are now done configuring the strategy:

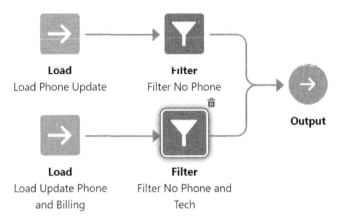

Figure 6.18 – Completed strategy

10. The only thing that remains is to make Next Best Action available on the **Case** page. Go to a case, click **Edit Page**, and add the **Einstein Next Best Action** component to the page components configured, as shown in the following screenshot:

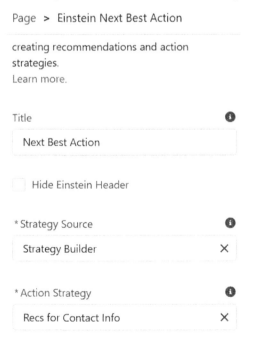

Figure 6.19 – Configure the Einstein Next Best Action component

Congratulations, you have now configured Einstein Next Best Action and will see the recommendations whenever you look at a case for a relevant account.

Pickled Plastics looks forward to much-improved account data in the future. If your configuration is correct, you should see the Lightning component on the case record page as in the following screenshot:

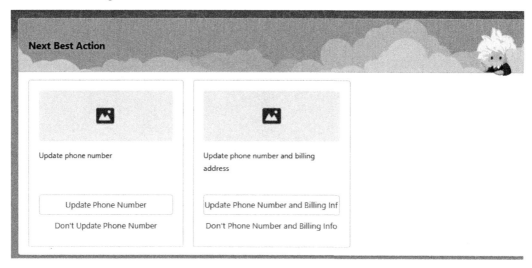

Figure 6.20 - Einstein Next Best Action component in action

In this example, we configured a Next Best Action strategy to help improve data quality for our accounts. This was a simple example, but the feature is nearly infinitely expandable and can integrate with advanced machine learning features to really make the feature shine.

We will now move on to Einstein Prediction Builder, the easiest way you will ever find to create a custom predictive model for your Salesforce data.

Predicting outcomes with Einstein Prediction Builder

Einstein Prediction Builder is often referred to in Salesforce documentation as *custom AI for admins*. This statement has some claim to truth, at least if you have well-populated data objects with fields that have relatively stable correlations between them. In the following sections, we will review the capabilities of this feature and attempt to build a basic prediction ourselves.

Overview of Einstein Prediction Builder

Einstein Prediction Builder works by analyzing historical data in Salesforce objects using machine learning under the hood. While we don't have access to the details of the model used, we could perhaps assume that it uses the same kind of model tournament to determine the optimal algorithm that we have seen in previous features.

While there is no data science degree required to configure Einstein Prediction Builder, you do need to define your use case and success metrics upfront, if you want to use this feature successfully. You can nearly always get a prediction that will work some of the time for some of the data, so unless you know what success looks like in advance, you may well be deceived.

Predictions are always made on the basis of the data contained in a single object and the predictions themselves are always stored in a field on that object. This makes them easy to activate with standard Salesforce features. However, there is also an Einstein Predictions Lightning component that you can use to understand the key factors underlying a prediction rather than just the prediction itself. However, this setup means that if you need to combine or wrangle data to make a prediction, the only way that can be achieved is by adding fields that replicate or transform the data you need directly on the object. That can be fine for small amounts of customization but quickly gets unwieldy.

You do, however, have some powerful configuration options at your disposal when defining the prediction. You can vary between binary classification and regression models and configure what fields are used for prediction. Additionally, you can segment your data and have separate predictive models for different segments.

Perhaps the most salient choice you have to make is the example set, which records are used for training, and optionally a prediction set that defines what records have values predicted for them. This choice is crucial in that a machine learning model is only as good as the data you feed it, so if you define a low-quality example set, your model will be bad.

Once you have created your model, you can review its results using a pre-built set of scorecards. This will break down the quality and expected results as well as letting you drill into what fields are key predictors in the generated model.

There are some limitations to be aware of, however. First, while you can start generating predictions using a trial version of the feature as soon as you want more than a single active prediction, you will need to pay for the requisite licensing. Unsurprisingly, you will also need a certain minimum amount of data – currently 400 records per segment that you want to predict for – in order to generate a prediction. Finally, while Prediction Builder works with all custom objects, the same is not true for the standard ones. You should check what objects are supported prior to suggesting the feature.

Einstein Prediction Builder can be a slightly addictive feature when you first try to use it. It is really good fun to build various models based on existing data and see what you can and can't predict. What you will tend to find is that it can be genuinely hard to get a high-quality prediction for most things you care about.

This fact to some extent summarizes the architectural view of this feature. If you, by some trial and error, can get a sufficiently high-quality prediction from Prediction Builder to be useful in practice, there is little reason to make another choice. However, more often than not, you need more advanced data wrangling and combinations of data that can be supported by a single Salesforce object in order to get a good prediction. In those cases, you will need to move to a more advanced feature to get what you want.

Having now considered the capabilities of Einstein Prediction Builder, we will go on to try a simple example from Pickled Plastics Ltd.

Einstein Prediction Builder at Pickled Plastics Ltd.

Pickled Plastics have been having some issues with their customer service in recent months. Many more cases have reached an escalation stage than in the past and it is starting to become an issue that is drawing attention from senior-level executives. The head of customer service has asked whether it would be possible to predict which cases are likely to escalate, so she can assign her best customer service agents to handle them proactively.

You have decided to try your hand at meeting this requirement using Einstein Prediction Builder. In the following steps, we will see how this is done:

1. First, go to **Setup | Einstein Prediction Builder** and click **New Prediction**.

2. Name the prediction `Predict Escalation` and click **Next** as shown in the following screenshot:

Name your prediction

Predicting the future is hard work, but Einstein will guide you every step of the way.

To get started, give your prediction a name.

*Prediction Name

Predict Escalation

*API Name

Predict_Escalation

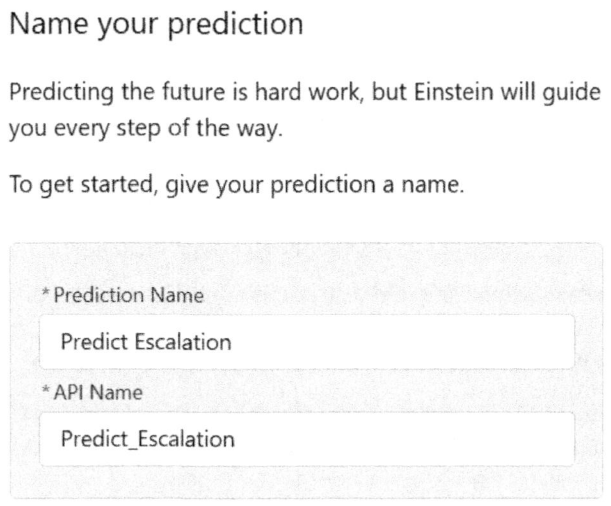

Figure 6.21 – Name prediction

3. Select **Case** under **Select an object to predict** as shown in the following screenshot. Leave the segment as is. Click **Check Data** on the right-hand side of the screen if you would like to confirm that your data is adequate.

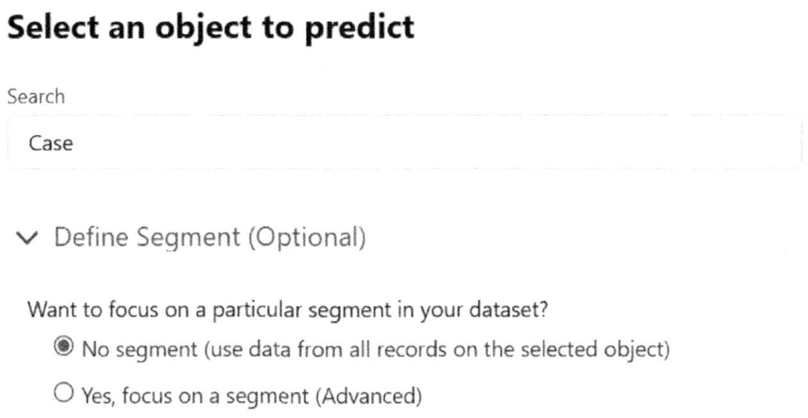

Select an object to predict

Search

Case

⌄ Define Segment (Optional)

Want to focus on a particular segment in your dataset?
- ⦿ No segment (use data from all records on the selected object)
- ◯ Yes, focus on a segment (Advanced)

Figure 6.22 – Select an object to predict

4. You are interested in knowing whether or not a case is likely to escalate, so on the following screen, select **Yes/No** as the type of prediction:

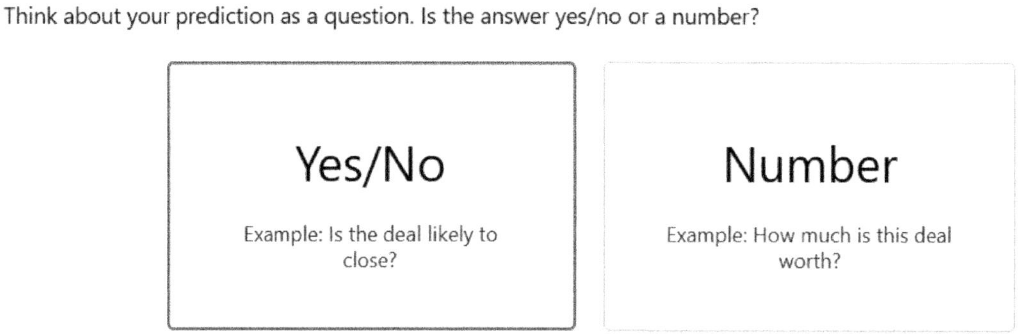

Think about your prediction as a question. Is the answer yes/no or a number?

Yes/No

Example: Is the deal likely to close?

Number

Example: How much is this deal worth?

Figure 6.23 – Select the type of prediction

5. On the next screen, answer **Field** as there is a field for escalation on the case already:

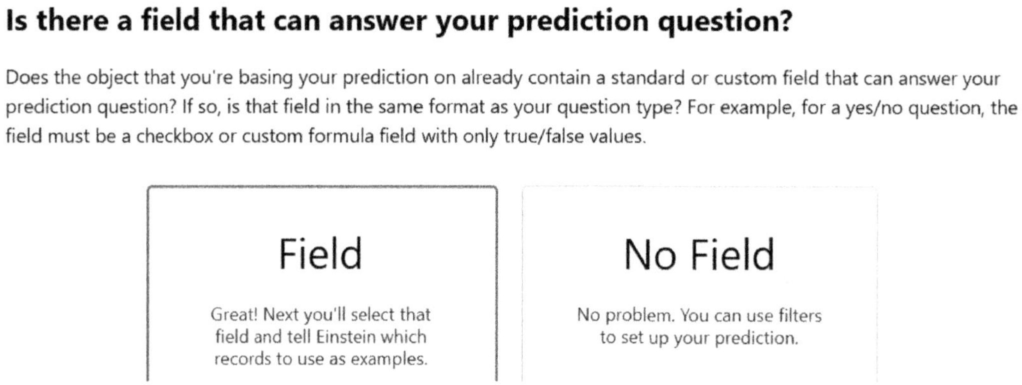

Is there a field that can answer your prediction question?

Does the object that you're basing your prediction on already contain a standard or custom field that can answer your prediction question? If so, is that field in the same format as your question type? For example, for a yes/no question, the field must be a checkbox or custom formula field with only true/false values.

Field

Great! Next you'll select that field and tell Einstein which records to use as examples.

No Field

No problem. You can use filters to set up your prediction.

Figure 6.24 – Answer for prediction

6. Now on the next screen, you should configure the field as per the following screenshot:

Select a field, example records, and prediction set

Search

| Escalated | ⊗ |

Which records should Einstein use as examples?

* Include Records That

| Meet All Conditions | ▼ |

* Field		* Operator		* Type		* Value		
Status	🔍	Equals	▼	Picklist ▼		Closed	▼	🗑

Figure 6.25 – Field configuration

7. On the next screen, deselect the **CSAT** field, the customer satisfaction score, as that may contaminate the prediction as the outcome is known only after completion. Do the same for the field **Date/Time Closed**.

–	Field Label ⌄	Field Name ⌄	Data Type ⌄
✔	Contact Phone	ContactPhone	Phone
✔	Created By	CreatedById	Lookup(User)
☐	CSAT	CSAT__c	Number(18, 0)
✔	Date/Time Closed	ClosedDate	Date/Time

Figure 6.26 – Field configuration cont.

8. Now you'll create the field that will hold the prediction. Call it `Likely to Escalate` and select **On** for **Show Top Predictors on Records**:

Choose how you want prediction results to display

If you turn on Show Top Predictors on Records, be sure to also add the Einstein Predictions component to your record page layouts. Predictors, which represent fields, display in this component regardless of field-level security. If you have fields you don't want users to see, go back one step and exclude those fields from your prediction.

Figure 6.27 – Create a prediction field

9. Now just review the information and when ready, click **Build Prediction**. It can take up to 24 hours for the prediction to build so you may want to take a break from it and get back to it later. First, however, let's add the **Einstein Predictions** component to the **Case** page.

10. Go to a case, click **Edit Page**, and add the **Einstein Predictions** component to the page components configured as shown in the following screenshot, leaving other values at their defaults:

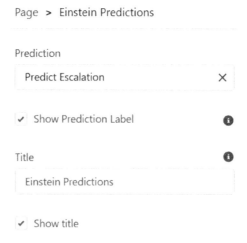

Figure 6.28 – Configure the predictions component

11. Congratulations, you have now configured the prediction the head of customer service asked for. Pat yourself on the back. If you have created the prediction correctly, you should be able to go back and enable your prediction after 24 hours. If all is well, you can select **View Scorecard** and it will look as in the following screenshot:

Figure 6.29 – Prediction scorecard

12. Note that there is a warning on the quality of the prediction, but you can proceed regardless. In practice, we would look at ways to improve it before activating the prediction. Click **Enable Prediction** to start generating values for your records, which will be stored on your case records.

We have now seen an example of how Einstein Prediction Builder can work to deliver fast value through a fast point-and-click configuration interface. Now, we will go on to our last declarative AI option, Einstein Discovery.

Generating insights with Einstein Discovery stories

Einstein Discovery is a part of the Tableau CRM suite that Salesforce provides for advanced analytics. Tableau CRM is a topic that deserves several book-length treatments in its own right, so we will only be able to scratch the surface here. However, because of the brilliant machine learning capabilities inherent in Einstein Discovery stories both from an analytical and predictive standpoint, we will cover as much as we can in the next section and then follow with a small configuration example.

Overview of Einstein Discovery

Einstein Discovery is an add-on to Tableau CRM that adds statistical modeling and machine learning to the analytical capabilities of the core product. It shares the ability with Einstein Prediction Builder to generate automated machine learning models on the basis of datasets, but because it is embedded in Tableau CRM, it can make use of the data wrangling tools found in that product, which overcomes many of the limitations found in Prediction Builder. As long as the data is synchronized to Tableau CRM, you can effectively combine and transform it into whatever you need for your model.

Einstein Discovery, however, is not just about prediction, but can also generate descriptive and prescriptive analytical models that can help you understand and improve your data. Based on the data and a question you ask in the form of a field, you will be able to see what factors stand out as potential explanations.

Stories are the principal components of Einstein Discovery. A **story** is a generated analytical and optionally predictive model that gives you insights into the factors that explain the outcomes that you see in your data. They can be created either on the basis of datasets or **lenses**—the Tableau CRM word for data analysis you have done on data. You can also create templates for stories, for instance, to deploy them across orgs.

Whether you create a story based on a dataset or a lens, you start by selecting the field you want to analyze. Think of this as asking a question along the lines of *what factors impact the outcomes I see in field X?* You can analyze based on occurrences of values in the field, for instance, how many times different categorizations occur. You can also analyze based on maximizing or minimizing an outcome such as maximizing a final price variable to see what factors let you charge more.

You have the option of either generating a model just for analysis or also generating a predictive model based on the dataset. Finally, you have the option of having Einstein Discovery automatically choose the fields to include for you in the model or specifying the fields to use for analysis yourself.

Once you have generated the model, you will be presented with a pre-built dashboard that shows you the key factors found by the analytical model. You can drill into these factors to get even more detail. If you have selected to create an analytical model, you can also test out your predictive model by specifying example values.

Predictive models can be activated in a number of different ways. You can write the values back to Salesforce objects in the way that Einstein Prediction Builder works. This can be hard to do in practice because you need to map all the fields in your predictive model to fields on the record, which is not always possible as there isn't always one-to-one correspondence between the datasets. You can also show them using the Einstein Predictions Lightning component.

Most interestingly, you can get predictions programmatically using either an API call or the `ConnectApi.SmartDataDiscovery.predict` method in Apex. That means the models can be incorporated in advanced use cases and so have a wider scope than most features we have looked at so far. Having now covered the very basics of Einstein Discovery, we will go on to show a simple example.

Einstein Discovery at Pickled Plastics Ltd.

The head of customer service was so impressed with your work on the prediction of case escalation that she has asked you to help her with a special project. A key goal for the customer service function is to resolve cases on the first contact. That is to say, if a customer calls, we want to solve their problem on the first call. If the customer sends an email, we want to reply to that email with a solution to their problem. Repeated and sustained correspondence is expensive, and we want to avoid it if at all possible. Your job is to help the head of customer service analyze what factors contribute to cases being resolved at first contact.

Based on your knowledge of the Einstein Platform, you have selected to address this requirement using an Einstein Discovery Story based on the pre-existing **First Contact Resolution** field on the case object. In the following steps, we will go through what is required to configure this story:

1. To start with, we need to import the data into Tableau CRM. There is a pre-configured dataflow for this purpose, but we need to add the **First Contact Resolution** field to the import. Go to **Analytics Studio | Data Manager | Dataflows & Recipes**. You should see three dataflows as in the following screenshot.

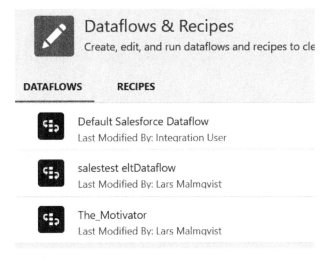

Figure 6.30 – Pre-configured dataflows

2. Open **salestest eltDataflow** and find the **Extract_Case** node as in the following screenshot:

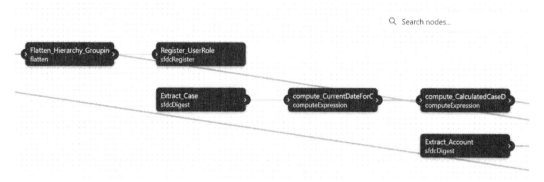

Figure 6.31 – Dataflow editing

3. Open the **Extract_Case** node, click on **Fields**, and add **First Contact Resolution** as follows:

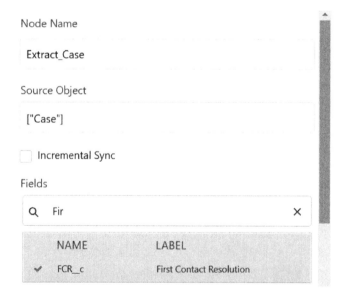

Figure 6.32 – Add the First Contact Resolution field

4. Click **Save**, then **Propagate**, and in the following popup, click **Update Dataflow**. You will get a warning but just click **Update Dataflow** again as shown here:

Figure 6.33 – Update dataflow? dialog

5. After the update is complete, click **Run Dataflow**. It will tell you that the dataflow has been put in the queue. Click **Go to Data Monitor** and wait until the dataflow has run completely, as shown in the next screenshot. The warning does not concern us for this scenario, so we move on happily.

Figure 6.34 – Data Monitor screenshot

Awesome, you now have the data you need to do the analysis. There are several ways to create an Einstein Discovery Story, but as this is a case-specific story, we will start it directly from the Case dataset:

1. Click **Data** and, on the right-hand menu for the **Case** dataset, click **Create Story** as shown in the following screenshot:

Name		Time Created	Created By	App	# of Rows	Data Refreshed	Last Queried	
	Opportunities	Jul 1, 2021 at 3:01 AM	Lars Malmqvist	salestest	706	Today at 5:40 AM	Jul 2, 2021 at 4:31 AM	▼
	Activities	Jul 1, 2021 at 3:01 AM	Lars Malmqvist	salestest	2193	Today at 5:40 AM	Jul 2, 2021 at 3:58 AM	▼
	Pipeline Trending	Jul 1, 2021 at 3:01 AM	Lars Malmqvist	salestest	1107	Today at 5:40 AM	Jul 2, 2021 at 3:47 AM	▼
	Cases	Jul 1, 2021 at 3:01 AM	Lars Malmqvist	salestest	1625	Today at 5:40 AM	Jul 2, 2021 at 3:42 AM	▼
	Oppty Products	Jul 1, 2021 at 3:01 AM	Lars Malmqvist	salestest	1496	Today at 5:40 AM	Jul 2, 2021	Edit Dataset
	Accounts	Jul 1, 2021 at 3:01 AM	Lars Malmqvist	salestest	1002	Today at 5:40 AM	Jul 2, 2021	Delete Dataset
	Users	Jul 1, 2021 at 3:01 AM	Lars Malmqvist	salestest	21	Today at 5:40 AM	Feb 1, 202	Create Story

Figure 6.35 – Create Story from the dataset

2. You now get the wizard for creating an Einstein Discovery Story. Select the **First Contact Resolution (true)** field and leave the remaining options in place as shown in the following screenshot:

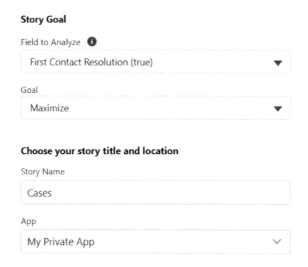

Figure 6.36 – Create Story wizard

3. In the next step, select **Insights Only** as shown in the following screenshot. We are only interested in analysis for the current use case. If we wanted to generate a predictive model to use via an API or to have the value written to Salesforce objects, then we would have selected **Insights & Predictions**.

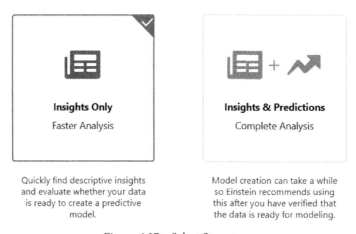

Figure 6.37 – Select Story type

4. You are not quite sure what factors are really important to **First Contact Resolution** at this point. So, you decide to go with **Automated** analysis and then refine it later. You can see this step in the next screenshot:

How would you like to select the fields for your story?

Automated

Einstein will automatically select
the fields that are most relevant
to your goal.

Manual

You manually select the fields
you want to include in your
story.

Figure 6.38 – Select the type of analysis

Einstein will now crunch the numbers and then bring you to the generated dashboard. It will look somewhat like the following screenshot:

Figure 6.39 – Einstein Discovery dashboard

5. From here, you can drill into the various factors that affect **First Contact Resolution**. For instance, pick **Case Subject** to see the following breakdown:

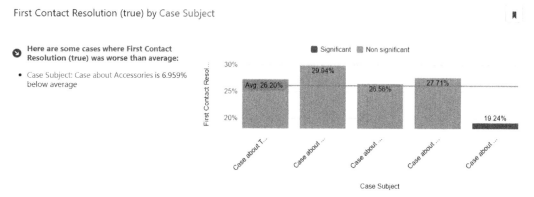

Figure 6.40 – Einstein Discovery drilldown

You can also have a look at the recommendations to improve your analysis as shown in the next screenshot:

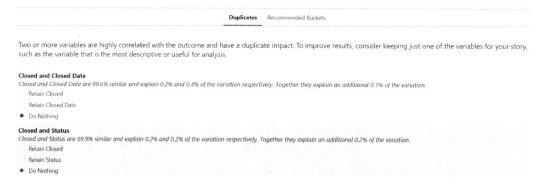

Figure 6.41 – Einstein Discovery recommendations

Have a play around. And when you're happy, share it with the head of customer service.

We have now completed our review of declarative AI features and in the next chapter, we will move on to advanced code-based use cases. First, we will briefly summarize what we've learned.

Summary

In this chapter, we have looked at declarative customization options for Salesforce AI. We have learned about Einstein Next Best Action and seen how it enables us to give in-context recommendations that can improve the way our users work with Salesforce either using simple rules or by generating advanced recommendations based on AI.

Then we looked at Einstein Prediction Builder, the proverbial "custom AI for admins" that can generate good predictions for fields on your objects, at least if you meet the general conditions. This feature can generate predictions easily but only works well if you have a lot of data with relatively stable relationships between the fields.

Finally, we had a very brief look at Einstein Discovery, a feature that deserves a much longer treatment than we can give it here. This is possibly the most powerful of the declarative features in our arsenal, but it does require Tableau CRM, which will disqualify it from being used in many organizations.

Overall, we have seen that by using these features, we have a degree of flexibility in deploying custom AI features without needing to resort to a programmatic solution. That will take us further than the built-in features and when they are a good fit, these features will likely have the fastest time to value compared to other approaches.

That being said, of course, there comes a time when you need to do something genuinely complex and tailored to your own organization, often requiring advanced features only available via APIs. When you reach this point, you need to use code and in the next chapter, we will start this journey by looking at Einstein Platform Services APIs.

Questions

1. What are the four key elements of Einstein Next Best Action?

2. Where can the data used for prediction by Einstein Prediction Builder be placed?

3. How can predictions from Einstein Discovery be activated?

7

Building AI Features with Einstein Platform Services

This will be a hands-on chapter that will take you through three examples of using the Einstein Platform Services APIs to create custom AI solutions for the platform. Along the way, it will discuss some of the architectural choices and trade-offs involved. The examples will move from an image classifier to a text recognizer to a sentiment analysis application, all integrated into a normal Salesforce Sales or Service workflow.

In this chapter, we're going to cover the following main topics:

- Introducing Einstein Platform Services
- Getting started with the Vision and Language Model Builder
- Classifying images with Einstein Vision
- Understanding text with Einstein Language

After completing this chapter, you will have gained an understanding of how to use Einstein Platform Services to build AI solutions on Salesforce using advanced API-based methods.

Technical requirements

To follow along with the examples in this chapter, please register an analytics-enabled developer org. This can be requested using the form at `https://developer.salesforce.com/promotions/orgs/analytics-de`.

You will also need to download the chapter's code files that can be found here: `https://github.com/PacktPublishing/Architecting-AI-Solutions-on-Salesforce/tree/main/Chapter07`.

The Code in Action (CiA) video for the chapter can be found at `https://bit.ly/3laT2ZK`.

Introducing Einstein Platform Services

In this chapter, we will become familiar with Einstein Platform Services, the deep learning-driven APIs that Salesforce provides to deliver advanced AI-driven experiences on the Salesforce platform. With these services, you can not only leverage existing deep learning models, but you can also train or at least fine-tune custom models on your data to get cutting-edge performance for your particular use case.

Einstein Platform Services is, at its foundation, a set of RESTful APIs that are consumed on a usage-based pricing model that can be accessed to tap into deep learning capabilities delivered by Salesforce. It has two pillars: Einstein Vision, which focuses on computer vision use cases, and Einstein Language, which focuses on use cases for text processing. There is an additional app available called **Einstein Vision and Language Model Builder** that provides some UI niceness on top of the APIs, but this is an unsupported feature, so it can't be considered core to the offering.

In general, it is best to think of Einstein Platform Services much like any other third-party APIs you may already be using, with the difference that it is tied to your particular Salesforce org rather than being generally available. With Einstein Vision and Language Model Builder, you get a layer on top that delivers another level of user experience, but it's best to remember that this is just a wrapper around the RESTful API. There is no deep integration of functionality and you cannot, in general, rely on standard Salesforce features to do the heavy lifting for you.

In this chapter, we will go through the main APIs with a focus on three practical examples. First, we will go through signing up and installing the Einstein Vision and Language Model Builder app.

Getting started with the Einstein Vision and Language Model Builder

Einstein Platform Services are, at their core, a set of RESTful APIs that can be accessed from any client that provides the appropriate credentials. However, while working in Salesforce, you have an option that slightly simplifies your life: the Einstein Vision and Language Model Builder.

This package started its life as a wrapper library on top of the REST services but is now a full-fledged exploratory UI and Apex library for working with Einstein Platform Services. It is available both as an AppExchange managed package, as shown in the following screenshot, and as an unmanaged package that you can deploy and customize based on your requirements:

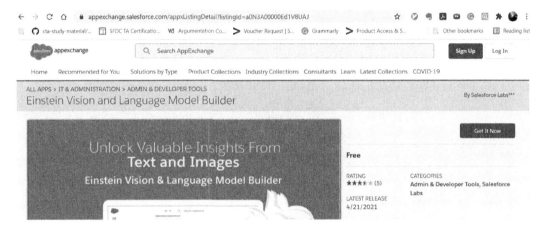

Figure 7.1 – Einstein Vision and Language Model Builder AppExchange listing

The package, once installed as explained ahead, gives you the following three key capabilities to make your life easier:

- Authentication is handled by the package's setup. This means you do not have to worry about the initial code to authenticate your callouts against the endpoints you use. This simplifies your code and reduces the time it takes to get started.

- You get an exploratory UI for building and testing models directly within Salesforce. This is extremely handy as machine learning models can be notoriously hard to validate, test, and debug. It also works as an excellent learning tool for understanding what capabilities are available within Einstein Platform Services.

- You can write Apex code against the REST services using the wrapper library provided. This library maps fairly closely to the underlying REST services, so you don't lose much fidelity by using it. That way, you avoid all the instrumentation code that comes with making HTTP callouts.

While there can be reasons for using the API directly, especially when doing large-scale development with proprietary instrumentation libraries, for any exploratory or **Proof of Concept** style work, you would be missing out by not using this excellent tool.

To set up Einstein Vision and Language Builder, follow these steps:

1. First, you need to sign up for an account at `api.einstein.ai/signup`. You must do this to be able to use Einstein Platform Services at all.

2. For this example, choose **SIGN UP USING SALESFORCE**, as shown in the following screenshot, and log in with the credentials for your Analytics-Enabled Developer Org:

Einstein Platform Services

Build smarter apps with Einstein Vision and Language

Lost your private key?

Figure 7.2 – Signing up for Einstein Platform Services

3. When asked, choose **Allow**, as shown in the following screenshot:

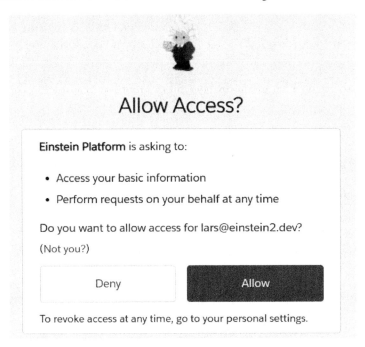

Figure 7.3 – Allowing access

4. You will now be given a private key. This is crucial, so please save it somewhere you won't lose it. Otherwise, you will have trouble later and may need to restart your setup from scratch.

5. An email will be sent to the account that you signed up with, as shown in the following screenshot. Once this email has arrived, you can continue installing the managed package for Einstein Vision and Language Model Builder.

6. Now, go to the listing for Einstein Vision and Language Model Builder at
    `https://appexchange.salesforce.com/appxListingDetail?`
    `listingId=a0N3A00000Ed1V8UAJ` and click **Get It Now**. You will be asked to
    log in or continue as a guest. In the following steps, I'll assume you have logged in,
    but if you want to continue as a guest, the steps are almost identical. Now, select the
    org where you want to install the package, as shown in the following screenshot:

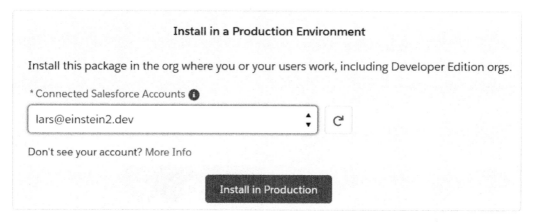

Figure 7.4 – Install in a Production Environment page

7. Confirm the installation of the package, as shown in the following screenshot:

Figure 7.5 – Installing the managed package

8. Now, choose **Install for All Users** on the next screen:

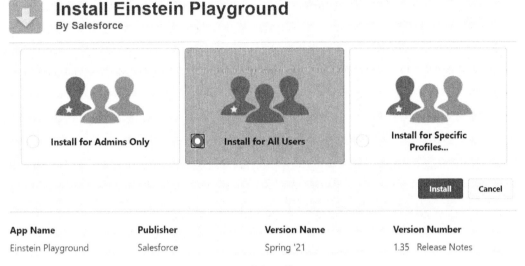

Figure 7.6 – Install for All Users option

9. The installer will ask you to confirm third-party access for the `einstein.ai` APIs. Note that although this is a Salesforce product, from the point of view of the core Salesforce clouds, you are still calling out to a third-party API.

Figure 7.7 – Approve Third-Party Access page

10. Now, the installation will begin. This will take a while, but once you get an email stating that the installation is complete, you can verify that the package has been installed correctly by navigating to **Installed Packages** in the setup, as shown in the following screenshot:

Figure 7.8 – Installed Packages page

11. Now, you will have a new app in App Launcher called **Einstein Playground**, the affectionate nickname given to Einstein Vision and Language Model Builder. Go to this app, click the **Einstein Admin** banner, then click **Setup and Configuration** to configure the package, as shown in the following screenshot:

Figure 7.9 – Einstein Vision and Language Model Builder configuration

12. Under **Account Settings**, type in the email you used to sign up for Einstein Platform Services and upload the PEM file with your private key that you previously downloaded, as shown in the following screenshot:

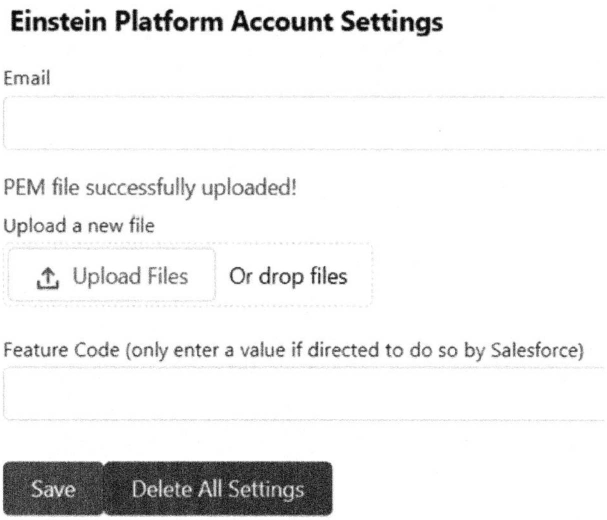

Einstein Platform Account Settings

Email

PEM file successfully uploaded!
Upload a new file

⬆ Upload Files   Or drop files

Feature Code (only enter a value if directed to do so by Salesforce)

Save   Delete All Settings

Figure 7.10 – Einstein Platform Account Settings

13. Click the **Save** button. Now, you can go back to the introduction screen by clicking on the banner and see that your account has been set up correctly. This is shown in the following screenshot:

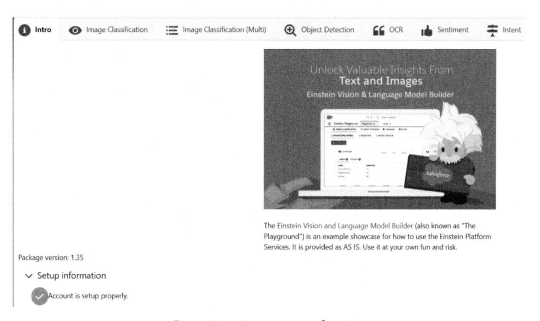

Figure 7.11 – Account set confirmation

We will use the Einstein and Language Model Builder in all the examples that we will be going through in this chapter, although in quite different ways. First, we will consider how to use Einstein Platform Services for computer vision tasks.

Classifying images with Einstein Vision

Einstein Vision is one of the two core pillars of Einstein Platform Services. In this section, we will briefly survey the elements that make up this offering and then move on to creating an image classifier while using our dataset for fine-tuning.

Overview of Einstein Vision

Einstein Vision is Salesforce's core offering in the computer vision space. It is less general-purpose than equivalent offerings from other vendors such as Google or Amazon and that is probably by design. Instead, it offers very deep functionality in areas that are core to CRM-type processes, including image classification, object detection, and OCR.

The three core APIs and their general capabilities are as follows:

- **Image classification**: The image classification API allows you to classify images. There are a set of pre-built models that allow you to classify food images, general images, scene images, and multi-label images, all of which can help you get started using the API. For more specific use cases, you can train your model, or more accurately fine-tune Salesforce's pre-built model, on your dataset. You simply provide a dataset with images categorized into labels that correspond to what you want to predict by structuring them into folders and providing them to the API in the right way. There are various requirements around format, quality, and size, but they are fairly wide and should be workable for most needs.

- **Object Detection**: The Object Detection API detects objects in images and provides the bounding box for where in the image the object has been detected. We talked about this API when discussing some functionality in Consumer Goods Cloud to track the goods displayed on shelves during site visits, as part of a retail compliance use case. And indeed, there is a special mode for retail execution that is tailored for this particular use case. If your use case isn't retail execution, the process is much the same as for image classification. Create your dataset for training with object detection, which will require you to specify bounding boxes around the objects you are looking to detect. Then, you must put the images in folders corresponding to their label, zip them up, and send them to the API. Once trained, you can use your particular model ID for future inference.

- **Optical Character Recognition (OCR):** The OCR model is a pre-built model provided by Salesforce to detect text in images. It has three pre-built modes that can be specified for recognition: one for general text, one for business cards, and one for tabular data. It also has pre-built capabilities for recognizing a range of standard US forms and identity documents, so if you are commonly accepting these, that could be a real time saver. In contrast to the other two APIs, you can't train your own OCR models.

Einstein Vision is a focused offering that offers a lot to the particular target audience it has in mind, but it may not quite have the breadth yet for adoption across a wide part of the Salesforce ecosystem. We will now focus on a particular example of its use at Pickled Plastics Ltd.

Einstein Vision at Pickled Plastics Ltd.

The marketing department has been wanting to participate proactively in conversations that involve a plastic box on social media. They are particularly interested in being able to comment when someone has a plastic box in an image on Instagram to position Pickled Plastics boxes in relation to what is shown.

The Head of Marketing has heard a lot about computer vision and has asked the CIO to look into whether this is something that could be supported by existing platforms. The CIO, in turn, has commissioned you to perform an investigation into the capabilities of Salesforce to support this requirement.

You have decided to conduct a proof of concept that will involve training an image classifier using Einstein Image Classification to identify whether an image contains a plastic box. If that turns out to be successful, you will report back and seek approval to continue with building a tool to help the marketing department meet its requirements.

To do this, you will need to perform the following steps:

1. Start by downloading the `dataset.zip` file from `https://github.com/PacktPublishing/Architecting-AI-Solutions-on-Salesforce/blob/main/Chapter07/dataset.zip`, if you have not already done so. This file contains 20 positive and 20 negative cases for the image classifier we want to train, structured in the way that Einstein Platform Services expects.

2. Now, navigate to the **Image Classification** tab in **Einstein Playground** and under **Datasets and Models**, click the **New** button, as shown in the following screenshot:

Figure 7.12 – Creating a new dataset

3. In the dialog that appears, choose **Create Dataset from File** and upload the `dataset.zip` file that you just downloaded. This is shown in the following screenshot:

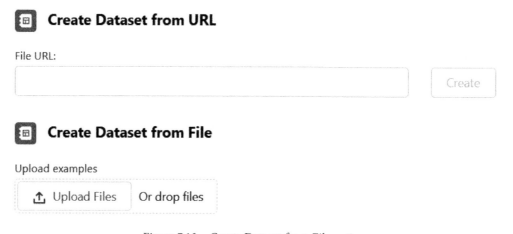

Figure 7.13 – Create Dataset from File option

4. You will now return to the previous tab and see that you have a new dataset with a status of **SUCCEEDED**, as shown in the following screenshot:

Figure 7.14 – Dataset created successfully

5. From the dropdown on this dataset, select **Train**. Be careful to only do this once and wait for a toast message to appear. This is shown in the following screenshot:

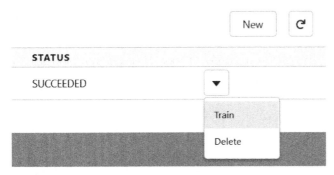

Figure 7.15 – Training the model

6. Once the model has been successfully created, you will see a toast message that lets you know your **model id**.

Figure 7.16 – Model training

7. Now, you have to wait for the model to train. This is quite a small dataset, so it shouldn't take more than a few minutes. When it's completed, it will appear on the screen, as shown in the following screenshot:

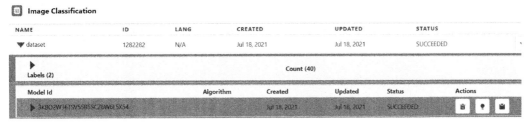

Figure 7.17 – Model successfully trained

Click the middle button with the lightbulb icon (at the bottom right) to test your model by making predictions. This will take you to the following screen:

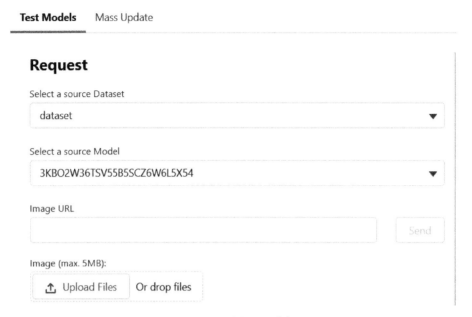

Figure 7.18 – Test Models

8. You can make predictions by uploading images to be classified. This book's GitHub repository contains an examples folder with some images to try. For instance, you can select the p1.jpg file and upload it to get a result similar to the following:

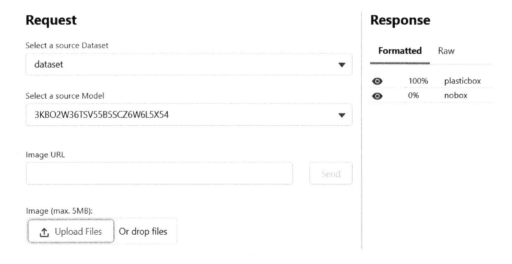

Figure 7.19 – Classification response

Wow. Our model is **100%** sure there's a **plasticbox** in this image. However, this isn't surprising as we've cheated and used an image that was already part of the training set. Try this with a few more images of your own and see what you get.

9. The model is now ready for use, but you want to be sure you can use it in code effectively, before reporting back to the CIO and the Head of Marketing. Open a **Developer Console** and start an execute anonymous session.

10. Copy and paste the code from the c7_exec_anom.apx file in this book's GitHub repository. You will need to adapt the ID to the one for your current model. The code in question is shown in the following section:

```
string imageURL = 'https://upload.wikimedia.org/
wikipedia/commons/6/6b/PP_box.jpg';

string modelID = '<your model id>';

einsteinplay.Einstein_PredictionService service = new
einsteinplay.Einstein_PredictionService(einsteinplay.
Einstein_PredictionService.Types.IMAGE);

einsteinplay.Einstein_PredictionResult predResult =
service.predictImageUrl(modelID, imageURL, 2, null);

system.debug('Probabilities: ' + predResult.
probabilities);
```

This code does three simple things:

I. It instantiates a prediction service of the right type – in this case, for image classification.

II. Then, it gets a prediction result for the image specified in the image URL. This is a picture of a plastic box from Wikipedia.

III. It then writes out the results to the debug log, allowing you to inspect the results.

When you're ready to run the code, your execute anonymous window should look as follows:

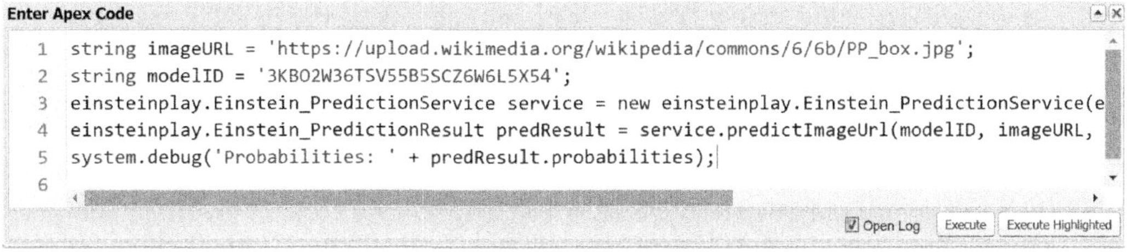

Enter Apex Code

```
1  string imageURL = 'https://upload.wikimedia.org/wikipedia/commons/6/6b/PP_box.jpg';
2  string modelID = '3KBO2W36TSV55B5SCZ6W6L5X54';
3  einsteinplay.Einstein_PredictionService service = new einsteinplay.Einstein_PredictionService(e
4  einsteinplay.Einstein_PredictionResult predResult = service.predictImageUrl(modelID, imageURL,
5  system.debug('Probabilities: ' + predResult.probabilities);
6
```

☑ Open Log   Execute   Execute Highlighted

Figure 7.20 – Execute anonymous window

You will see that an **Einstein_PredictionResult** is returned, which is a set of probabilities over the possible labels – in this case, **plasticbox** or **nobox**. If all has gone well, your model should be fairly sure there's a plastic box in this particular image.

With that, you have completed the initial task set out for you by the CIO and Head of Marketing. While there are various ways this example can be expanded, for now, we will move on to the language part of Einstein Platform Services.

Understanding text with Einstein Language

Einstein Language is the second pillar of Einstein Platform Services and focuses on APIs that allow you to extract structured information from unstructured text. From a research perspective, Salesforce is a leading player in publishing cutting-edge academic research on Natural Language Processing and Einstein Language is the way you, as a user of Salesforce, can tap into that. As for Einstein Vision, we will start by providing a quick overview of the APIs and then move on to the examples.

Overview of Einstein Language

If you were to summarize the Einstein Language APIs in a sentence, you'd say that they were all about understanding what a customer is trying to accomplish and how they might be feeling about it. As with Einstein Vision, this is a small subset of the total universe of **Natural Language Processing** (**NLP**) tasks that are available via various AI vendors beyond Salesforce, but it is a subset that is highly relevant to what the Salesforce platform is good at.

Like Einstein Vision, there are three main APIs on the language side, which are summarized as follows:

- **Intent**: The intent API is all about programmatically understanding what a customer is trying to achieve, for instance, to route an incoming message to the right department or figure out what topics are particularly salient in a conversation. To do this, you must upload a CSV file of examples using the API, for instance, *I don't understand my invoice*, mapped to a label, say *billing-related*, and train the model based on these examples. The AI is clever enough to extrapolate quite a bit from your examples, so the list you provide does not have to be exhaustive. However, as always with machine learning, the more data you provide, the better the results will be. Once the model has been trained, which happens in the same way as it does for Einstein Vision, you will be able to call the API with the model ID and some text and get the relevant intent labels back.

- **Sentiment**: Sentiment models attempt to determine how people are feeling about something at a given point in time by examining the text they write. For instance, we will be looking at classifying how people feel about the support they are receiving in our sentiment analysis example. The Sentiment API comes with a **CommunitySentiment** model that applies a generic sentiment model that works well across a range of text. However, you will get better results by creating a dataset that contains specific examples from your context, along with labels describing the sentiment encountered. When you call the Sentiment API, you get a scoring system across the three principal labels – positive, neutral, and negative – that are used by the model. Not everything will be classified correctly as the API might not catch things such as irony or sarcasm in all cases. You can then use this sentiment information to drive your business use cases normally.

- **Named Entity Recognition** (**NER**): NER is a classic NLP use case that seeks to identify structured entities in unstructured text. For instance, in the headline *SFDC to spend $1B on AI research*, the NER API would be able to identify SFDC as an organization and $1B as an amount of money. Currently, the API, which at the time of writing is still in beta, can identify date/time, duration, email, location, money, number, organization, percent, person, phone number, and URL. NER is rarely a goal in and of itself, but can substantially enrich other AI use cases by adding structure to text data.

Einstein Language is a powerful addition to your arsenal for building deeply customer-centric solutions on the Salesforce platform. For instance, you could combine these two services to extract text from a scanned image with OCR and then extract named entities from the text with NER. It may require more thought and planning to implement well than was the case for Einstein Vision, as the use cases tend to be more involved on the language side and therefore also more technically complex.

Now, let's look at an example of using the CommunitySentiment model to understand how customers might be feeling about the support they are receiving.

Einstein sentiment analysis at Pickled Plastics Ltd.

Customer satisfaction is key to Pickled Plastics Ltd. and unfortunately, it hasn't been trending upward in recent quarters. The Head of Customer Service is interested in understanding whether AI could help him proactively find and address cases that are going off track. He has heard about sentiment analysis and would like to explore it using that as part of the solution. In particular, he would like to know if the conversation on a particular **Case** takes a negative turn, as reflected in the case's comments.

You have explored the options for delivering sentiment analysis solutions using Einstein Platform Services, and you have hit upon what you consider a simple and elegant solution that employs a pre-built Apex action that comes with Einstein Vision and Language Model Builder.

You have also designed a flow-based solution around this action, which will aggregate information from the **Case Comment** object and send it for classification with Einstein Platform Services using the Apex action. Pickled Plastics is a long-term user of Salesforce and has historically always used the **Case Comment** object rather than the newer **Case Feed** object to keep track of their **Case**-related conversations.

You can implement this solution by performing the following steps:

1. You need to add two new custom fields to the **Case** object. The first is to hold the aggregated **Case Comment** text. Configure the long text area, as shown in the following screenshot. There's no need to add to the page layout.

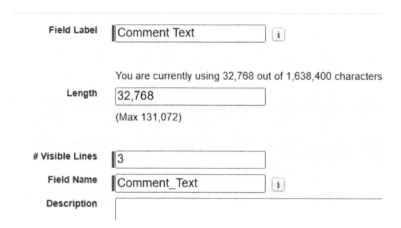

Figure 7.21 – Comment Text field

2. The second is to hold the predicted sentiment, which will be positive, neutral, or negative. Configure a text field, as shown in the following screenshot. There's no need to add to the page layout for this one either:

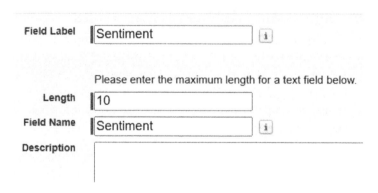

Figure 7.22 – Sentiment field

3. Now, go to **Flows** and create a **Record-Triggered Flow**. Set the object to **Case Comment** and run the flow once it's been created, as shown in the following screenshot:

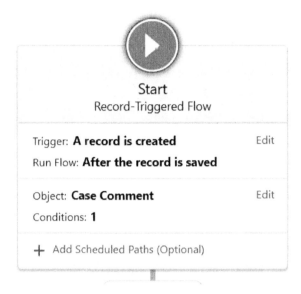

Figure 7.23 – Case Comment flow

4. Configure the filter conditions, as shown in the following screenshot:

Figure 7.24 – Conditions for the Case Comment flow

5. Now, add a **Get Records** element, called `Assign text`, call it `Get Case`, and configure it, as follows:

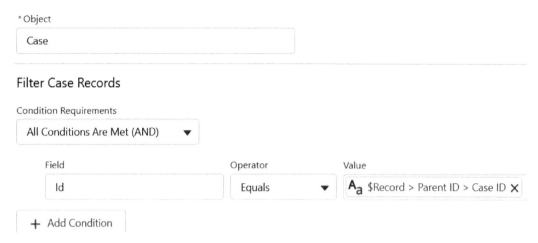

Figure 7.25 – Get parent case

6. Now, add an **Assignment** element to add the text from the new comment to the field of the parent record:

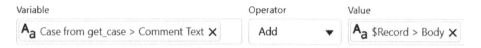

Figure 7.26 – Adding a comment to the parent

7. Then, add an **Update Records** element, called `Update case`, and configure it, as shown in the following screenshot:

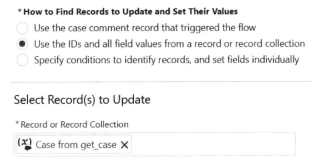

* How to Find Records to Update and Set Their Values
- ◯ Use the case comment record that triggered the flow
- ⦿ Use the IDs and all field values from a record or record collection
- ◯ Specify conditions to identify records, and set fields individually

Select Record(s) to Update

* Record or Record Collection

(𝑥) Case from get_case ✕

Figure 7.27 – Updating the parent case

Now let's move on to predicting the sentiment.

8. We then, save and activate the flow. With that, you have set up the part that aggregates the comment text so that we can send it for classification. You can see the final flow in the following screenshot:

Figure 7.28 Update Comment Text flow

9. Create another **Record-Triggered Flow**, this time on **Case**. Execute it when a record is created or updated and once the record has been saved. This should look as follows:

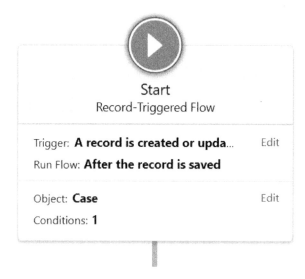

Figure 7.29 – Case record triggered flow

10. Unfortunately, we can't use a long text area in a filter condition, so we will simply execute this flow every time there's a change, as shown in the following screenshot. Should you want to use this example in production, I would advise that you change this to something more suitable.

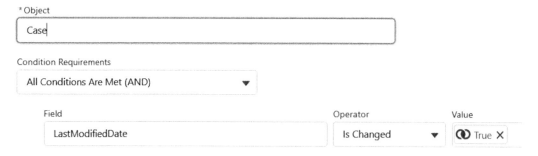

Figure 7.30 – Filter conditions for the Case flow

11. Now, add an **Apex action** element and search for `Einstein Text Prediction - Language`. This action can be used for various text processing tasks, including sentiment analysis. Configure the element as shown in the following screenshot, call it `Predict Sentiment`:

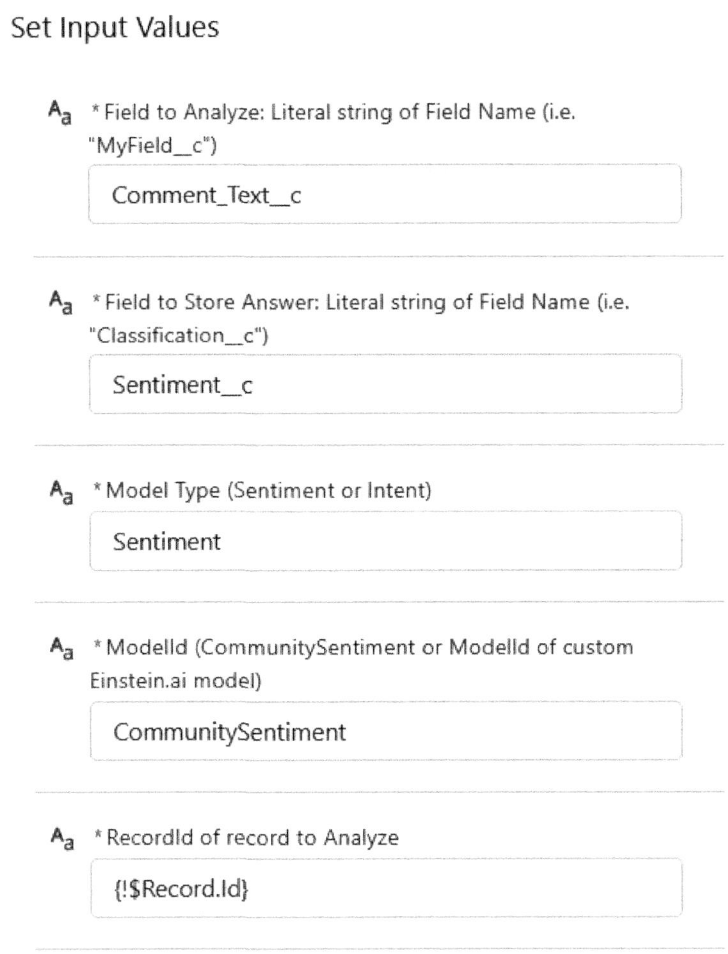

Set Input Values

A_a * Field to Analyze: Literal string of Field Name (i.e. "MyField__c")

> Comment_Text__c

A_a * Field to Store Answer: Literal string of Field Name (i.e. "Classification__c")

> Sentiment__c

A_a * Model Type (Sentiment or Intent)

> Sentiment

A_a * ModelId (CommunitySentiment or ModelId of custom Einstein.ai model)

> CommunitySentiment

A_a * RecordId of record to Analyze

> {!$Record.Id}

Figure 7.31 – Configuring the text prediction element

12. Now, save and activate the flow. With that, you have a working solution! You can see the final flow in the following screenshot:

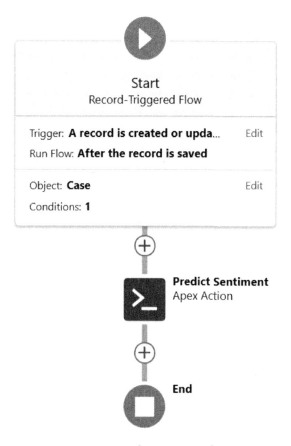

Figure 7.32 Predict sentiment flow

The only thing we need to do now is show the sentiment on the case layout, which we'll do by adding it to the highlight panel.

13. To do so, go to the **Case** object | **Compact Layouts** and create a new compact layout, as shown in the following screenshot:

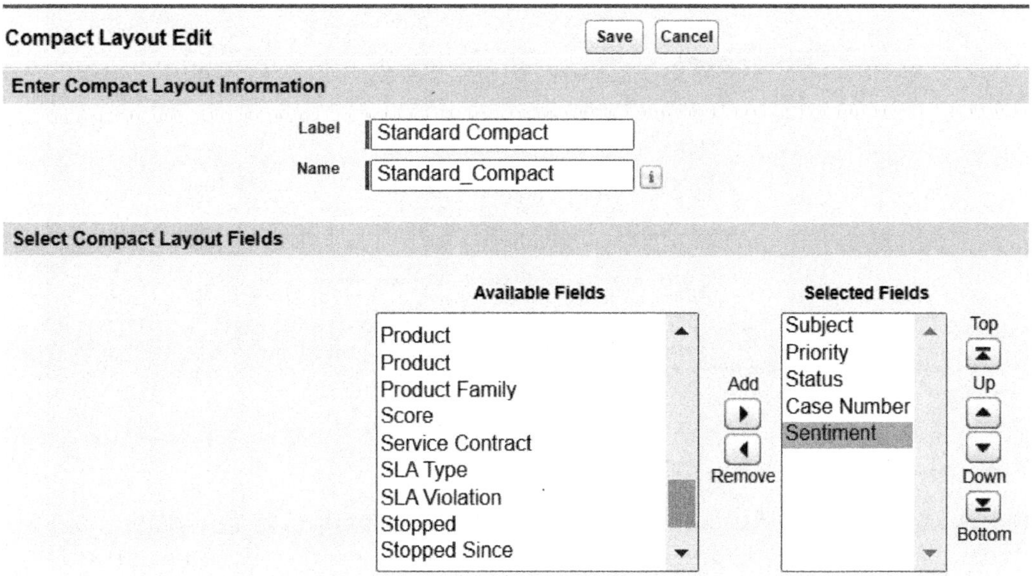

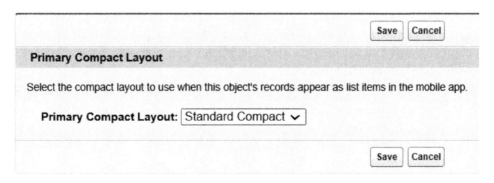

Figure 7.33 – Configuring the compact layout

14. Save it and click **Manage Assignments**. Then, make the new layout the primary for the org, as shown in the following screenshot:

Figure 7.34 – Setting the primary layout

15. Now, navigate to a **Case**, add a **Case Comment**, and sit back and enjoy as the sentiment is shown in the highlight panel, as shown in the following screenshot:

Figure 7.35 – Sentiment of the Case layout

Having completed our look at sentiment analysis, we will move on to the final example in this chapter, where we will look at Einstein OCR, a feature that blends both vision and language elements.

Einstein OCR at Pickled Plastics Ltd.

The Head of Customer Service is quite pleased with the sentiment feature you implemented for him, and he has asked you to take on another project using Einstein Platform Services. Many of the queries that tend to go wrong involve invoices that have disputes on them.

Unfortunately, many of the small businesses Pickled Plastics deal with rely exclusively on paper invoices, and Pickled Plastics, therefore, have trouble reconciling with the information in their finance system. Due to this, the Head of Customer Service has asked if there is a way to extract information from scanned invoices principally so that the identifiers can be copied between systems, but in the future potentially to facilitate some level of Robotic Process Automation.

You have looked at Einstein OCR and think that it just might be doable, at least if you keep it simple. You have designed a feature that allows users to upload an invoice, run it through OCR, and store the raw output into a field that the Customer Service Agents can use to copy and paste information into other systems.

First, you must create an Apex class called `ExtractInvoiceText` in the Developer Console to house the logic for calling the OCR endpoint.

The following code describes an Apex action that takes a list of IDs of the content version records as input. This is necessary for the flow we'll build later, although for this example, we will only accept one input, ignoring the rest:

ExtractInvoiceText.cls

```
global without sharing class ExtractInvoiceText {
    private static string task   = 'text';
    private static string modelID = 'OCRModel';


    @InvocableMethod
    public static List<String>
      extractText(List<List<String>> e) {
```

The logic selects the binary content from that content version record, encodes it as base64, and sends it for classification with the OCR service by using the appropriate prediction service and classification method:

```
    ContentVersion base64Content = [SELECT Title,
      VersionData FROM ContentVersion where Id =
      :e[0][0] ORDER BY Title LIMIT 1];
    Blob fileBody =base64Content.VersionData;
    String fileAsString =
      EncodingUtil.base64Encode(fileBody);
    einsteinplay.Einstein_PredictionService service =
      new einsteinplay.Einstein_PredictionService
      (einsteinplay.Einstein_PredictionService.Types
      .OCR);
```

Once it gets the result back, it iterates over the returned probabilities and aggregates the probable labels – in this case, those that correspond to the recognized text – into a single string that is returned to the calling flow:

```
    einsteinplay.Einstein_PredictionResult predResult =
      service.predictOcrBase64(modelID, fileAsString,
      task, 2, null);
    system.debug('Probabilities: ' +
      predResult.probabilities);
```

```
    string retStr = '';

    for (einsteinplay.Einstein_Probability p :
        predResult.probabilities){
        retStr += p.label + '\n';
    }

    return new List<String>{retStr};
}

global class ExtractVar {
    @InvocableVariable(label='contentVersionId'
        required=true)
    global Id contentVersionID;
}
}
```

Now, you can implement the rest of the feature by performing the following steps:

1. Start by creating a field on the **Case** object that holds the text that's been extracted from the invoice, as shown in the following screenshot. Add this field to the page layout.

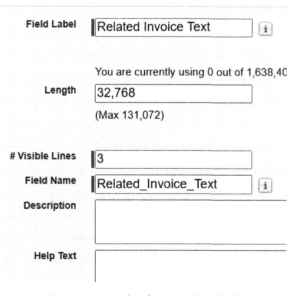

Figure 7.36 – Related Invoice Text field

2. Go to **Flow Builder** and create a new screen flow. Then, add a **Screen element** with the properties shown in the following screenshot:

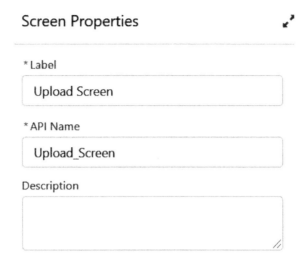

Figure 7.37 – Upload screen

3. Add a variable called `recordId` that's available for input.

4. Drag in a file upload component and configure it with **API Name** set to `UploadFile`, **File Upload Label** set to `Upload`, **Allow Multiple Files** set to `{!$GlobalConstants.False}`, and **Related Record Id** set to `{!recordId}`. This should look like the following:

Figure 7.38 – Upload screen – continued

5.   Then, you need to create a variable to hold the text that's returned by the Apex
     action. To do this, create the following variable:

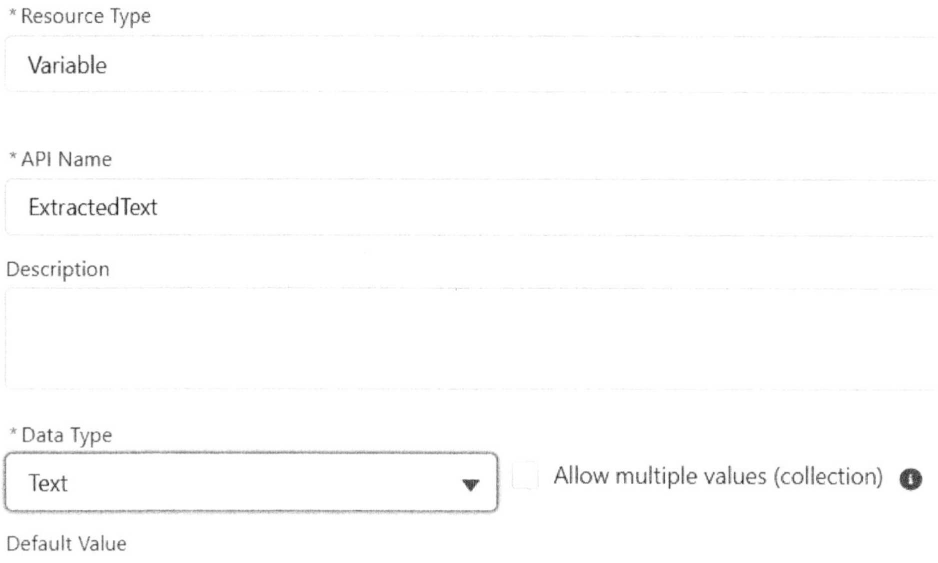

* Resource Type

> Variable

* API Name

> ExtractedText

Description

>

* Data Type

> Text   ▼   ☐ Allow multiple values (collection) ⓘ

Default Value

Figure 7.39 – Extracted text variable

6.   Now, add an Apex action of the **ExtractInvoiceText** type, call it `Extract Text`,
     and configure it like so:

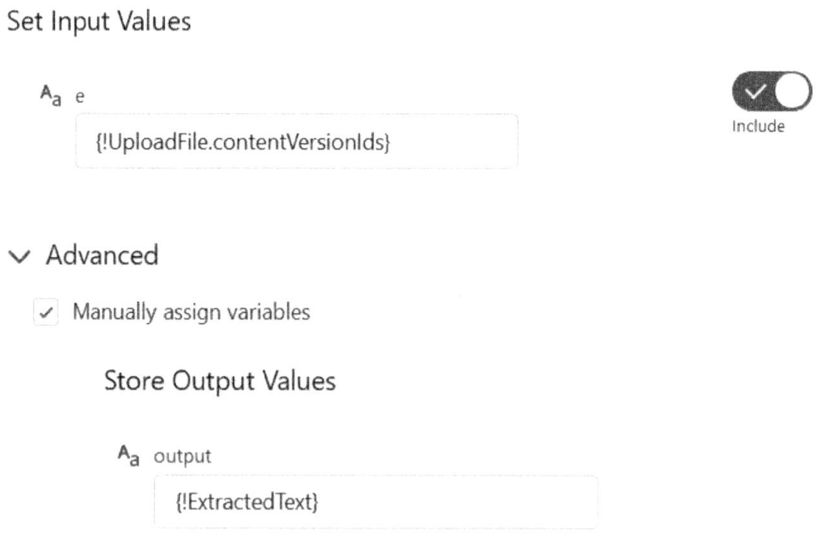

Set Input Values

A_a e

> {!UploadFile.contentVersionIds}

✓◯
Include

∨ Advanced

☑ Manually assign variables

Store Output Values

A_a output

> {!ExtractedText}

Figure 7.40 – Extracting the text action

7. You can get the related case by using a **Get Records** element, called Get case, configured as in the next screenshot:

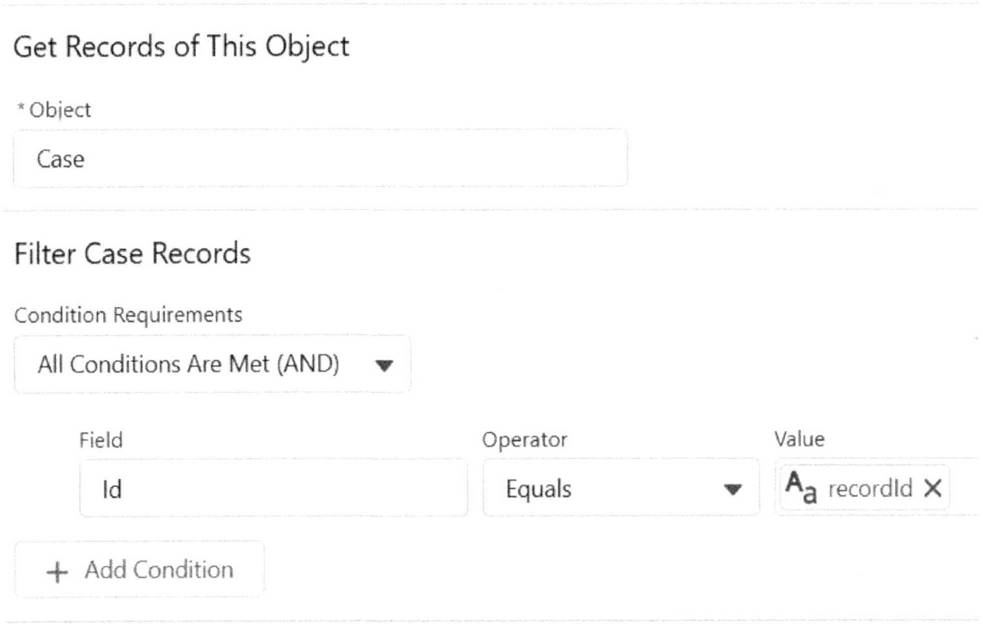

Get Records of This Object

* Object

> Case

Filter Case Records

Condition Requirements

> All Conditions Are Met (AND)   ▼

Field	Operator	Value
Id	Equals ▼	A_a recordId ✕

> ＋ Add Condition

Figure 7.41 – Getting a related case

8. Add an **Assignment** element, called Assign Extracted Text, and configure it as follows to update the case with the extracted text, adding it to the Related Comment Text field:

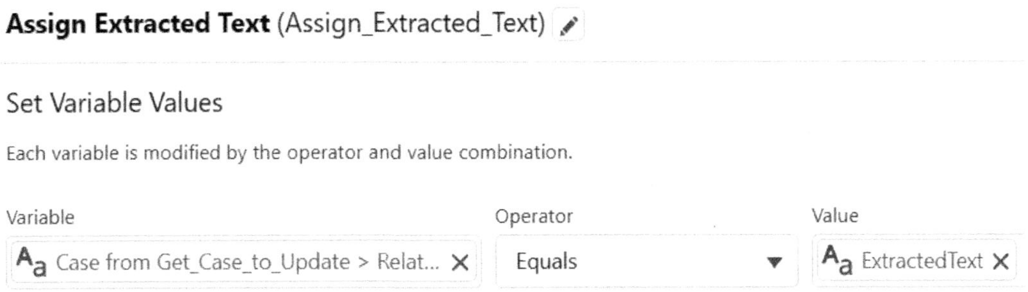

Assign Extracted Text (Assign_Extracted_Text) ✎

Set Variable Values

Each variable is modified by the operator and value combination.

Variable	Operator	Value
A_a Case from Get_Case_to_Update > Relat... ✕	Equals ▼	A_a ExtractedText ✕

Figure 7.42 – Assign Extracted Text page

9. To finish the flow, add an **Update Records** element, called `Update case`, to update the case, as shown in the following screenshot:

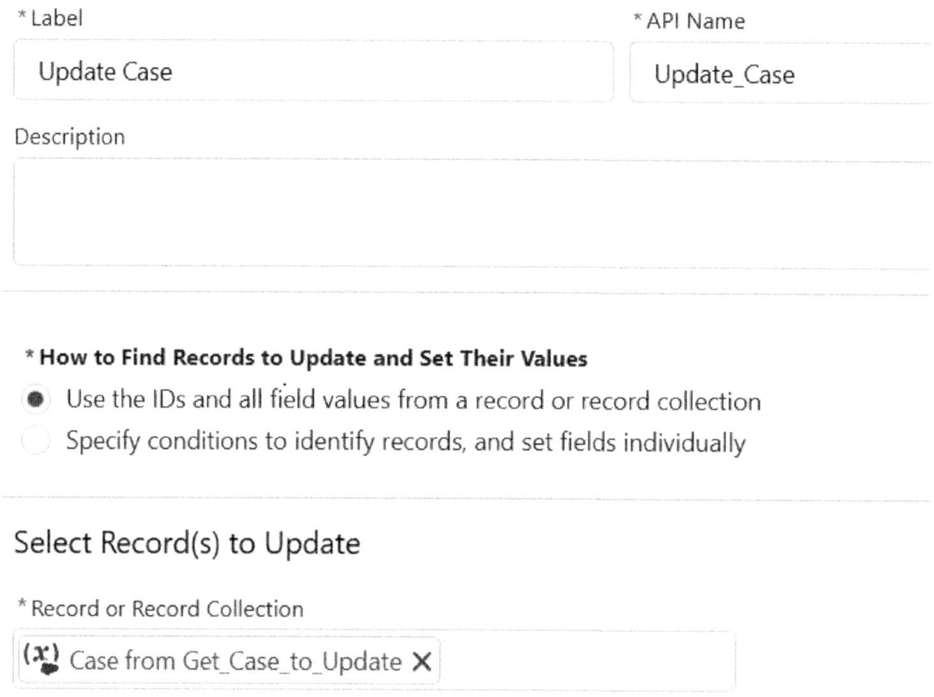

* Label

Update Case

* API Name

Update_Case

Description

* **How to Find Records to Update and Set Their Values**

⦿ Use the IDs and all field values from a record or record collection

◯ Specify conditions to identify records, and set fields individually

Select Record(s) to Update

* Record or Record Collection

(x) Case from Get_Case_to_Update ✕

Figure 7.43 – Updating the related case

10. Save and activate the flow. Well done – the flow and code are now complete! Save and activate the flow. You can see the final flow in the following screenshot:

Figure 7.44 Extract Invoice Text flow

All that remains is to add a button to launch a screen flow from the **Case** record. Go to **Object Manager | Case | Buttons, Links, and Actions | New Action** and create an action with the configuration shown in the following screenshot:

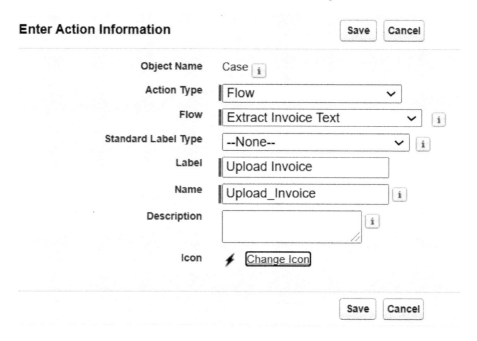

Figure 7.45 – Configuring the Upload Invoice action

Add the action to the **Case** layout, upload the invoice document from `https://github.com/PacktPublishing/Architecting-AI-Solutions-on-Salesforce/blob/main/Chapter07/invoice.png`, and see the extracted text appear in the **Related Invoice Text** field. Note that if you have feed tracking enabled for case the action will appear in the feed and not as a button.

Congratulations! With that, you have completed the examples for this chapter. That was not an easy task. This also completes the main technical section of this book, so in the next chapter, we will focus on what to do when you have to go off platform and integrate third-party APIs. First, however, let's summarize what we've learned in this chapter.

Summary

In this chapter, we have looked at Einstein Platform Services, the APIs Salesforce provides to allow you to tap into their AI capabilities at a foundational level. We looked at three examples of how this technology can be used within the CRM, but to be honest, we've only been able to scratch the surface.

The APIs provide an impressive capacity to be tailored using customer-specific data and for customers to build their own set of models on top of the core technology provided by Salesforce. This is also the main reason to go in this direction, architecturally speaking. You should use Einstein Platform Services if you have a relatively advanced use case that requires a level of customized data to perform well and you have the necessary technical capacity to implement it.

One thing worth noting is that Einstein Platform Services is not an all-encompassing set of AI services in the style provided by Amazon, Microsoft, or Google. Rather, it is a focused niche offering that adds value in the key places typically required by CRM-like use cases. If you are looking for a commodity service that delivers the highest bang for the buck, you are probably better off with one of the other three mentioned providers. If, however, you are looking to add a custom bit of functionality to a core CRM process and no out-of-the-box features will do the trick, Einstein Platform Services should be your first port of call.

The fact that Einstein Platform Services has limited scope inherently means that occasionally, you will have to go to third-party vendors to meet your requirements. We will see how this can be done in the next chapter.

Questions

1. What feature might I use if I wanted to automatically detect whether my brand's products are on a shelf?

2. Why might I want to train my own sentiment model rather than use the pre-built one?

3. What is a limitation of Einstein OCR in comparison with other Einstein Platform Services?

8
Integrating Third-Party AI Services

This, too, will be a hands-on chapter that takes you through three examples of custom development. In this case, we are using external third-party services as part of normal Sales/Service workflows on Salesforce. The first example will train a custom prediction model to predict the likelihood of a support case resulting in legal liability using Amazon SageMaker, the second will extract key phrases from a case, and the third will bring in automated translations with the Google Translation API. As part of each feature discussion, it will reference the Pickled Plastics Ltd. scenario that is used throughout the book to give a real-world grounding.

In this chapter, we're going to cover the following main topics:

- Introducing the examples
- Predicting with a custom model using AWS SageMaker
- Extracting key phrases with Azure Text Analytics
- Translating text with Google Translate

After completing this chapter, you will have gained practical knowledge of how to integrate third-party AI solutions into Salesforce.

Technical requirements

To follow along with the examples in this chapter, please register an analytics-enabled developer org. This can be requested by using the form here: `https://developer.salesforce.com/promotions/orgs/analytics-de`.

You will also need to download the chapter's files from GitHub at `https://github.com/PacktPublishing/Architecting-AI-Solutions-on-Salesforce/tree/main/Chapter08`.

Furthermore, you will need to sign up for free accounts with AWS, Google Cloud, and Microsoft Azure, using the following links:

- `https://aws.amazon.com/free`
- `https://azure.microsoft.com/en-us/free`
- `https://cloud.google.com/free`

We will not be providing instructions on the basic sign-up process. The following examples will assume that you are working from a newly created account on the respective platforms.

The Code in Action (CiA) video for the chapter can be found at `https://bit.ly/2Yk00mU`.

Introducing the examples

In this chapter, we will encounter three examples from three different cloud providers to see how to integrate third-party services into a Salesforce AI solution. All three of these providers offer a comprehensive suite of AI services and we will not attempt to survey these as each would require book-length treatment in their own right.

Instead, the examples are meant to teach you just enough about the services to understand what would be required were you to decide to adopt these third-party services as part of your application. They will also provide you with a solid understanding that you can use as a baseline for extending your own research in various directions.

The examples span three platforms:

- Amazon Web Services
- Microsoft Azure
- Google Cloud Platform

These are the largest and most comprehensive cloud AI service providers in existence and odds are if you need something, one or more of these platforms will have what you are looking for.

Of course, there are a plethora of other AI service providers in existence that might have the offering you are looking for in a given scenario, but as a starting point, these three platforms are likely the best port of call

The examples are intentionally simple and simplified. We do not seek to be all-encompassing, and we leave out the error-handling, instrumentation, bulkification, and so on that you would need to add were you to use the examples in a production context. That is done both to prevent this book from running into thousands of pages and to ensure that we focus on the salient details for the implementation rather than a broader technical and architectural discussion.

The first example, calling a custom machine learning model on AWS, is both the longest and the most complex. The other two involve relatively simple API applications in comparison. However, between these three examples, you should learn enough about how to integrate third-party AI services to be confident to start including them in your own designs.

With that preamble out of the way, let's dive right into the first example: creating a custom machine learning model and using it from Salesforce.

Predicting with a custom model using AWS SageMaker

Amazon Web Services (**AWS**) is the biggest player in the cloud marketplace and that includes AI services. In this section, we will be using four different services:

- **AWS SageMaker**: A managed service for custom machine learning models
- **S3**: The object storage layer of AWS
- **AWS Lambda**: Serverless functions running in the cloud
- **API Gateway**: The way you expose external APIs on AWS

The purpose of this example is to teach you the basics of using a custom machine learning model from Salesforce. To fit within the available amount of space, we will be skipping several elements that would normally be considered best practice, so don't use this example directly in a production environment. However, you will get an appreciation of how these elements can be formed into a solution should you need to architect one in the future.

As always, we return to our Pickled Plastics Ltd. scenario for our requirements. The legal department is increasingly concerned about the number of cases that are resulting in legal liability. You have previously introduced a field, `potential_liability__c`, that captures an agent's best guess at this. However, this guess has proven quite unreliable and the legal department would now like you to create an automated solution using machine learning and historical data to provide the solution.

You have decided that you will address this by creating a custom model on AWS that is based on the historical data provided by the legal team. You will access this from Salesforce by activating a quick action that will launch a screen flow to do the callout and get a response from the custom model. You will therefore need to provide a suitable API on AWS that can be called from Salesforce.

We will start the process of meeting these requirements by training a custom model on AWS SageMaker using Jupyter Notebooks, a data science environment, and creating an endpoint that can be called for prediction. To do that, we perform the following steps:

1. Click **All services | Amazon SageMaker** as shown in the following screenshot. This is the same way we will navigate between AWS services in future steps.

Figure 8.1 – Navigating AWS services

2. Expand **Notebook** in the menu and select **Notebook instances** as in the following screenshot. This will get you to the place where we can spin up the notebook we will be using for the training and deployment of our model.

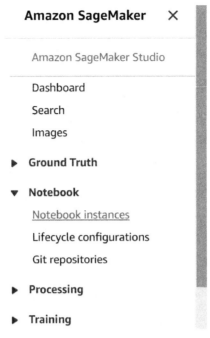

Figure 8.2 – Selecting Notebook instances

3. From there, click on **Create notebook instance** and fill in the options as per the following screenshot:

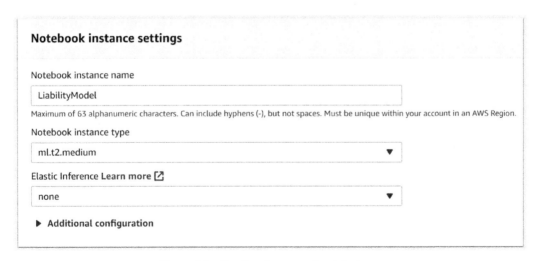

Figure 8.3 – Configuring a notebook instance

4. Scroll down to the **Permissions and encryption** section and go to **Create an IAM role** to match the following screenshot:

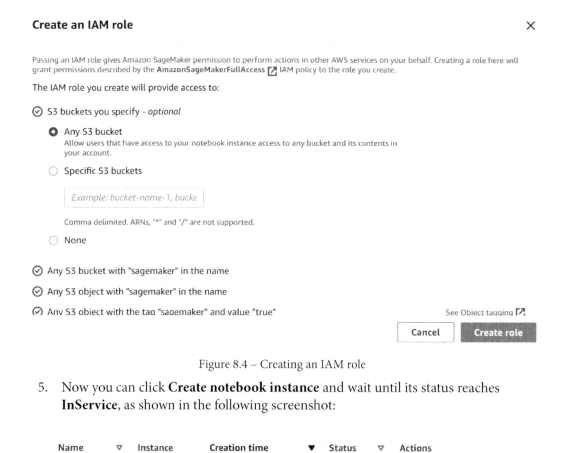

Figure 8.4 – Creating an IAM role

5. Now you can click **Create notebook instance** and wait until its status reaches **InService**, as shown in the following screenshot:

Name		Instance	Creation time		Status		Actions
○ LiabilityModel	▽	ml.t2.medium	Jul 19, 2021 14:57 UTC	▼	⊘ InService	▽	Open Jupyter | Open JupyterLab

Figure 8.5 – Notebook instance

6. Now, click **Open JupyterLab**, which will allow us to enter the code required for the example.

Jupyter Notebooks is a common development environment for data analytics and machine learning that we will be leveraging to train and deploy our model. We cannot give even a cursory introduction to it in this book without it spilling into many pages, but if you're interested, there are many good introductions available online. For example, you can try this one by George Seif: `https://towardsdatascience.com/a-beginners-tutorial-to-jupyter-notebooks-1b2f8705888a`.

The same is true of the Python programming language, in which the sample application is written. Before proceeding with the step-by-step instructions, we will be going through the code we are about to run in the next section. If you don't understand Python, don't worry as you won't need to change much and can just follow along with the textual narrative.

Coding the machine learning model

The following section describes the machine learning model we are using. The first thing we'll do is import some utility libraries. These are just dependencies that need to be in place for our code to run:

```
# import libraries
import boto3, re, sys, math, json, os, sagemaker, urllib.
request
from sagemaker import get_execution_role
import numpy as np
import pandas as pd
import matplotlib.pyplot as plt
from IPython.display import Image
from IPython.display import display
from time import gmtime, strftime
from sagemaker.predictor import csv_serializer
```

The next section creates the base image that we will use to train our model in the right AWS region. We are using a model called xgboost, which is a variant of a machine learning algorithm called **Gradient Boosting Machines**, which exhibits very strong performance on structured datasets:

```
#create the estimator image
region = boto3.session.Session().region_name # set the region
of the instance
xgboost_container = sagemaker.image_uris.retrieve("xgboost",
my_region, "latest")
```

We now come to the only place where you will need to modify the code. This section creates an S3 bucket for storing our training data. S3 buckets must have unique names, so you will need to come up with something suitable for your own case:

```
#create an S3 bucket to hold your training dat
#please give this a unique name
bucket_name = 'liabilitybucket123147576575'
```

```
s3 = boto3.resource('s3')
try:
    if  region == 'us-east-1':
       s3.create_bucket(Bucket=bucket_name)
    else:
       s3.create_bucket(Bucket=bucket_name,
          CreateBucketConfiguration={ 'LocationConstraint':
          region })
    print('Training data bucket created')
except Exception as e:
    print('Error encountered during bucket creation: ',e)
```

The next section loads the training data you will be uploading to the instance into a data frame that allows it to be processed:

```
#load data
try:
  model_data = pd.read_csv('./liability.csv')
  print('Success: Data loaded into dataframe.')
except Exception as e:
    print('Data load error: ',e)
```

We now need to split the dataset into one part for training and one part for testing our results. We do this in a ratio of 80/20:

```
#train/test split
train_data, test_data = np.split(model_data.sample(frac=1,
random_state=432), [int(0.8 * len(model_data))])
print(train_data.shape, test_data.shape)
```

Now we take our training data and convert it into the canonical format expected by AWS SageMaker models. As we do that, the data is also uploaded to S3, from where it can be loaded by the model that we will be launching in a second:

```
#define input data in right format
prefix = "PACKT-DEMO"
model_data.to_csv('train.csv', index=False, header=False)
boto3.Session().resource('s3').Bucket(bucket_name).Object(os.
path.join(prefix, 'train/train.csv')).upload_file('train.csv')
```

```
s3_input_train = sagemaker.inputs.TrainingInput(s3_data='s3://
{}/{}/train'.format(bucket_name, prefix), content_type='csv')
```

Now we set up the estimator, which is what the entity that we use to train our models with is called in AWS SageMaker terminology. Don't worry about the specific parameters here; they are set as per reasonable defaults:

```
#set up estimator
role = get_execution_role()
sess = sagemaker.Session()
xgb = sagemaker.estimator.Estimator(xgboost_container,role,
instance_count=1, instance_type='ml.m4.xlarge',output_path='
s3://{}/{}/output'.format(bucket_name, prefix),sagemaker_
session=sess)
xgb.set_hyperparameters(gamma=2,min_child_
weight=3,subsample=0.8,silent=0,objective='binary:logistic',
num_round=50)
```

We now train our model, which is one with a single line:

```
#train model
xgb.fit({'train': s3_input_train})
```

Finally, once our model is trained, we deploy it as a callable endpoint with another single-line command:

```
#deploy
xgb_predictor = xgb.deploy(initial_instance_count=1,instance_
type='ml.m4.xlarge')
```

And that is all there is to the core part of training and deploying a machine learning model. Let's now go and do it for real. Follow these steps next:

1. From your newly open JupyterLab environment, click the upload button shown in the following screenshot and select the two files, chapter 8 - example. ipynb and liability.csv, from your folder containing Chapter08 files:

Figure 8.6 – Uploading via JupyterLab

2. Once uploaded, open the `chapter 8 - example.ipynb` file. This should bring you to a screen like the following screenshot:

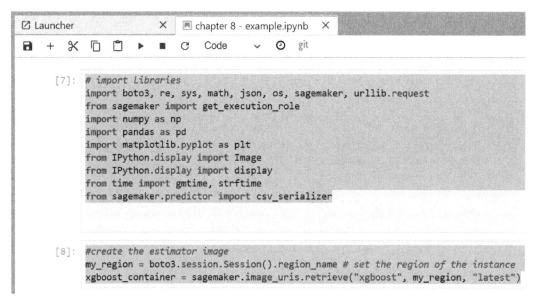

Figure 8.7 – IPython notebook

3. From the **Run** menu, select **Run All Cells** as shown in the following screenshot and go and have a cup of coffee as it will take a while to execute:

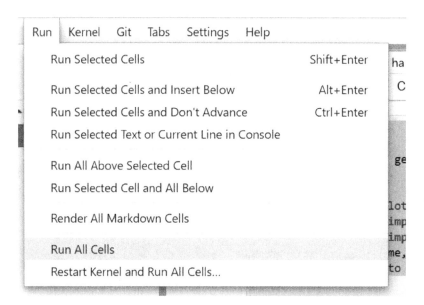

Figure 8.8 – Run All Cells

4. When everything has been completed, you will have a successfully trained model and an endpoint you can use for inference. This brings us to the second part of the task: creating a Lambda function to call the endpoint and exposing that externally via API Gateway.

5. Navigate to AWS Lambda using **Services | Lambda**.

6. Click **Create function** and select **Use a blueprint**, as shown in the following screenshot:

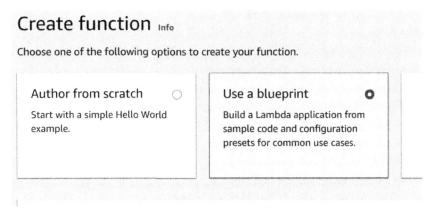

Figure 8.9 – Creating a Lambda function

7. As shown in the following screenshot, pick the blueprint named **microservice-http-endpoint-python**. This blueprint will set up a Lambda function and an associated API Gateway configuration at the same time.

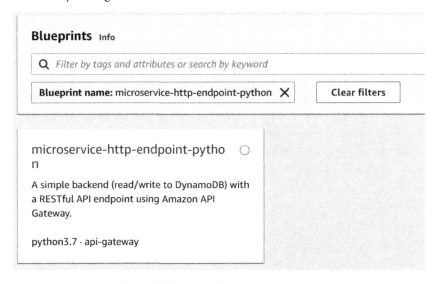

Figure 8.10 – Lambda function blueprint

There are two parts to the configuration of the Lambda function that you need to attend to. First, as shown in the following screenshot, you need to provide a function name and an execution role:

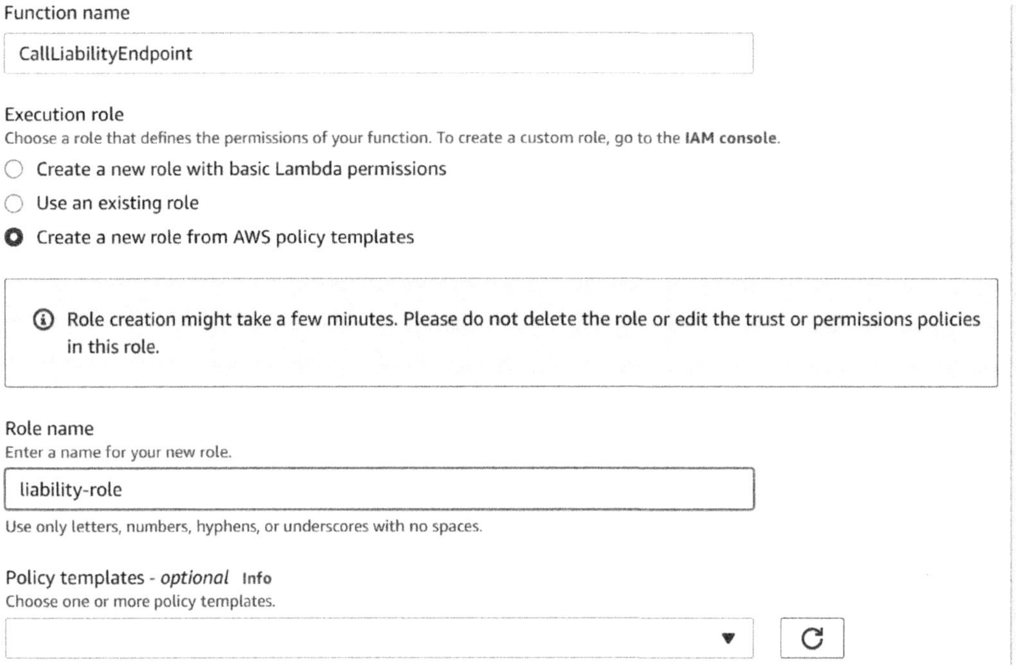

Function name

> CallLiabilityEndpoint

Execution role
Choose a role that defines the permissions of your function. To create a custom role, go to the **IAM console**.

○ Create a new role with basic Lambda permissions

○ Use an existing role

● Create a new role from AWS policy templates

> ⓘ Role creation might take a few minutes. Please do not delete the role or edit the trust or permissions policies in this role.

Role name
Enter a name for your new role.

> liability-role

Use only letters, numbers, hyphens, or underscores with no spaces.

Policy templates - *optional* Info
Choose one or more policy templates.

Figure 8.11 – Lambda function configuration

8. Then, as shown in the following screenshot, you need to configure the API Gateway that you will use. Note that we are going to leave the API open to the world, which is not generally good practice, but it saves us having to address the details of security configuration on AWS, which is a big topic that we do not have space for here.

API Gateway trigger   [Remove]

Add an API to your Lambda function to create an HTTP endpoint that invokes your function. API Gateway supports two
types of RESTful APIs: HTTP APIs and REST APIs. Learn more

API
Create a new API or attach an existing one.

[Create an API   ▼]

API type

( ) HTTP API   (●) REST API
      Create an HTTP API.   Create a REST API.

Security
Configure the security mechanism for your API endpoint.

[Open   ▼]

Don't add any authorization or authentication requirements. Any user can invoke your function with an HTTP call.

Figure 8.12 – API Gateway configuration

9. You can now create the function and wait until everything is ready. The Lambda
    function itself is another simple Python script that simply calls the inference
    endpoint with the right input format. For reference, the code is in the following
    screenshot, but you don't need to understand the details. Just copy/paste this code
    from the `lambda_handler.py` file in the `chapter 8` folder into the **Code
    source** window in AWS Lambda.

Code source Info

```
10
11   def lambda_handler(event, context):
12
13       data = json.loads(json.dumps(event))
14       payload = json.loads(data['body'])['data']
15
16       response = runtime.invoke_endpoint(EndpointName=ENDPOINT_NAME,
17                                          ContentType='text/csv',
18                                          Body=payload)
19
20       result = json.loads(response['Body'].read().decode())
21       return {
22           "isBase64Encoded": False,
23           "statusCode": '200',
24           "headers": {},
25           "body": "{\"result\":\"" + str(result) + "\"}"
26       }
27
```

Figure 8.13 – Lambda function

10. Now, go into the **Configuration | Environment variables** section of the Lambda function and type in the name of the endpoint that was created in SageMaker, when you set up your model, as an environment variable. You can see this under **AWS SageMaker | Inference | Endpoints**. The configuration should look like the following screenshot:

Figure 8.14 – Lambda configuration

11. Now, go to **Configuration | Triggers** and click **Details** on the API Gateway node as shown in the following screenshot. Make a note of the **API endpoint** as that is what you'll be calling from Salesforce to use the API.

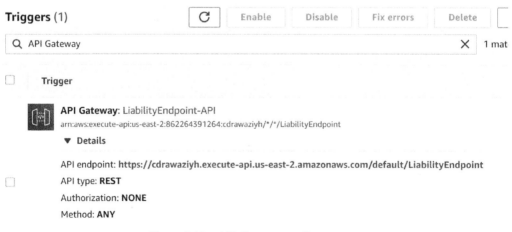

Figure 8.15 – API Gateway configuration

Well done! You have completed the second step of this example and we are now ready to move off AWS and back into Salesforce.

The Salesforce part of the solution will consist of a screen flow that will be launched by a quick action on the **Case** layout. The cornerstone of this screen flow is the Apex action that actually does the callout to AWS to get the result. We will therefore start by reviewing the salient parts of this code, available in the `AWSSageMakerCallout.cls` file in the `chapter 8` files folder.

First, we note that you will have to change the value of the endpoint variable to whatever you noted down from the API Gateway configuration. There are also some constants whose purpose will become clear further on:

```
//replace with your own endpoint
    private static string endpoint =
      'https://cdrawaziyh.execute-api.us-east-
      2.amazonaws.com/prod/LiabilityEndpoint';


    //constants representing ordering of arguments
    private static Integer ORIGIN    = 0;
    private static Integer PRIORITY  = 1;
    private static Integer PRODUCT   = 2;
    private static Integer REASON    = 3;
    private static Integer CASETYPE  = 4;
```

As you may have noticed, if you looked at the dataset we trained on in AWS SageMaker, all values have to be numeric. The inputs, in this case, are a number of picklist fields on inherently textual cases. We therefore map these into numbers by converting them to the index that the picklist value has in Salesforce under its default ordering. The following Apex function accomplishes this goal:

```
    //method to get index of picklist value
    private static Integer getPicklistIndex(SObject sobj,
      String fieldName, String pickVal){
          Schema.DescribeFieldResult fieldResult =
            sobj.getSobjectType().getDescribe().
            fields.getMap().get(fieldName).getDescribe();
List<Schema.PicklistEntry> ple = fieldResult.
getPicklistValues();
Integer i=0;
Map<String,Integer> mapStat=new Map<String,Integer>();
        for(Schema.PicklistEntry pp:ple){
```

```
                        mapStat.put(pp.getValue(),i++);
        }
        return mapStat.get(pickVal);
}
```

The main function in the Apex action takes the inputs, which are provided as text strings, and maps them into numeric values for the callout using the preceding function. It then converts this into the JSON format expected by the API:

```
@InvocableMethod
    public static List<String>
        getLiabilityState(List<List<String>> inputs) {
        //setup input to callout
        List<String> inputList = inputs[0];

        //convert inputs to indices for processing
        List<Integer> intInputs = new List<Integer>();

        intInputs.add(getPicklistIndex((SObject)new Case(),
            'Origin', inputList[ORIGIN]));
        intInputs.add(getPicklistIndex((SObject)new Case(),
            'Priority', inputList[PRIORITY]));
        intInputs.add(getPicklistIndex((SObject)new Case(),
            'Product__c', inputList[PRODUCT]));
        intInputs.add(getPicklistIndex((SObject)new Case(),
            'Reason', inputList[REASON]));
        intInputs.add(getPicklistIndex((SObject)new Case(),
            'Type', inputList[CASETYPE]));
    String dataVals = String.join(intInputs, ',');
        string body = '{"data":"' + dataVals + '"}';
```

The rest is fairly boilerplate Apex code that sets up the callout to AWS, sends it off, parses the response, and returns it to the calling flow:

```
    //setup callout
        Http h = new Http();
        HttpRequest req = new HttpRequest();
        req.setHeader('Content-Type', 'application/json');
```

```
        req.setEndpoint(endpoint);
        req.setMethod('POST');
req.setBody(body);


        // send the request, and return a response
        HttpResponse res = h.send(req);
        String resBody = res.getBody();
Map<String, Object> parsedRes = (Map<String,
Object>)JSON.deserializeUntyped(resBody);
        List<String> retVar = new List<String>();
        retVar.add((String)parsedRes.get('result'));
        return retVar;
}
```

Because we left the API open, we can just call and get a response at this point. This lets us move on to configuring the screen flow, which you do by performing the following steps:

1. Before you do anything else, you need to register a remote site with the URL that you noted in the API builder.

2. Once done, go to **Flow Builder** and create a new screen flow.

3. Add five picklist choice sets to the resources section for the **Case** fields – **Origin**, **Case Reason**, **Priority**, **Type**, and **Product__c**, each configured as in the following screenshot. The picklist values will be taken from these fields.

Figure 8.16 – Configuring choices

4. Also create a text variable named `recordId`, available for input, to receive the ID of the context case.

5.   Create a **Get Records** element configured as in the following screenshot:

Figure 8.17 – Configuring Get Records

6.   Now create a screen element, call it `Liability Callout Screen`, and add five picklists corresponding to the choice sets previously configured. See the following screenshot as an example. All picklists should be required as the API will not work without all the data.

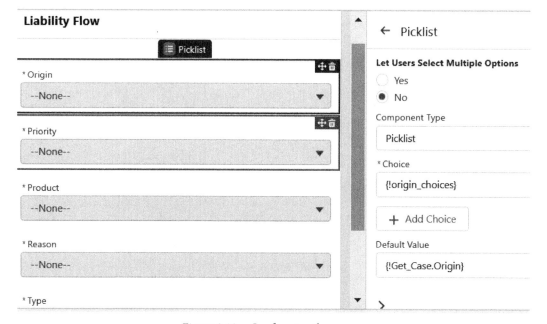

Figure 8.18 – Configuring the screen

7. Now create a collection variable of the `text` type and call it `SageMaker_inputs`. This will be used for the parameters sent to the Apex action.

8. Create an **Assignment** element and map 10 variables, as shown in the following screenshot, to update both **Case** and the collection of model parameters.

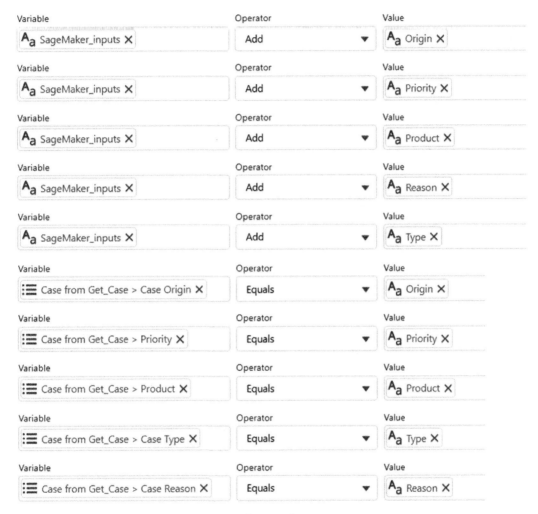

Figure 8.19 – Configuring the assignment step

9. Create a text variable called `result_text` to hold the output of the callout to AWS.

10. Now, add an Apex action step of the type **AWSSageMakerCallout**, call it `Callout to Sagemaker`, and configure it as shown in the following screenshot:

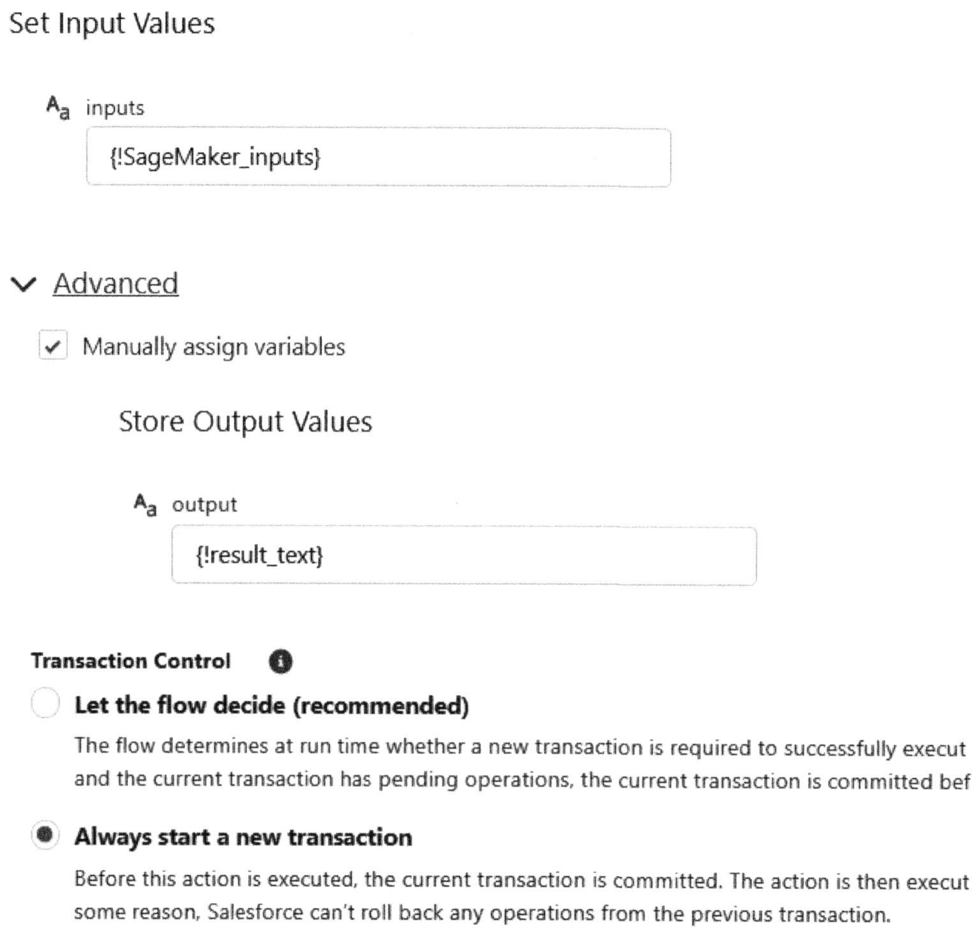

Set Input Values

A_a inputs

{!SageMaker_inputs}

∨ Advanced

☑ Manually assign variables

Store Output Values

A_a output

{!result_text}

Transaction Control

◯ **Let the flow decide (recommended)**

The flow determines at run time whether a new transaction is required to successfully execut and the current transaction has pending operations, the current transaction is committed bef

◉ **Always start a new transaction**

Before this action is executed, the current transaction is committed. The action is then execut some reason, Salesforce can't roll back any operations from the previous transaction.

Figure 8.20 – Callout inputs

11. Now create a formula variable called `result_as_float` that has the formula `VALUE(result_text)`, which will convert the text result into a numeric value.

12. We will use this value to determine whether we should set potential liability to yes or no based on a 0.5 threshold. Add a decision node and configure it as shown in the following screenshot:

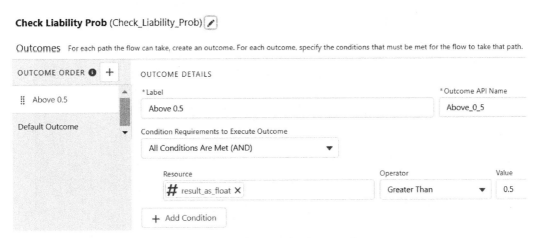

Figure 8.21 – Configuring the decision element

13. On the **Above 0.5** branch, create an assignment step setting the potential liability to **Yes**, as shown in the following screenshot. Create an equivalent step on the default branch with a value of **No**:

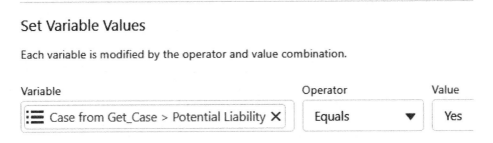

Figure 8.22 – Assigning potential liability

14. Now update the case using an **Update Records** node configured as in the following screenshot and, after you save and activate, you're done. All that remains is to create an action and add it to the page layout.

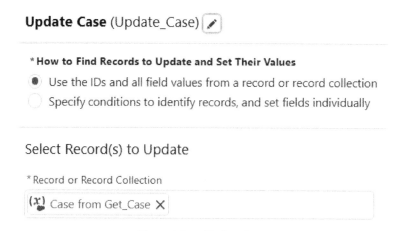

Figure 8.23 – Update Case

15. Add a quick action as in the following screenshot and add it to the **Case** layout:

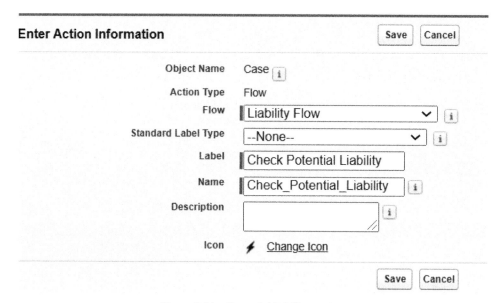

Figure 8.24 – Potential liability action

16. Go to **Case** and try out your new action. An example is shown in the following screenshot:

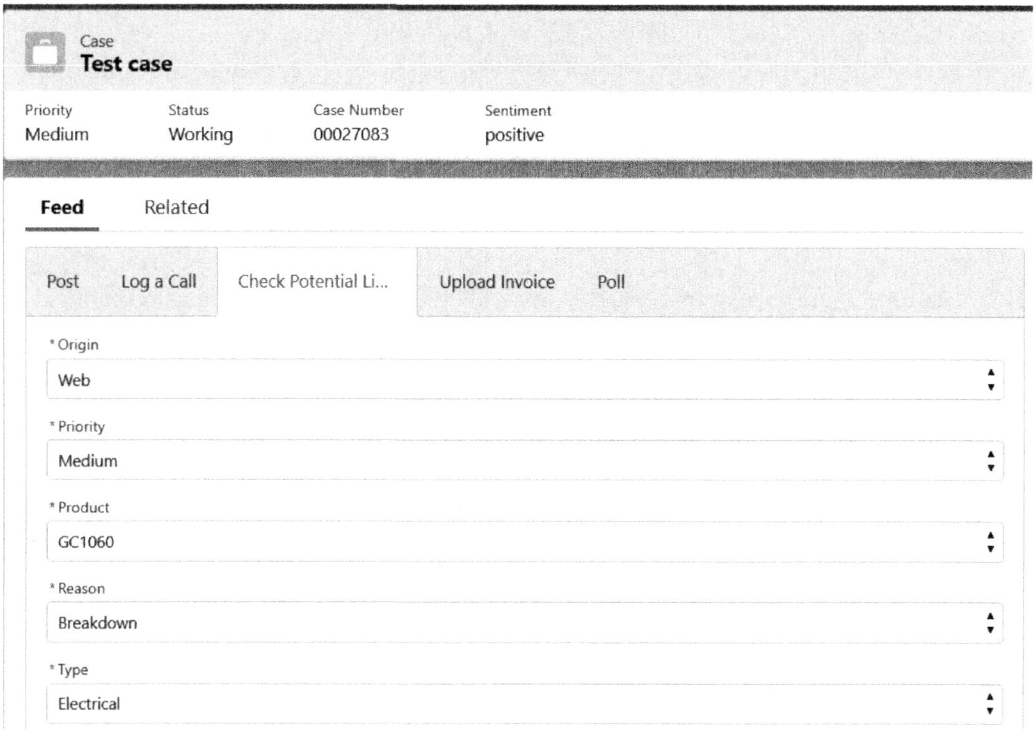

Figure 8.25 – Potential liability action in action

Congratulations! You have now completed the longest and most difficult scenario in this book.

The ability to use a custom model from AWS is a capability that can be stretched to meet any requirement, where other means fail. Therefore, it is highly useful to know how to do this in practice. However, you should now also have an appreciation for why this isn't something to do lightly. We only scratched the surface here and even that is a complex procedure.

Now that you have completed the example, it is important to clean up the AWS account so that you don't incur any running charges. When you are completely done with this example, go to your account and delete all files in S3, and then delete the S3 bucket. After that, stop your notebook instance, delete it, and also delete the associated endpoint. The Lambda function and API Gateway do not incur running charges, so you can leave those if you like.

With all that done, we can now move on to a much simpler example, extracting key phrases from our case conversation.

Extracting key phrases with Azure Text Analytics

Azure is Microsoft's general platform within which they provide an extensive array of AI services via APIs. In this example, we will be making use of the **Text Analytics** component, a subcomponent of the wider Cognitive Services offering that contains most of the AI services on offer. This subcomponent contains a range of APIs related to **Natural Language Processing** (**NLP**), which can be used for a variety of purposes, some of which overlaps with the offerings from Einstein Platform Services that we examined in *Chapter 7, Building AI Features with Einstein Platform Services*.

However, for the purpose of this example, we will be using a service that has no such equivalence on the Salesforce platform. This is the Key Phrases API, which extracts key phrases from unstructured text documents. It works by you posting a set of JSON formatted text documents to the API endpoint identified by an index and getting in return a set of key phrases characteristic of those input documents, again formatted in JSON.

We do this to meet yet another requirement from the head of customer services. She has had a report from her service managers that because of the high volume of cases at the moment, they are having trouble keeping up with what their customer service agents are doing on the cases they are handling. They have asked whether they could have an *at a glance* summary of the conversation happening on a given case. After thinking a bit, you have come up with a solution based on the Azure Key Phrases API.

In designing your solution to this requirement, you have decided to build on the example from *Chapter 7, Building AI Features with Einstein Platform Services*, which used **Case Comments** to gauge the sentiment of a given case. Effectively, you will be using the same aggregated text that you produced in this chapter and use a new screen flow to call out to Azure for the key phrases.

The first thing you will need to do is configure the endpoint on Azure that you will be calling from Salesforce. To do so, follow these steps:

1. Log in to your Azure account.

2. Now, go to **Create Cognitive Services | Text Analytics**. This will create a particular version of this service for your use.

3. There are two bits to configure, first, **Project details**. Create a new resource and give it a unique name. Select **Free Trial** under **Subscription** as shown in the following screenshot:

Create ...
Text Analytics

---

* **Basics**   Tags   Review + create

Unlock insights from unstructured text using advanced natural language processing. Use sentiment analysis to find out what customers think of your brand. Find topic-relevant phrases using key phrase extraction and identify the language of the text with language detection. Detect and categorize entities in your text with named entity recognition. Learn more ☑

Project details

Select the subscription to manage deployed resources and costs. Use resource groups like folders to organize and manage all your resources.

Subscription * ⓘ | Free Trial   ⌄ |

└──── Resource group * ⓘ | (New) Packt   ⌄ |
                                     Create new

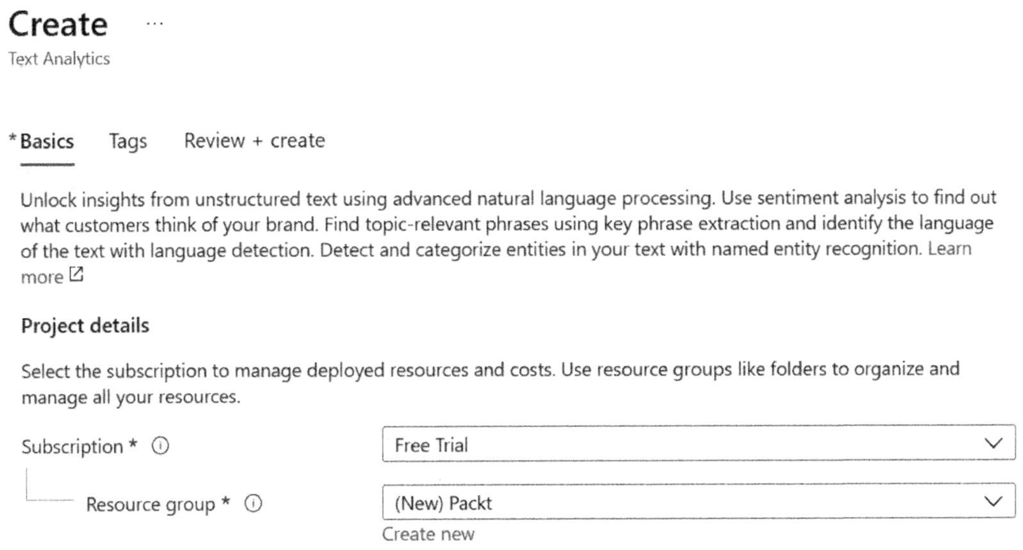

Figure 8.26 – Creating a Text Analytics service

4. Second, you need to fill in **Instance details**. Do so in the way shown in the following screenshot, using your unique name:

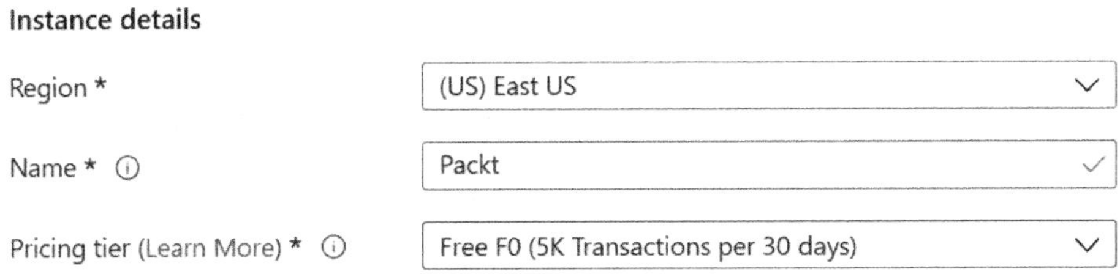

Instance details

Region * | (US) East US   ⌄ |

Name * ⓘ | Packt   ✓ |

Pricing tier (Learn More) * ⓘ | Free F0 (5K Transactions per 30 days)   ⌄ |

Figure 8.27 – Configuring the Text Analytics service

Now you will have to wait for your resources to deploy. Once everything is ready, the screen will look something like the following:

Figure 8.28 – Completed Text Analytics deployment

5. Now you need to get your API key and endpoint, which you can get to from the **Manage keys** menu option. You should note down either of the two API keys and the endpoint URL as you will need these later to configure the Apex action we'll use for the callout.

Well done. This is all that needs to be done on the Azure side in order to be able to complete this example. We will now proceed to look at the code required on Salesforce to complete this example.

Coding the example on Salesforce

In this section, we will have a look at the code for the key Apex action that will be calling out to Azure and getting a response back. As always, remember that the code is structured to be easy to follow and not take hundreds of pages to explain, so adapt as appropriate if you want to use this in production. The code can be found in the `AzureKeyPhrasesCallout.cls` file in the `chapter 8` files folder and you can use that to create a new Apex class in Developer Console.

The code starts by defining the two bits of information you just got from Azure. This is the only place you'll need to customize the code, so insert your own values here:

```
//replace with your own endpoint
private static string endpoint = '<YOUR ENDPOINT
                                HERE>';
//replace with you API key
private static string API_KEY = '<YOUR API KEY HERE>';
```

The logic in **InvocableMethod** that is the core of an Apex action is divided into four parts. The first part, shown in the following code listing, sets up the input to the callout by formatting the input given to the method into a JSON string that meets the expectations of the Azure endpoint:

```
//setup input to callout
        //only accepting one string for this example,
        //bulkify if you want to use
        if (inputs == null || inputs.size() <= 0 ||
                inputs[0].length() == 0){
            return new List<String>{'No output'};
        }
        String inputStr = inputs[0];
        string body = '{"documents":[{"language":"en",
                "id":"1", "text": "' + inputStr + '"}]}';
```

The second part sets up and does the actual callout. Note that the way we authenticate ourselves is simply by including the suitable API key header. Otherwise, this is boilerplate Salesforce code that makes a callout using the `Http*` standard classes:

```
    //setup callout
    Http h = new Http();
    HttpRequest req = new HttpRequest();
    req.setHeader('Content-Type', 'application/json');
    req.setEndpoint(endpoint);
    req.setHeader('Ocp-Apim-Subscription-Key',
            API_KEY);
    req.setMethod('POST');
    req.setBody(body);

    // send the request, and return a response
    HttpResponse res = h.send(req);
```

The response comes back as JSON and that needs to be parsed into something that is easier to work with. That is the purpose of the following piece of code that uses untyped JSON parsing to get the actual text key phrase values returned by the API:

```
    //get response and process JSON
    String resBody = res.getBody();
    Map<String, Object> parsedRes = (Map<String,
```

```
        Object>)JSON.deserializeUntyped(resBody);
    List<Object> docs =
        (List<Object>)parsedRes.get('documents');
    List<Object> keyPhrases =
        (List<Object>)((Map<String,
        Object>)docs[0]).get('keyPhrases');
```

The final part of the code converts this return information into the format that we need for our flow, namely, a single comma-separated return string that can be put into a relevant field on the **Case** object:

```
//combine returned phrases into single return string
    List<String> tmpRes = new List<String>();
    for (Object o : keyPhrases){
        tmpRes.add((String)o);
    }
    List<String> retVar = new List<String>();
    retVar.add(String.join(tmpRes, ','));
    return retVar;
    }
```

Now, with the heart of the solution built, let's create the screen flow that will call the Azure API and store the output on the case. We do that by performing the following steps:

1. First, go to **Remote Site Settings** and add a remote site for your Azure endpoint, along the lines of the following screenshot:

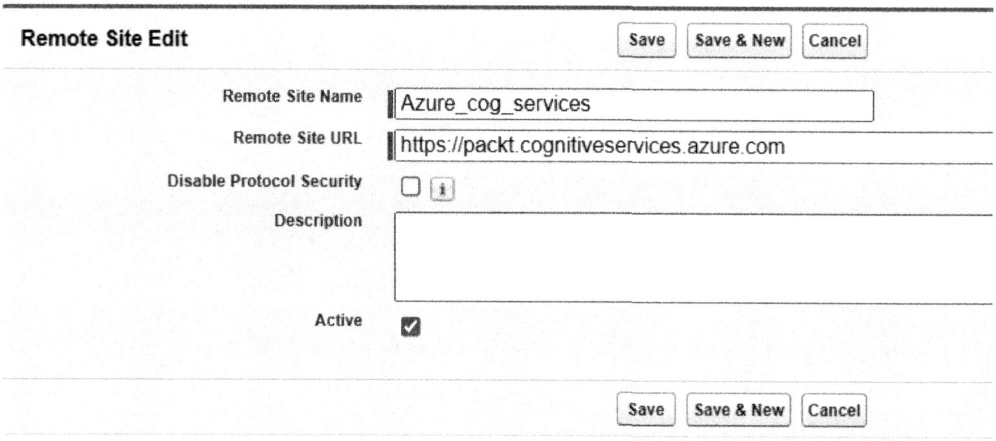

Figure 8.29 – Azure remote site

2. Next, let's create the field that will hold the text. Configure it as in the following screenshot and add it to the page layout:

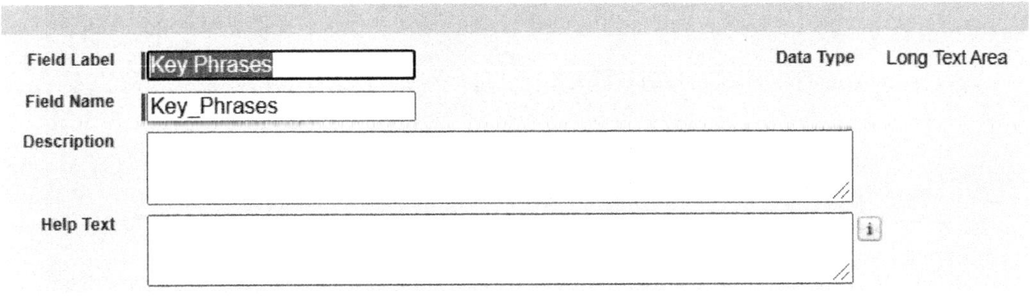

Field Label	Key Phrases		Data Type	Long Text Area
Field Name	Key_Phrases			
Description				
Help Text				

Figure 8.30 – Key phrases field

3. Now, go to **Flow Builder**, create a new screen flow, and add a variable called recordId of the text type available for input.

4. Add a **Get Records** element, **Get Case**, and configure it as in the following screenshot:

* Object

Case

Filter Case Records

Condition Requirements

All Conditions Are Met (AND) ▼

Field	Operator	Value
Id	Equals ▼	A_a recordId X

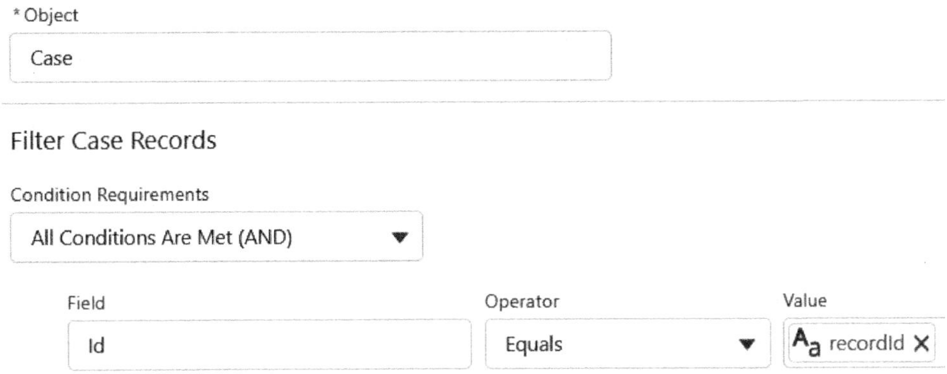

Figure 8.31 – Configuring Get Case

- Add an Apex action of the **AzureKeyPhrasesCallout** type, call it Callout to Azure, and configure the inputs as in the following screenshot:

Callout to Azure (Callout_to_Azure) ✎

Set Input Values

A_a inputs

{!Get_Case.Comment_Text__c}

Include

Figure 8.32 – Configuring the Apex action

5.   Now, add an **Assignment** node that assigns the output of the callout to the key phrases field on **Case**, as shown in the following screenshot:

Set Variable Values

Each variable is modified by the operator and value combination.

Variable	Operator	Value
A_a Case from Get_Case > Key Phrases ✕	Equals ▼	A_a Text from Callout_to_Azure ✕

Figure 8.33 – Configuring the assignment

6.   Then, add an **Update Records** element, **Update Case**, configured as in the following screenshot:

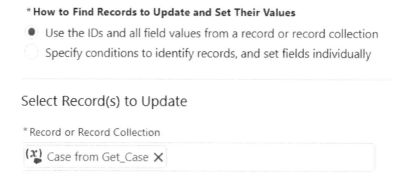

* **How to Find Records to Update and Set Their Values**

⦿ Use the IDs and all field values from a record or record collection

○ Specify conditions to identify records, and set fields individually

Select Record(s) to Update

* Record or Record Collection

(x) Case from Get_Case ✕

Figure 8.34 – Updating records for the Azure screen flow

7.   Finally, create a quick action to launch the flow as in the following screenshot and add the action to the **Case** layout:

Enter Action Information
Save
Cancel
Object Name
Case
Action Type
Flow
Flow
Azure Callout Flow
Standard Label Type
--None--
Label
Get Key Phrases
Name
Get_Key_Phrases
Description
Icon
Change Icon

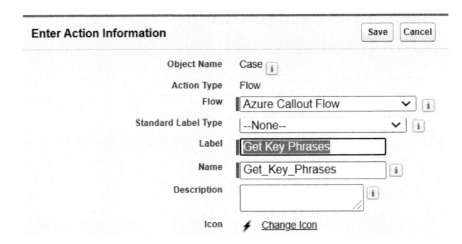

Figure 8.35 – Action for the callout to Azure

8. Now go and test your action by going to a case with a large amount of meaningful text in its text comments and clicking on your new callout button. Your **Key Phrases** field will get populated with the information from the API, as exemplified in the following screenshot:

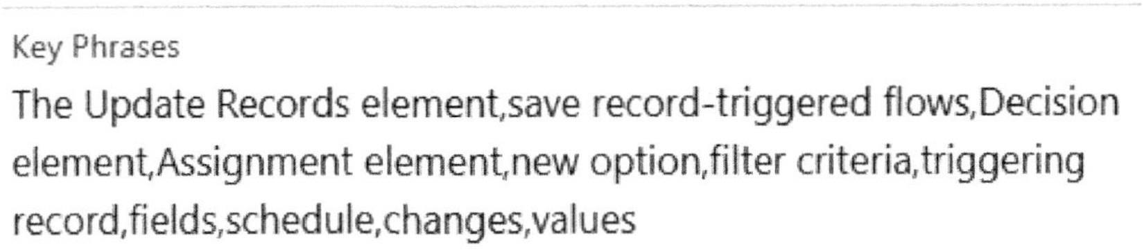

Key Phrases
The Update Records element,save record-triggered flows,Decision element,Assignment element,new option,filter criteria,triggering record,fields,schedule,changes,values

Figure 8.36 – Key phrases from API

Well done! You have now completed the second example in this chapter and worked with your second third-party platform.

Azure services are vast and comprehensive and are worth detailed study. For many other cognitive services, the process to connect and use them effectively is the same as we've seen in this chapter. Now you know how to consider these in your own solutions.

For our final example, we will be using one of the most pervasive AI technologies on the internet – Google Translate.

Translating text with Google Translate

For our last example, we will be using one of the AI applications almost everyone is aware of – Google Translate. Due to its use within the Chrome browser and the Google search engine, most people are aware of the vast capabilities of this technology to translate between languages. What fewer people are aware of is that this technology is available as an API that you can incorporate into your own application.

This is the API we will be working with for this example. Google, like Microsoft and AWS, has a substantial range of leading-edge AI services that you can access via APIs. Looking into these on your own after completing this example will repay the effort as you will understand the basics of how to interact with them after having completed this section.

This time, our requirements from Pickled Plastics Ltd. come from a happy place. The head of sales has just closed a new major deal with a Chinese reseller, not least due to the improvements in customer service that you, among others, have been working so hard on. The only problem is that the product catalog has not yet been translated into Chinese. You have people working on this, but it's a big job and in the meantime, the head of sales has asked you to come up with a tactical solution that allows sales reps to translate product descriptions automatically on demand.

You have thought about it, but Google Translate being the market leader in automated translation, you pretty quickly settled on using it. You have designed a simple solution that lets a sales rep translate the English product description via a quick action on the product page that calls out to the Google Translate API.

To accomplish this task, you first need to go to Google Cloud Platform and perform a few steps along the lines of the following:

1. First, you need to enable the Google Translate API. Go to your default project and then select **APIs & Services | Library**.

2. Search for `Translate` and select **Cloud Translation API**. This will bring you to a page like the following screenshot, where you should click **ENABLE**:

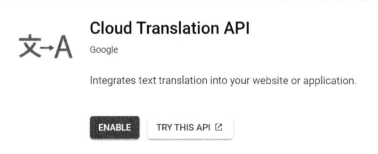

Figure 8.37 – Enabling the Cloud Translation API

3. Next, go to **APIs & Services | Credentials** and click **CREATE CREDENTIALS** to create a new API key, as in the following screenshot:

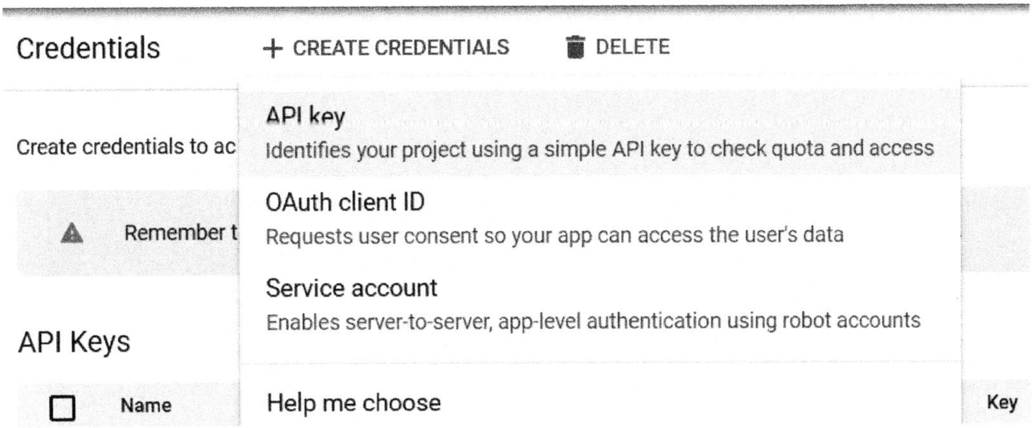

Credentials   + CREATE CREDENTIALS   🗑 DELETE

Create credentials to ac	**API key** Identifies your project using a simple API key to check quota and access
⚠ Remember t	**OAuth client ID** Requests user consent so your app can access the user's data
API Keys	**Service account** Enables server-to-server, app-level authentication using robot accounts
☐ Name	Help me choose Key

Figure 8.38 – Creating an API key

Note down the API key that is provided as you will need that to connect to the API from Salesforce. We should note that Google recommends the use of OAuth-based service accounts for authentication and you should follow that advice if you want to work with Google APIs in a production context.

We are now ready to start doing things on Salesforce, but once again before proceeding, we will have a look at the code that drives the functionality. Once again, this is found in the form of an Apex action that is invoked from a screen flow. The code can be found in the `chapter 8` files folder in the `GoogleTranslateAPICallout.cls` file.

If you have already completed the example on using the Azure Key Phrases API, you will see a lot of similarities. The structure of preparing the input in JSON format, sending it to the API endpoint, getting a JSON response back, parsing it, and returning it in the right format for a flow, is exactly the same. But there is, of course, a substantial difference in how this is done. Let's see how.

First, as always, we need to specify the endpoint and API key. Note that for the Google Translate API, you don't need to change anything on the endpoint, only the API key:

```
//fixed endpoint
private static string endpoint =
'https://translation.googleapis.com/language/translate/v2';


//replace with you API key
private static string API_KEY = '<YOUR API KEY>';
```

Preparing the input is done by taking the input string passed by the screen flow and putting that into the right JSON template for the callout. Here we have hardcoded translation to Chinese and are only including a single string to translate. Both can be amended should you wish to go further:

```
//setup input to callout
        //only accepting one string for this example,
        //bulkify if you want to use
        String inputStr = inputs[0];
        string body = '{"q":["' + inputStr + '"],
                        "target":"zh"}';
```

The callout is once again just boilerplate code that should be adapted to whatever frameworks you use for managing API callouts if you want to use it in production. Note that the Google Translate API accepts the API key in the query string rather than the header, which is different from the other example we've seen:

```
//setup callout
        Http h = new Http();
        HttpRequest req = new HttpRequest();
        req.setHeader('Content-Type', 'application/json');
        req.setEndpoint(endpoint + '?key=' + API_KEY);
        req.setMethod('POST');
        req.setBody(body);


        // send the request, and return a response
        HttpResponse res = h.send(req);
```

Parsing the response and generating the return string to the calling flow is a bit of JSON parsing work. The API returns a list of translations wrapped in a generic data object, so we're just going to extract the translated text, which is all we're interested in for this example. Then we'll put it into our return array that makes it accessible to the flow:

```
//get response and process JSON
        String resBody = res.getBody();


        Map<String, Object> parsedRes = (Map<String,
            Object>)JSON.deserializeUntyped(resBody);
        Map<String, Object> data = (Map<String,
```

```
            Object>)parsedRes.get('data');
   List<Object> translations =
            (List<Object>)data.get('translations');

   //generate response
   Map<String, Object> retTrans = (Map<String,
            Object>)translations[0];
   List<String> retVar = new List<String>();
   retVar.add((String)retTrans.get('translatedText'));
   return retVar;
```

Now that you understand the code, you should create the class via Developer Console in your own Salesforce org and move on to the next stage of the solution, creating the screen flow.

To do so, perform the following steps:

1. First, go and create a remote site setting for the Google API endpoint.

2. Now, we need to add the field on **Product2** that will hold the Chinese translation. Do that as per the following screenshot and add the field to the page layout:

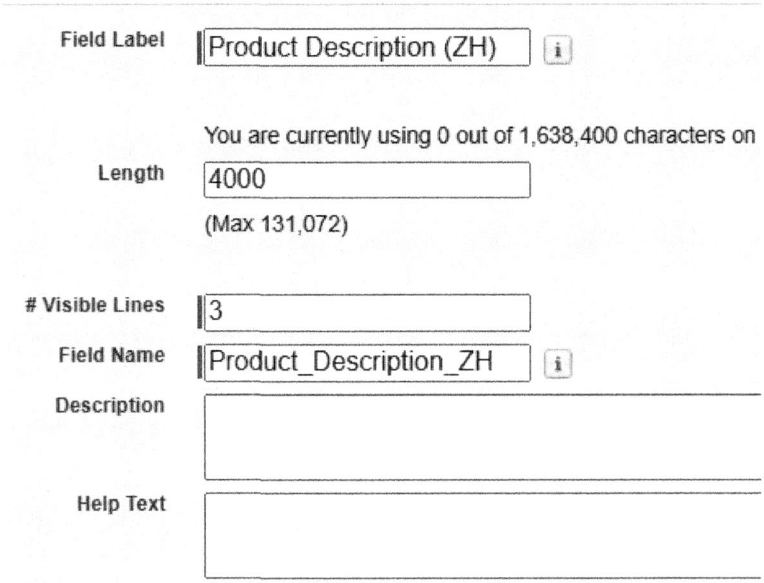

Field Label	Product Description (ZH) [i]
Length	You are currently using 0 out of 1,638,400 characters on 4000 (Max 131,072)
# Visible Lines	3
Field Name	Product_Description_ZH [i]
Description	
Help Text	

Figure 8.39 – Adding a field for the product description

3. Go to **Flow Builder** and create a new screen flow.

4. Add a text variable called recordId, available for the input.

5. Add a **Get Records Of This Object** element, call it Product, and configure it as per the following screenshot:

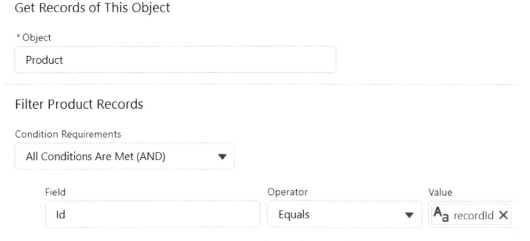

Figure 8.40 – Getting the product to update

6. Create an Apex action of the **GoogleTranslateAPICallout** type, call it Callout to Google, and configure it as in the following screenshot:

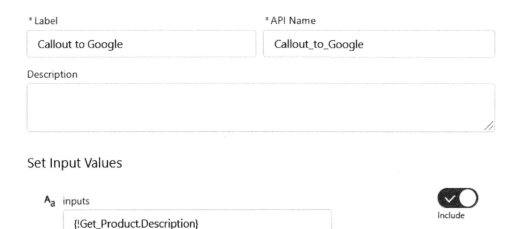

Figure 8.41 – Callout to Google

7. Create an assignment element and configure it as in the following screenshot:

Figure 8.42 – Assigning the result

8. Finally, create an **Update Records** element, configured as in the following screenshot:

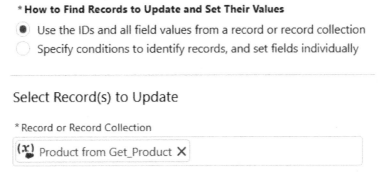

Figure 8.43 – Updating the product

9. Save and activate the flow.

10. We now need to add a quick action, so go to the **Product2** object and add a quick action configured as in the following screenshot:

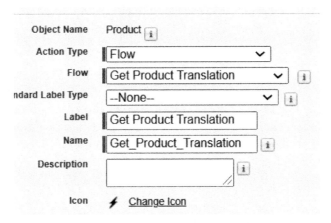

Figure 8.44 – Action for product translation

11. Now, add the action to the page layout and go try it out on a product with a long description. You may have to copy/paste something from elsewhere to get a good result. When successful, it should look something like the following screenshot:

Product Description

Plastic Box is a compilation box set by the post-punk band Public Image Ltd released in 1999 as a limited edition, but re-released for a standard release on 14 December 2009. It comprises four discs covering the band's activity from their debut in 1978 until their hiatus beginning in 1992.

Product Description (ZH)

Plastic Box 是后朋克乐队 Public Image Ltd 于 1999 年发行的限量版编辑盒，但于 2009 年 12 月 14 日重新发行为标准发行版。它包含四张唱片，涵盖乐队自 1978 年首次亮相以来的活动直到他们从 1992 年开始中断。

Figure 8.45 – Translated text on page layout

Congratulations! You have completed all the examples in this chapter, which also concludes the examples from this book. Google Translate is just one of many API offerings from Google Cloud Platform, but at least this gives you a basic familiarity with the process of integrating these services when you have a need to do so.

In our next chapter, we will try to bring together various strands from what we have learned to construct a decision guide to help you in deciding when to use what AI feature. First, however, we will briefly summarize the work we've done in this chapter.

Summary

In this chapter, we have looked at how to integrate third-party AI services into our Salesforce solutions. We worked through a lot of material, but hopefully, by doing the hands-on work, you now have a real appreciation of what it takes to build this kind of solution, even if on a very simplified basis.

One key learning point is the substantial difference in complexity between deploying and accessing your own custom models and using third-party services. We spent by far the longest on the first task, and while this is a technique that can be used to meet any requirement, it puts all the onus on you to come up with the right data, model, and integration pattern. This is a big ask and while you can do it if the occasion calls for it, you should be cautious about overuse. This should also make you appreciate just how useful the ability to fine-tune existing models with your own data that we saw in Einstein Platform Services is.

In contrast, the other two services were integrated with a minimum of fuss. Integrating point solutions for specific requirements via third-party APIs is often an investment that has a much better ROI than trying to do something yourself, even if that requires going off the Salesforce platform.

Overall, the message of this chapter is that you need to know your options and understand the real complexity involved when designing solutions. We hope the examples have helped get you on the path to that goal.

Now, we will move on to the penultimate chapter, where we will synthesize the lessons we've learned from an architectural point-of-view into a decision guide for choosing the right kind of AI service at the right time.

Questions

1. Why would you need to use a custom-built AI model?
2. Should you always seek to avoid third-party APIs?
3. What are some of the major cloud providers where you might have a look for good AI services?

Section 4:
Making the
Right Decision

This section will consolidate the information from previous sections into a format that can be used by architects to make decisions about what technologies to use in a given real-world situation. In *Chapter 9, A Salesforce AI Decision Guide*, we develop a decision guide that helps you ask the right questions about the solutions you're architecting. Finally, *Chapter 10, Conclusion*, reviews the overall lessons from the book, as well as giving pointers for further exploration.

This section comprises the following chapters:

- *Chapter 9, A Salesforce AI Decision Guide*
- *Chapter 10, Conclusion*

9
A Salesforce AI Decision Guide

This chapter will present a summary of all the key architectural decisions and trade-offs that are relevant to the technologies discussed in this book. We will start by introducing the guide and how to use it, then move on to discussing how to approach the decision-making process from three perspectives:

- A functional perspective grounded in common use cases
- A structural perspective grounded in technical and non-functional requirements
- A strategic perspective grounded in the long-term evolution of a company's enterprise architecture

In this chapter, we're going to cover the following main topics:

- Using the decision guide
- Choosing the right feature based on functional factors
- Choosing the right feature based on structural factors
- Choosing the right feature based on strategic factors
- Applying the framework in practice

After completing this chapter, you will have learned how to make an informed architectural decision about what AI features to use in a Salesforce project.

Using the decision guide

This chapter is structured as a decision-making guide to help you ask the right questions and make the right decisions, given your specific requirements. It contains three sections with factors that should be considered during the solution design phase of your AI project.

These factors will guide you based on the type of features we have considered in this book. In general, we can consider the features along a spectrum of more out-of-the-box to more custom, as shown in the following diagram:

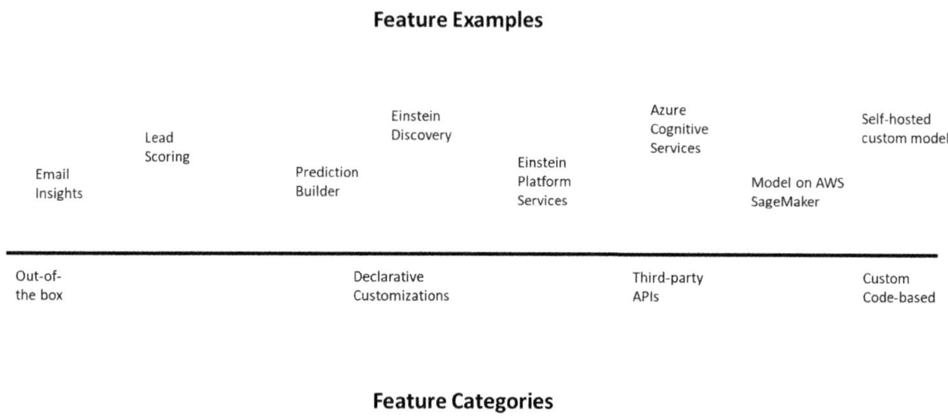

Feature Examples

	Lead Scoring		Einstein Discovery		Azure Cognitive Services	Self-hosted custom model
Email Insights		Prediction Builder		Einstein Platform Services	Model on AWS SageMaker	

Out-of-the box		Declarative Customizations		Third-party APIs	Custom Code-based

Feature Categories

Figure 9.1 – AI feature spectrum

At the far left, we have pure out-of-the-box features such as **Email Insights**, while at the far right, we have entirely **Custom Code-based** solutions. For this guide, we will group these into four categories: out-of-the-box, declarative customizations, third-party APIs, and custom code-based solutions.

To use this guide, make a shortlist of different solution options that you might consider for implementation. For instance, if you need to implement a lead scoring solution, you could consider the built-in **Einstein Lead Scoring model**, a model based on Einstein Discovery, or a custom model built on **AWS SageMaker**. For each option, consider going through the following factors and evaluate the consequences of each choice. Then, combine these into a complete evaluation, along with any normal due diligence you would do for any solution design, whether it's AI-related or not. The answer may be clear, or it may not, but that is why you will need to give it detailed architectural attention in the first place. The following diagram shows the overall framework:

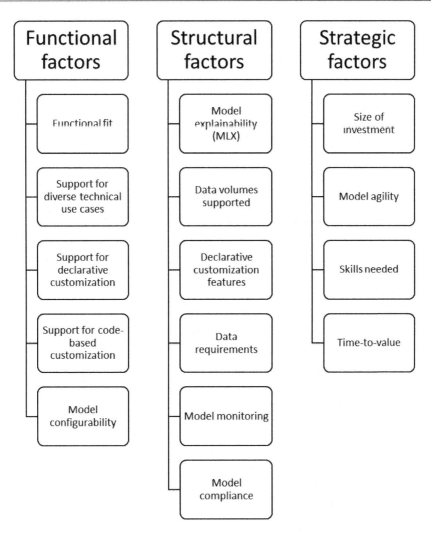

Figure 9.2 – Decision guide framework

We will start by considering the functional factors that should be considered as part of an evaluation.

Choosing the right feature based on functional factors

Functional factors include everything that is needed to implement the actual user experience of a given AI feature. That is both the UI, the data model, and the associated automation and code that is required for the whole process to work. In the following section, we will go through some of the key concerns that you may have, as an architect, in terms of functional factors and discuss how the different types of AI solutions stack up.

We will start by looking at functional fit, which is an obvious starting point for evaluating a feature to see if you wish to include it in your solution.

The following diagram shows where we are in the overall framework:

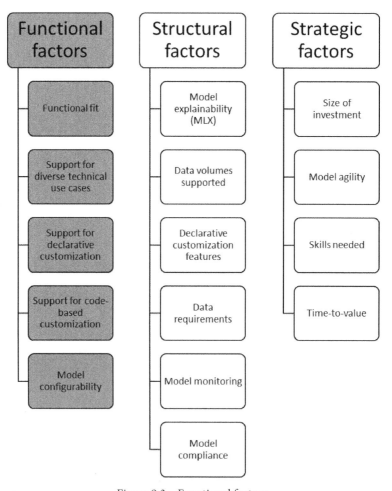

Figure 9.3 – Functional factors

Functional fit

By **functional fit**, we mean how well a given feature supports the use case that you want to apply it to. For instance, if you are considering a lead scoring requirement, you would evaluate the out-of-the-box Einstein Lead Scoring feature against the business requirements and figure out whether it is close. If it isn't, you might look at custom or third-party lead scoring solutions as well. You might still end up back with the original out-of-the-box feature for other reasons, such as cost or a commitment to using standard functionality, but the evaluation for functional fit should be done regardless.

In general, when we look at our different categories of solutions, we find the following:

- **Out-of-the-box solutions** tend to support the lowest number of specific requirements, which is not surprising as creating general-purpose machine learning models is extremely hard. From a return-on-investment and time-to-value perspective, they should always be considered, but in many cases, they may not support the detailed business requirements you need.

- **Declarative customization** will support most specific requirements at the UI and business process level but may not always support detailed requirements for how the model should perform.

- **Third-party API-based solutions** have similar issues to out-of-the-box solutions, but there are more of them from more vendors, so you are more likely to find a fit for your specific use case than by restricting yourself to Salesforce features. If you do find a fit, it is worth considering a custom solution.

- **Custom machine learning models** will fit any requirements you have the data to support and do so in the way you want. This means that if they're built to the specification, they will always have the highest functional fit. However, this comes at a significant expense.

Some key questions to consider regarding functional fit are as follows:

- How complex are our user requirements? Can they be simplified to fit with a more standard feature?

- Do we need to have control of the technical implementation of the machine learning layer?

- If we look more broadly, can we find a service that is a good fit for our user requirements?

Having considered functional fit, we will now move on to the next factor, which is support for diverse technical use cases.

Support for diverse technical use cases

By *support for diverse technical use cases*, we mean whether the feature supports usage in different kinds of technical setups. Specifically, we would look for whether the feature can be used synchronously to get a real-time response, asynchronously to get a response in a separate transaction, and whether it offers batch support for doing mass updates of large volume.

We consider this a functional factor as the user requirements will usually be quite specific on whether a response is expected now, in a bit, or at some point. We consider it different from functional fit as the users will rarely have strong opinions about the specific technical way to address their requirements.

Looking across our categories, we find the following:

- **Out-of-the-box solutions** will tend to only do things one way. That way, they will be well defined and may have good service levels, but there will be little scope to tailor things in most cases.

- **Declarative customization features** can be used to support any of the required technical setups. With the increasing power of flows, this is only likely to become more the case going forward.

- **Third-party APIs** can almost always be used both synchronously and asynchronously, but not all APIs support batching or bulking effectively. If you are looking at a batch-based implementation, you should ensure your selected API supports it.

- **Custom code-based solutions** can support any scenario you like, but you may be responsible for additional work on the API side if you decide to implement something more elaborate than what you get as standard from your platform of choice.

To evaluate a feature based on support for diverse technical use cases, you might ask yourself the following questions:

- Will our solution need to answer in near real time?

- Do we need control over when calculations are done?

- Is there a need, either as part of normal operations or to support some back-office process, to process large amounts of records in bulk?

With that considered, let's look at our third functional factor, support for declarative customization.

Support for declarative customization

The ability to customize features using clicks rather than code is a major reason that the Salesforce Platform has become as popular as it is. Therefore, we need to consider to what extent our proposed solution can support such customization, both now and in the future.

Considering this for our feature categories, we find the following:

- **Out-of-the-box features** will tend to have low configurability, but what can be configured will be configured in a declarative way. You will need to assess whether this flexibility is sufficient for your cases.

- **Declarative customization features**, by their nature, excel in this area and can generally support a very extensive degree of customization using standard Salesforce features.

- **Third-party APIs and custom code-based solutions** can have their UIs built using declarative features on Salesforce, but that's where it ends. Anything beyond that will not be possible using core Salesforce features, although you can buy **Mulesoft** as a way to improve this scenario if you use a lot of APIs.

When considering this factor, ask yourself the following questions:

- Do we need configurators or administrators to be able to configure the solution going forward?

- Do we have any design principles that steer us toward declarative solutions?

- What level of ongoing change are we expecting for the UI and business process requirements?

Having considered declarative customization options, next, we will consider code-based customization options.

Support for code-based customization

While most organizations prefer declarative customizations, when possible, it is no secret that most end up needing a certain amount of code for advanced customization as well. This is even more true when it comes to areas such as AI, where many services are reached via integration and requirements are often at the cutting edge of the possible. This means that over time, as our use of AI features becomes more complex, we are increasingly likely to need to add some code to the mix. Therefore, we should also consider how easy code-based customization is for the features we are considering.

Using our four categories, we find the following:

- **Out-of-the-box features** with very few exceptions have zero options for code-based customization. Of course, you can still use the output of such models in code; for example, the score generated by Einstein Lead Scoring that is stored on the Lead record. But if you need to extend the process with code, you are, generally speaking, out of luck.

- **The declarative customization features** mostly play well with code-based solutions. Einstein Prediction Builder does not offer many options, but both Einstein Next Best Action and Einstein Discovery can be integrated effectively with code-based extensions of various sorts.

- **Third-party APIs** have vastly differing levels of customizability. While they are accessed via code or middleware, there is no general answer to how easy they are to use in various extension scenarios. Therefore, you need to research in light of your current and expected requirements if you go down this route.

- **Code-based customization features** are, of course, infinitely extensible with code. You can either create algorithms directly in Apex, call third-party APIs, or generate a model and API, as we did in *Chapter 8, Integrating Third-Party AI Services*. The problem, as always, is that you will need to write, test, and maintain that code.

When considering code-based customization features, you should ask yourself the following questions:

- Can we meet the current requirements without writing a line of code?

- Will this still be true for requirements 6 or 12 months into the future?

- How likely is it that we will need to create a unique model or algorithm around this feature to accommodate business needs?

After considering code-based customization, we will conclude our discussion of functional factors with a discussion on model configurability.

Model configurability

We use the term model configurability to denote the ability of you and your organization to change the parameters of the machine learning models used by your AI features. This includes elements such as selecting the choice of algorithm, customizing the dataset used for training, choosing thresholds, setting hyperparameters, configuring the retraining frequency, and so on.

Most of the other factors we have discussed in this section have applicability beyond the world of AI, although we've considered them from that perspective. Model configurability, however, addresses your organization's need to be in control of the actual model that's used as the engine for the higher-level feature.

Considering our categories once again, we find the following:

- **Out-of-the-box features** have low to moderate configurability and very few options for changing the deep structure of the model itself.

- This is, to a large extent, true for third-party APIs as well, except those platforms such as **Einstein Platform Services**, which allow you to fine-tune a pre-existing model with your data so that you have more options.

- **Declarative customization features** also have at best moderate configurability. Einstein Discovery does let you wrangle your dataset and select an algorithm from a restricted set, but even then, you don't get granular control of the learning process.

- Your only real option, if you need detailed control of your machine learning model, is to build it yourself. This is unsurprising but needs to be stated explicitly. The need to control the detailed features of the model you use is one of the principal reasons you would choose to build a Salesforce AI solution based on custom code.

When considering model configurability, ask yourself the following questions:

- Is there a reason why we need to control the algorithm and learning parameters for the feature we're building?

- Would we be able to transform data into a format that could be supported by a simpler implementation choice?

- Could fine-tuning an existing model with our data be sufficient to get us the results we need?

This concludes our discussion of functional factors. We will now move on to the next grouping, structural factors.

Choosing the right feature based on structural factors

Structural factors include technical and non-functional requirements that don't directly stem from the functional requirements of business users. In a broader setup, this includes things such as performance, maintainability, testability, and many more. However, in contrast to our discussion of functional factors, we will limit ourselves to items that are of special relevance to AI features.

Don't think this means you shouldn't consider performance, maintainability, or testability when designing for AI; we just don't want this guide to go on for hundreds of pages. Also, most of the considerations for these non-functional requirements are the same when you're designing for AI as when you're designing other complex features. You can see where we are in the overall framework in the following diagram:

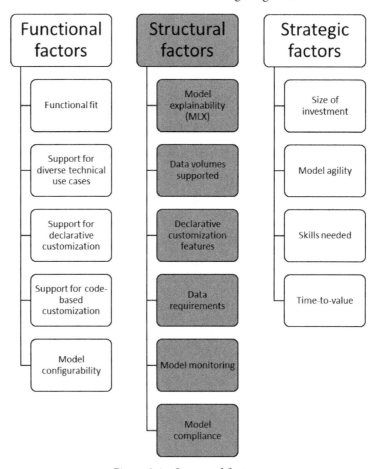

Figure 9.4 – Structural factors

We will start by considering the need for model explainability.

Model explainability

Model explainability (MLX) refers to the ability to explain how a machine learning model comes to its decision, given a set of inputs. For instance, why did a particular lead get that particular lead score? Some models such as linear regression or decision trees are relatively easy to explain, while others such as deep neural networks are much harder. However, in many scenarios, it may be strictly necessary to give an account of why a decision was made, whether it be for legal, practical, or ethical reasons.

When we consider our four categories, we find the following:

- **Out-of-the-box Salesforce features** tend to perform well in terms of explainability. Salesforce tends to put a lot of effort into identifying the reasons behind a certain outcome and making this available for users. This is not universally true, but for most built-in features, we can understand the outcome fairly well.

- The same pattern is true for declarative customization features, with both **Einstein Prediction Builder** and **Einstein Discovery** scoring highly on this point.

- The explainability of third-party APIs varies by API, so we can't generalize on this point. However, it is fair to say that Salesforce is at the forefront in providing explainable AI features and that most other providers tend to provide less explainability overall.

- When building a custom model, the level of explainability is up to you. If you pick a complex neural network model, you will have to do a lot of work to make it explainable, whereas a simple decision tree might be nearly self-explanatory. You need to plan for the effort required in any case.

When considering this factor, ask yourself these questions:

- Are there people who might have a legal or ethical claim to an explanation for the decisions made by our AI?

- Can we easily identify the factors that drive the outcomes of your model?

- Would we have the confidence to trust the model if an explanation isn't readily possible?

Having considered MLX, we will move on to the data volumes supported by different features.

Data volumes supported

Machine learning models live or die based on the data you feed them. A worse model with better data is nearly always preferable to a better model with worse data. The same tends to be true about data volumes – more is nearly always better, although, of course, diminishing returns set in at some point. The amount of data that can be processed by a given feature implementation option is, therefore, a relevant consideration, especially for large organizations with large datasets.

Considering our feature categories, we find the following:

- **Out-of-the-box Salesforce features** vary in the number of records supported, ranging from tens of thousands to a few million in most cases. This means that if you need to process truly massive datasets, this option may not be suitable. However, in general, the best practice is to only keep operational data live on Salesforce. For long-term historical analysis or modeling, a purely on-platform approach is rarely advisable.

- **Declarative customization features** are a mixed bag when it comes to this question. Einstein Prediction Builder will largely have the same issues as the built-in features. **Einstein Next Best Action** can be made to generate options based on external data, which would overcome any limitations at the cost of extra complexity. The row limit for all datasets in Einstein Analytics is 10 billion, which should suffice for all but the largest implementations. However, Einstein Discovery can only process up to 20 million rows for a single analysis, which is low enough to be a concern in some cases.

- **Third-party API** features that support fine-tuning tend to have relatively conservative dataset limits. For instance, Einstein Platform Services has a maximum total dataset size of 2 GB. However, when using fine-tuning, it is common to use relatively small datasets, so this may not be a significant constraint in practice.

- **Custom code-based solutions** can handle as much data as your architecture will cope with. As always, this comes at extra cost and effort relative to the other solution options.

When considering data volumes, ask yourself these questions:

- How much data will we need to process once my feature has been fully developed?

- Is there a point of diminishing returns on adding more data to our scenario?

- Do the benefits of adding more data or more types of data outweigh the extra complexity of implementation and maintenance?

Data volumes are an important topic because data is so essential to machine learning models. Therefore, we will proceed along the same lines and consider data requirements.

Data requirements

There is a minimum amount of data needed to say anything intelligent about a question that you would like to answer. That is as true in life as it is in machine learning. Different types of models require different amounts of data to generalize well. **Simple regression models** can often work well with only hundreds of data points, while a general-purpose language model may require billions of pages of text to work well. Therefore, you must consider whether the data you have available is adequate for the type of feature you are planning to implement. Being overambitious will only lead to worse results. Favor a simpler approach if you have relatively little data available.

In terms of our feature categories, we find the following:

- **Out-of-the-box Salesforce features** tend to require a minimum of a few hundred records to function and a few thousand records to function well. The limits and recommendations vary, so check the documentation for the specific feature you are considering.

- **Declarative customization features** largely have the same minimum limits as the built-in features, which is to say 400 records in a dataset segment to create a predictive model. You should use several thousand at least if you can.

- **Third-part API features** don't typically require additional data. For those supporting fine-tuning, you should plan to use a few hundred to a few thousand records at least.

- **Custom code-based features** can support as much or as little as you want. Here, the key consideration is to be realistic about what kind of model complexity will be supported, given your data volumes and quality. This can be more of an art than a science in some cases, so plan for some trial and error.

When considering data requirements, ask yourself the following questions:

- How much quality data do we have available?

- Can we, somehow, get hold of more if necessary?

- Is the model we want to use going to work, given our data constraints?

Now, having considered the data requirements, we will move on to the next topic, model monitoring.

Model monitoring

Performance, in the practice of a machine learning model, can often be less than what it is in test conditions. That is partly because there will tend to be greater variability in the types of input that your model sees in the wild than during model training and testing, and partially because the world changes, and what was a good prediction yesterday need not remain so tomorrow. The ability to monitor your model after it has gone into production is, therefore, a critical component to any AI feature deployment, and you need to include it in your design from the beginning.

Considering our feature categories, we find the following:

- **Out-of-the-box features** mostly have great monitoring capabilities as Salesforce provides us with pre-built dashboards. As always, check your specific feature, but in general, this is an area where the pre-built features are strong.

- The same is by and large true for the declarative features as we have pre-built ways of monitoring models created by both Einstein Prediction Builder and Einstein Discovery.

- **Third-party APIs** are highly variable on this point but compared to the Salesforce monitoring offering, they mostly fall a bit behind.

- When considering a custom code solution, the monitoring process is generally as good as you make it. Some platforms do give you something for free when you use their toolkits to create your model, so investigate that to save some effort.

When considering monitoring, ask yourself the following questions:

- What are the key metrics we need to track for this model?

- How will we judge our model's success or failure?

- Who do we need to view and understand the model's performance?

Now that we've considered the monitoring requirements you might encounter, we will finish looking at structural factors by considering model compliance.

Model compliance

Compliance is a concern for nearly all large organizations. Whether privacy-related, such as complying with GDPR, or security-related, such as complying with ISO27001, you will need to consider how your AI feature will check the boxes. Two particular concerns are worth highlighting. First, legislation such as GDPR gives individuals both a right to an explanation of an automated decision and an opt-out from any automated decision-making. These are requirements that need to be met by your solution if you are using automated decision-making in any process. Second, some security standards require very specific controls to be in place that may or may not be supported by the specific feature you are considering. You may not always have the option of creating custom controls or getting exceptions for the features you are building.

In general, considering our categories, we find the following:

- **Salesforce features**, both built-in and declarative, will tend to have strong compliance controls present, but very few options for customizing them if your standards require something that they do not support. In most cases, compliance will be adequate, but it will tend to take it or leave it. For individual rights related to individual decision-making, you will need to engineer the processes yourself around the way the standard features work. This is fundamentally a business process question, but crucial to the operation of the feature.

- **Third-party APIs** will have varying levels of compliance based on the specific platform in question. You will need to do individual assessments of the fit to your requirements for each platform and API you use.

- **Custom code-based solutions** will be able to leverage the compliance options of the platform they are based on, and you also have a relatively broad range of options to engineer your controls. Hard compliance requirements can be another good reason to choose a custom solution in some cases.

You should ask yourself the following questions when considering model compliance:

- What are the specific controls that we have to comply with to meet our organizational compliance requirements?

- Does the default platform control of the feature we're using meet those requirements?

- Will this feature make automated decisions that affect individuals in an area with strict data protection legislations, such as the EU?

This concludes our discussion of structural factors. We will now move on and consider the high-level strategic factors relevant to our AI features.

Choosing the right feature based on strategic factors

By strategic factors, we mean the high-level business-related considerations that we need to consider when designing an AI feature. AI projects are rarely small or inexpensive, and considering the business consequences of the decisions we're making is a necessary corrective for any conclusions we might draw from our functional or structural analysis. You can see where we are in the overall framework in the following diagram:

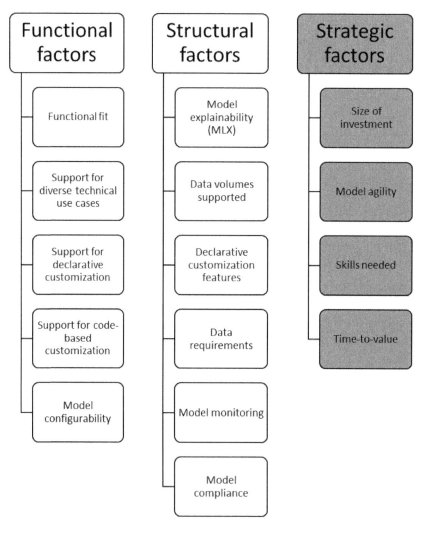

Figure 9.5 – Strategic factors

We will begin this analysis by considering the size of investment required to implement different types of features.

Size of investment

The initial investment covers the amount of effort and money, including licensing costs, that will be required to implement an AI feature. We will include in this the full life cycle cost of the implementation and the ongoing maintenance cost of running the solution.

Considering our feature categories, we can generalize the investment size in the following way:

- **Out-of-the-box features** will tend to have the lowest initial implementation cost and the lowest cost of maintaining the solution, but the highest ongoing licensing costs as special licensing is required for nearly all the built-in features we've discussed.

- **The declarative customization features** have higher implementation and maintenance costs than the out-of-the-box features but also require special licensing. Therefore, they can be relatively expensive in terms of the total cost.

- **Third-party APIs** tend to be priced on a usage basis, so depending on how many times you call them, they may be expensive or not. They will have a higher implementation and maintenance cost than a declarative solution on average, but less than a fully custom solution.

- **Custom-code solutions** will have the highest initial implementation and ongoing maintenance costs, but most likely the lowest licensing costs as you will just be paying for normal API calls rather than including a service premium.

When considering the size of the investment, ask yourself the following questions:

- Do we understand the full scope of the requirements well enough to estimate the cost of various options?

- How much usage is this feature likely to get if it is successful?

- Does our organization tend to prefer large capital expenditure over increased operational expenses or the other way around?

We will now move on from our discussion of investment and consider the question of model agility.

Model agility

Model agility refers to the ability of the capacity of the model underlying your AI feature's ability to adapt and change over time to meet new requirements. This includes whether you can incorporate changes in data formats or incorporate new kinds of data, whether you can change the output to a different format if required, or whether you can create a variant model that solves a closely related problem.

Considering the categories we use for our features, we find the following:

- **Out-of-the-box features** have overwhelmingly low agility and if you are expecting considerable evolution of the feature over time, they may not be appropriate. While some models can be tweaked, they generally can't be substantially changed.

- **Declarative customization features** have higher agility and can evolve to a greater degree than out-of-the-box features. The reengineering required to make major changes can be substantial in some cases, but it is generally possible to make these changes.

- **Third-party APIs** will generally not allow you to change much, although they may provide different options via parameters that you can pass. However, you may be able to introduce an abstraction layer that would allow you to switch out the specific API you're using without affecting the rest of the functionality. This may be an option to consider if you're expecting substantial evolution over time.

- **Custom code-based solutions** can evolve to fit new requirements, so long as your architecture and design accommodate them. Making it flexible to future changes will probably increase initial costs of implementation and this should be considered during planning.

When considering model agility, you should ask yourself the following questions:

- How much do we expect the model requirements to change over time?

- What provisions do we need to make for flexibility in the model setup?

- If our model cannot accommodate future changes, is the level of sunk cost at an acceptable level?

Now that we've considered model agility, we will look at the skills needed for implementing different features.

Skills needed

The skills required to implement an AI solution can be a major factor in deciding whether to go with a given solution design or not. It is, for obvious reasons, impossible to go with a cutting-edge, custom-built machine learning model without having cutting-edge developers and data scientists to build it. These can be hard skills to find, even in the open market.

Considering our four categories of features, the following general statements can be made:

- **Out-of-the-box features** can be implemented with just normal Salesforce configurator skills and an adequate level of data literacy. This is within the scope of most organizations.

- **Declarative customization features** require a greater need for data skills and a better understanding of how to build workable models. It is, however, within the grasp of many experienced Salesforce professionals.

- **Third-party APIs** typically require an integration developer with an understanding of integration patterns on Salesforce, although middleware can make this easier. The level of data skills required is relatively moderate for this category.

- **For custom-built solutions**, you will need developers and usually, they are of an entirely different type than those you would normally use for Salesforce. If you have high demands for your model, these may need to be very specialized. For instance, if you want to have a unique market-leading solution for generating automated email replies to your customers, you would probably need to hire someone with a PhD in Natural Language Processing with relevant research experience and a development team to support him or her.

In general, ask the following questions when considering what skills are needed for your AI project:

- Given the complexity of the solution we're proposing, are we confident we can find the necessary skills either in-house or with our preferred suppliers?

- Can we realistically support and maintain the proposed solution with the skills we have in-house?

- What training or development do we need to provide to make this happen?

Now that we've considered the skills requirements in the context of our design, we are ready to move on to one of the most crucial strategic factors: time-to-value.

Time-to-value

Time-to-value is the term used to describe how long it takes from starting a project for it to deliver real business value. This doesn't necessarily mean completing the project. In a world that is increasingly driven by agile, incremental processes, it may just be the first **Minimum Viable Product** (**MVP**) drop of a feature. Business change is often very dependent on momentum, and delivering value quickly can be essential to the success and failure of a project, whatever else their merits might be.

When considering our four categories in terms of time-to-value, we find the following:

- **Out-of-the-box solutions** deliver value the fastest if they are a good fit for the business requirements, which should be fairly self-explanatory, given the easier implementation for these features.

- **Declarative customization features** deliver fast value if you design them well as there isn't the overhead associated with a code-based solution.

- **Third-party API solutions** can deliver value very quickly if you have strong middleware and integration frameworks in place. Otherwise, they are fairly heavyweight options.

- **Custom code-based solutions** can deliver value quickly in some cases, where you can base your work on open source examples or common practices. If you can't do this, it may be a quite difficult and lengthy process to get to the value you need.

When considering time-to-value, ask yourself the following questions:

- Does our organization typically allow for long value realization cycles?

- Can we deliver enough value in a short time for it to be meaningful to the business?

- Are there third-party options available that would change the value equation if included?

This concludes our consideration of time-to-value and our decision guide. We will now move on and quickly consider how this framework might be used.

Applying the framework in practice

The most important thing to understand about applying this framework for decision-making is that you will never have a perfect fit. There will be different considerations pointing in different directions and you need to assess which factors are the most important.

For instance, when considering a credit scoring use case, you might find that a third-party API provides you with a near-perfect functional fit and a very strong time-to-value. You might even have the skills to implement it. However, on closer examination, the model may not meet your compliance and explainability criteria and thus have to be discarded for legal reasons.

Additionally, you may run up against general architecture and security guidelines within your organization that may override the best fit based on this framework. For instance, you may have strong architecture governance against heavy customization that prohibits a heavily code-based approach, or you may be unable to use certain pre-built solutions such as Einstein Activity Capture because your security organization does not permit the use of AWS.

You should perform the following steps to use this framework in practice:

1. Write down the requirements clearly and succinctly, supported by any additional diagrams that are necessary for you to keep a clear mental picture of how the solution should work.

2. Generate a rough list of options that you will decide between. These can be sketched at a high level as there is no need to proceed with options that can be disqualified early.

3. Then, review the factors in the decision model and decide which ones have high importance for your use case.

4. Work through these factors one by one and pick out the best fit among your options and any alternatives that would work, but not be ideal. Also, note when an option seems to be ruled out by a given factor.

5. Now, pick your two or three best-fit options based on this analysis. Assess these against your overall architecture governance principles, security guidelines, and other enterprise frameworks you need to consider.

6. If you have a clear winner, well done. Now, all you have to do is document it and convince the business users and other stakeholders that your recommendation is right. However, you may need to return and iterate some of the previous steps to get to a conclusion.

This process is, of course, somewhat idealized and in practice, you rarely have the luxury of coming up with a design without having to consider the needs of many other stakeholders. Also, there is the risk that you won't find a good fit solution, in which case you have to go back and talk to people in your organization about what compromises might be acceptable. That being said, trying to think of the architecture and design process in a structured manner will only help you in getting to a good outcome. Having covered the application of the framework, we will now proceed to the summary.

Summary

In this chapter, we looked at 14 factors that are important in deciding what kind of AI feature to use. By going through these, you will avoid the common pitfalls that haunt many AI feature implementations and ensure that you get to the right solution for your organization.

We saw that factors will often point in different directions. For instance, you may have very detailed and complex user requirements coupled with hard compliance requirements pointing toward a custom code-based solution built on a cloud platform. However, you may not have the necessary skills to implement this, nor the requirements to be able to realize value cannot be met with a custom solution that takes all requirements into account.

While that can be dispiriting if you are an architect, that is your job. You need to make the difficult trade-offs between competing technical and business considerations that result in a solution that is, if not perfect, at least adequate to the needs of your organization both now and in the future. Hopefully, this guide has shown you some of the ways you can do this.

We will now move on to our next and final chapter, where we will conclude our time together, reflect on what we've learned, and examine where we might go next. There, you will reexamine some of the key points from previous chapters. We will also point out links to resources that can help you develop further.

Questions

1. What are the different kinds of factors to consider in relation to AI feature decisions?

2. Before evaluating different feature designs, what should you do?

3. Having a limited budget for implementation is relevant to what factor?

10
Conclusion

This chapter will conclude our time together learning about **artificial intelligence (AI)** on Salesforce. We will go through some of the main points we have learned and draw out some key lessons to take away for the future. Then, we will have a look at additional areas that you can continue to explore after you finish this book.

In this chapter, we're going to cover the following main topics:

- Using the power of built-in features
- Extending with declarative features
- Knowing when to go beyond declarative features
- Choosing where to go from here

After completing this chapter, you will understand what you have learned from working through this book and where to go to get a deeper understanding of the various areas discussed.

Using the power of built-in features

We started this book by looking at the built-in features in the core Salesforce clouds. No clouds are more used than Sales Cloud and Service Cloud, so it made sense to start our exploration there. What we saw was a range of pre-built features such as **Einstein Lead Scoring**, **Einstein Forecasting**, and **Einstein Case Classification** that use powerful and simple pre-built **machine learning** (**ML**) models to accomplish very specific tasks that help optimize sales or service processes.

In general, the lesson of the first few chapters is that there is a lot of value in the out-of-the-box features, and this can be realized quickly if these features happen to be a good fit for your business requirements and you don't have significant compliance or enterprise architecture constraints in terms of what you can implement. You can see a selection flow in the following diagram:

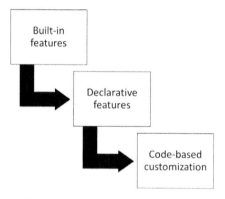

Figure 10.1 – Feature selection flow

Some features such as **Einstein Reply Recommendations** can be harder to implement successfully because of large data requirements or problems with update cycles. Finally, other features such as **Einstein Bots** are worlds unto themselves and can be used for a range of scenarios well beyond the scope of this book.

We then moved on to look at the wealth of AI features in Marketing Cloud. It is fair to say that the amount of value you get out of the box in Marketing Cloud exceeds any of the Salesforce core clouds. This includes both analytical capabilities such as **Einstein Email Insights**, the several ways of leveraging AI in a journey builder such as **Send Time Optimization** and **Einstein Engagement Scoring**, and the powerful capabilities of **Einstein Email Recommendations**.

Unfortunately, the huge value you get out of the box in Marketing Cloud is somewhat offset by the fewer capabilities you have for customization within this cloud. You will more frequently be forced to adopt a code-based approach if you need something unique in Marketing Cloud rather than in the core clouds.

Commerce Cloud is another world unto itself, and while we touched on some of the AI capabilities in this cloud, this is an area you should devote more time to study if you want to start implementing AI features in practice. The architecture of Commerce Cloud is very different from the core cloud services and also less tightly integrated than Marketing Cloud, so the technical scenarios will often be more complex.

We also had a look across the Salesforce industry clouds, which often have quite detailed and deep AI or analytical capabilities within a narrow space. Industry clouds are a major area of focus for Salesforce at the moment and if your company is in one of the verticals where Salesforce is bringing out unique cloud offerings, it is worth following closely what gets released within your space. While not everything in industry clouds is relevant to everyone, it is often extremely relevant to the right target audience and can save a lot of time in custom implementation efforts.

After getting familiar with the built-in offerings, we moved on to looking at ways of extending them with declarative features. We will revisit the main points from this area next.

Extending with declarative features

The three declarative features we covered in *Chapter 6, Declarative Customization Options* (**Einstein Next Best Action**, **Einstein Prediction Builder**, and **Einstein Discovery**) can be used along with the standard Salesforce platform features such as flows and Lightning pages to create advanced custom solutions for your AI business requirements.

Einstein Next Best Action provides a framework for providing in-context recommendations for what to do next. A combination of a declarative strategy builder and the ability to extend the built-in functionality with Apex at various points of the flow means that you can find ways of bending this feature to do far-flung things if you feel so inclined.

For instance, you could decide to create recommendations linked to different screen flows, each representing a different layout for filling out the core record and replacing the normal page layout mechanism. That would be a bad idea, as you already have Lightning pages and page layouts at your disposal. Instead, use the incredible power of this feature wisely to guide your team to make the best possible choice at the best possible time.

Einstein Prediction Builder is the easiest way to create a custom AI prediction model that is currently available anywhere else on the market. If you can live with the restrictions of needing all the data in one object and having Salesforce pick the algorithm for you, this feature is a winner.

If you need a bit more power but are not ready to go for a full-blown custom model, use Einstein Discovery. This feature is not as widely used as it should be, considering its enormous power, and I would encourage you not to overlook it. With Tableau CRM you have advanced data-wrangling capabilities at your disposal, and with Einstein Discovery you can tweak the ML model sufficiently for most purposes and even make the result available for inference via an **application programming interface** (**API**). If your organization uses Tableau CRM, make Einstein Discovery the first place you look to create new models.

Of course, as we have also seen, not everything can be solved on a platform and we explored a number of options for going beyond Salesforce core to solve our requirements. We'll look at some of the key lessons from that discussion next.

Knowing when to go beyond declarative features

Throughout this book, we have highlighted a range of scenarios that might mean you can't—or shouldn't—go forward with a standard or even a declarative solution. Whether for compliance or goodness of fit, or due to a need for detailed algorithmic control, a third-party or custom solution can in many cases be the right decision. Just because you have good features on a platform, this doesn't mean these features can solve every requirement well.

First, it is worth noting that Einstein Platform Services, while developed by Salesforce, is actually from an architectural point of view more or less equivalent to a third-party API solution just with a bit of additional tooling added to make your life easier. You should therefore evaluate these alongside other third-party APIs in most cases.

Third-party API solutions in general can add substantial value if they are a close fit to business requirements. They are often not very difficult to implement and if you have good frameworks or middleware already in place, they can be a fast path to value for a number of generic use cases.

While custom code-based solutions are both expensive and risky and require specialized skills to create, they are sometimes the only approach that will get you where you need to go. If you are dealing with an important business requirement that merits substantial investment, has a custom dataset, and where the results have to be state of the art, then you are probably looking at going in this direction. Platforms such as **Amazon Web Services** (**AWS**) SageMaker can make your life easier, but ultimately, we're talking about a custom ML model and custom code, so it will never be simple.

Now, having reviewed some of our key lessons from the book, let's have a look into the future and examine where you might go next to grow your knowledge.

Choosing where to go from here

Working through this book, you will no doubt have noted a number of different areas where you might want to deepen your knowledge. This book surveys a vast field of functionality, and unfortunately, we can't cover everything about everything. In the following sections, we will propose a few different ways you can extend the foundation you have gotten from this book. The following diagram shows some paths you can take:

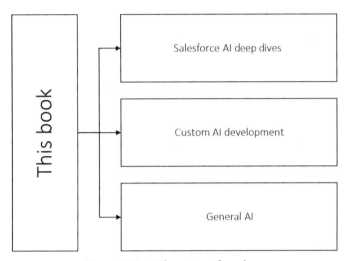

Figure 10.2 – Where to go from here

First, we will look at ways to extend your knowledge of Salesforce AI features.

Salesforce AI features

We now list some of the most relevant resources to extend your knowledge of Salesforce AI features:

- For a solid deep dive into the Einstein platform from a Salesforce perspective, you can follow the *Get Smart with Salesforce Einstein* trail on *Trailhead*, which can be found at this link: `https://trailhead.salesforce.com/en/content/learn/trails/get_smart_einstein`.

- To learn more about Service Cloud Einstein, you can follow the *Make Service Cloud Smarter* trail. This can be found here: `https://trailhead.salesforce.com/en/content/learn/trails/service_einstein`.

- To understand more about Marketing Cloud Einstein, you can follow the *Evolve Your Marketing Strategy with Artificial Intelligence* trail. This can be found at the following link: `https://trailhead.salesforce.com/en/content/learn/trails/einstein-and-the-modern-marketer`.

- If you want to dive deeper into Commerce Cloud Einstein, you can do so using the *Deploy Commerce Cloud Einstein* trail. You can find it at this link: `https://trailhead.salesforce.com/en/content/learn/trails/deploy-commerce-cloud-einstein`.

- The best way to get more knowledge of Einstein Prediction Builder is by using the *Filter-Based Predictions with Einstein Prediction Builder* module, found here: `https://trailhead.salesforce.com/en/content/learn/modules/filter-based-predictions-with-einstein-prediction-builder`.

- Einstein Next Best Action has an excellent deep-dive module on *Trailhead*, entitled *Recommendation Automation with Einstein Next Best Action*. This can be found here: `https://trailhead.salesforce.com/en/content/learn/modules/recommendation-automation-next-best-action`.

- You can learn a lot more about Einstein Discovery in the *Gain Insight with Einstein Discovery* trail. You can find it here: `https://trailhead.salesforce.com/en/content/learn/trails/wave_analytics_einstein_discovery`.

- Finally, you can understand the details of Einstein Platform Services by following the guides on the main documentation site, which can be found here: `https://metamind.readme.io/docs`.

We will now have a look at the resources you might consult if you wanted to learn more about custom AI feature development on Salesforce.

Custom AI feature development

Here are some of the most relevant resources to extend your knowledge of custom AI feature development on Salesforce:

- Most custom AI development on Salesforce requires knowledge of integration scenarios, therefore you may want to consider the *Integration Architecture Designer* Salesforce certification. You can study for it using the following trailmix: `https://trailhead.salesforce.com/en/users/strailhead/trailmixes/architect-integration-architecture`.

- To get a better understanding of how you can use Microsoft Cognitive Services as part of your solution, you can consult the book *Learning Microsoft Cognitive Services* by *Leif Larsen*. It's available at the following link: `https://www.packtpub.com/product/learning-microsoft-cognitive-services-third-edition/9781789800616`.

- If you are interested in learning more about how to use the AWS AI solutions in your setup, consult the book *Hands-On Artificial Intelligence on Amazon Web Services* by *Subhashini Tripuraneni* and *Charles Song*. You can have a look at the following link: `https://www.packtpub.com/product/hands-on-artificial-intelligence-on-amazon-web-services/9781789534146`.

- To learn more about the AI services available on **Google Cloud Platform** (**GCP**) and how they can be used in your solution, you can look at *Google Cloud AI Services Quick Start Guide* by *Arvind Ravulavaru*. You can see more details here: `https://www.packtpub.com/product/google-cloud-ai-services-quick-start-guide/9781788626613`.

We will conclude our review of resources with a few of a more general nature.

General AI background

Here are some of the most relevant resources to extend your general AI knowledge:

- The *Coursera* course by Andrew Ng is one of the best-known and most respected resources for learning the basics of ML. You can find it here: `https://www.coursera.org/learn/machine-learning`.

- For a deeper view of Jupyter Notebook and data science, you can consult the Packt Publishing book *Jupyter for Data Science* by *Dan Toomey*. You can find it here: `https://www.packtpub.com/product/jupyter-for-data-science/9781785880070`.

- For an in-depth study of chatbot design, you can consult *Voicebot and Chatbot Design* by *Rachel Batish*, which you can view at the following link: `https://www.packtpub.com/product/voicebot-and-chatbot-design/9781789139624`.

This concludes our presentation of ways in which you might start to grow your knowledge in this field. Now, we will conclude with a summary.

Summary

Congratulations! You have made it to the end of the book. Sprinkle yourself with gold stars and get ready to implement some Salesforce AI solutions. On a more serious note, while you now have the foundation to understand the architecture and design of AI features on Salesforce, this is a fast-moving area and you should prepare to keep up to date—for instance, by looking at some of the additional resources we have suggested.

Overall, the key message of this book is that you as an architect have an impressive array of options at your disposal when creating solutions for AI requirements on Salesforce. However, the sheer number of powerful options you have available and the many detailed limitations and considerations that pertain to them means that your job gets harder, not easier.

You have to make the right engineering trade-offs between the different features at your disposal in order to satisfy both your business users and the various organizational constraints you are working under. One of the things that we tried to convey in *Chapter 9, A Salesforce AI Decision Guide*, was that you will most likely not find a single solution that is optimal from all perspectives. You will need to sacrifice something, whether functionally, structurally, or strategically, and you need to make the right call for your particular case.

This book has been a step in the direction of enabling you to make these decisions in the right way and we hope that you now feel confident in thinking through the options for architecting AI solutions on Salesforce. Ultimately, when the choice becomes yours to make, you will need to bring everything together with your experience of making great solutions on the Salesforce platform, combining AI with other requirements to meet your organization's business needs. We wish you the best of luck with this endeavor and hope this book will be a place you can return to for continuing inspiration as you grow in your abilities to architect new Salesforce AI solutions.

Questions

1. What are the main approaches to implementing the AI features discussed in this book?

2. What paths can you take to enhance your knowledge of architecting AI features on Salesforce?

3. How do you envisage the process of coming up with the right architecture for an AI feature?

Assessments

Chapter 1

1. To leverage the value of intelligent CRM data, automate routine processes, and better connect with your customers on a personal basis

2. Pre-built solutions; Lightning Platform; Tableau CRM; declarative platform services; and programmatic platform services

3. Probabilistic in nature, as well as model-based, data-dependent, autonomous, opaque, evolving, and ethically valent

Chapter 2

1. Einstein Lead Scoring

2. AWS

3. North America

Chapter 3

1. Einstein Article Recommendations

2. Message; rule; action; question

3. Once when you turn the feature on and once when you hit 10,000 chat transcripts

Chapter 4

1. To automatically schedule the best time to send an email

2. In Journey Builder

3. Market basket analysis

Chapter 5

1. Pre-built analytics apps

2. Einstein Discovery

3. Intelligent document automation

Chapter 6

1. Screen flows; recommendation records; strategies; and the Einstein Next Best Action lightning component

2. On a single Salesforce object, exclusively

3. Using write-back, with the Einstein Discovery lightning component, or using the API

Chapter 7

1. Einstein Object Detection.

2. Because I am dealing with a specific domain with its own jargon.

3. You can't fine-tune your own model.

Chapter 8

1. Because your requirements in one dimension or another go beyond what's available on the platform.

2. No, often they can offer an excellent functional fit with a short time-to-value.

3. Azure; AWS; Google Cloud Platform.

Chapter 9

1. Functional, structural, and strategic.

2. Ensure that you have a good grasp of the requirements.

3. The size of the investment.

Chapter 10

1. Using built-in features, using declarative features, and using code-based customization

2. Diving deeply into specific features, expanding your general AI knowledge, and improving your overall AI development skills

3. As a process of balancing trade-offs in an optimal manner

Packt.com

Subscribe to our online digital library for full access to over 7,000 books and videos, as well as industry leading tools to help you plan your personal development and advance your career. For more information, please visit our website.

Why subscribe?

- Spend less time learning and more time coding with practical eBooks and Videos from over 4,000 industry professionals

- Improve your learning with Skill Plans built especially for you

- Get a free eBook or video every month

- Fully searchable for easy access to vital information

- Copy and paste, print, and bookmark content

Did you know that Packt offers eBook versions of every book published, with PDF and ePub files available? You can upgrade to the eBook version at packt.com and as a print book customer, you are entitled to a discount on the eBook copy. Get in touch with us at customercare@packtpub.com for more details.

At www.packt.com, you can also read a collection of free technical articles, sign up for a range of free newsletters, and receive exclusive discounts and offers on Packt books and eBooks.

Other Books You May Enjoy

If you enjoyed this book, you may be interested in these other books by Packt:

Becoming a Salesforce Certified Technical Architect

Tameem Bahri

ISBN: 978-1-80056-875-4

- Explore data lifecycle management and apply it effectively in the Salesforce ecosystem
- Design appropriate enterprise integration interfaces to build your connected solution
- Understand the essential concepts of identity and access management
- Develop scalable Salesforce data and system architecture
- Design the project environment and release strategy for your solution
- Articulate the benefits, limitations, and design considerations relating to your solution
- Discover tips, tricks, and strategies to prepare for the Salesforce CTA review board exam

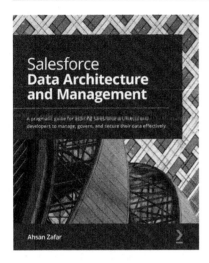

Salesforce Data Architecture and Management

Ahsan Zafar

ISBN: 978-1-80107-324-0

- Understand the Salesforce data architecture

- Explore various data backup and archival strategies

- Understand how the Salesforce platform is designed and how it is different from other relational databases

- Uncover tools that can help in data management that minimize data trust issues in your Salesforce org

- Focus on the Salesforce Customer 360 platform, its key components, and how it can help organizations in connecting with customers

- Discover how Salesforce can be used for GDPR compliance

- Measure and monitor the performance of your Salesforce org

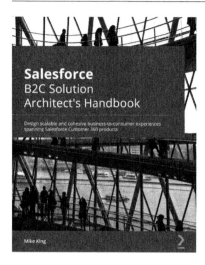

Salesforce B2C Solution Architect's Handbook

Mike King

ISBN: 978-1-80181-703-5

- Explore key Customer 360 products and their integration options
- Choose the optimum integration architecture to unify data and experiences
- Architect a single view of the customer to support service, marketing, and commerce
- Plan for critical requirements, design decisions, and implementation sequences to avoid sub-optimal solutions
- Integrate Customer 360 solutions into a single source of truth solution such as a Master Data Model
- Support business needs that require functionality from more than one component by orchestrating data and user flows

Packt is searching for authors like you

If you're interested in becoming an author for Packt, please visit `authors.packtpub.com` and apply today. We have worked with thousands of developers and tech professionals, just like you, to help them share their insight with the global tech community. You can make a general application, apply for a specific hot topic that we are recruiting an author for, or submit your own idea.

Share Your Thoughts

Now you've finished *Architecting AI Solutions on Salesforce*, we'd love to hear your thoughts! Scan the QR code below to go straight to the Amazon review page for this book and share your feedback or leave a review on the site that you purchased it from.

https://packt.link/r/1801076014

Your review is important to us and the tech community and will help us make sure we're delivering excellent quality content.

Index

Einstein Social Insights 135, 136
Einstein Splits
  about 15, 116-119
  variants 116
Einstein Vision
  about 8, 20, 198
  at Pickled Plastics Ltd. 207-211
  capabilities 206
  images, classifying with 206
  overview 206, 207
  working with 199-206
Einstein Vision for Social Studio
  about 136, 137
  classifiers 136
Einstein Visit Recommendations 158, 159
Einstein Visit Task
    Recommendations 158, 159
Einstein Web Recommendations 133-135
Email Insights 276

F

Financial Services Cloud 17
Financial Services Einstein
  Analytics for Insurance 151, 152
  Analytics for Mortgage 153
  Analytics for Retail Banking 152
  Analytics for Wealth
    Management 150, 151
  Client Segmentation 153
  Consumer Banking Starter
    Analytics 152
  implementing 150
  Tableau CRM for 150
  Wealth Starter Analytics 153
framework
  applying, in practice 294, 295

functional factors
  feature, selecting based on 278
  functional fit 279
  model configurability 282, 283
  support, for code-based
    customization 281, 282
  support, for declarative
    customization 281
  support, for diverse technical
    use cases 280
functional fit 279
Fundraising Analytics template 160
Fundraising Performance
    Analytics template 160

G

general AI knowledge
  resources 303
Google Translate
  text, translating with 264-270
Gradient Boosting Machines 51, 239

H

Health Cloud 17
Health Cloud Einstein
  Analytics for Healthcare 145-147
  using 144

I

Industry Clouds
  Einstein for 144
Intelligent Document Automation
    and Form Reader 155
intents 74

Einstein sentiment analysis 213-222
Einstein Vision 207-211
lead scoring model 40
Platform Services layer 8
Portable Document Format (PDF) 37
Programmatic Platform Services
  about 20
  Einstein Language 20, 21
  Einstein Vision 20
Proof-of-Concept (PoC) 78, 200

Q

quality assurance (QA) 45

R

Retail Compliance
  optimizing, with Consumer
    Goods Cloud Einstein 157

S

Sales Cloud Einstein
  about 32, 33
  components 32
  setting up 42-44
Sales Cloud Einstein Readiness Assessor
  running 40-42
Salesforce
  example, coding on 258-263
Salesforce AI
  components 7
Salesforce AI features
  resources 301, 302
Salesforce Einstein
  elements 9

Salesforce Einstein, elements
  about 9
  Declarative Platform Services 18
  Einstein for Commerce 15
  Einstein for Industry Clouds 17
  Einstein for Marketing 13
  Einstein for sales 10
  Einstein for Service 12
  Programmatic Platform Services 20
Salesforce org
  technical requirements 33
Service 12
Service Cloud Einstein
  about 68
  Einstein Article Recommendations 68
  Einstein Bots 68
  Einstein Case Classification 68
  Einstein Reply Recommendations 68
simple regression models 287
Stock Keeping Unit (SKU) 78
strategic factors
  about 290, 291
  feature, selecting based on 290, 291
  model agility 292
  size of investment 291
  skills requirements 293
  time-to-value 294
structural factors
  about 284
  data requirements 287
  data volumes supported 286, 287
  feature, selecting based on 284, 285
  model compliance 289
  model explainability (MLX) 285
  model monitoring 288

T

Tableau CRM
  about 8
  for Financial Services Einstein 150
Tableau CRM for Manufacturing 156, 157
text
  translating, with Google
      Translate 264-270
Text Analytics 256
time-to-value 294

U

use cases, Einstein Bots
  deflection 71
  qualification 70
  routing 71
user experience (UX) 51
user interface (UI) 34

V

variables 74
View View Last Cart 130

W

waterfall predictions 130
Wealth Starter Analytics 153